Contents

KT-590-931

Acknowledgments

We are greatly indebted to staff and residents in the cities of Manchester and Newcastle who have been willing to share their invaluable experiences and knowledge with us over nearly five years. The contributions of Jill Preston, Community and Housing Director in Newcastle, Eamonn Boylan, Deputy Chief Executive in Manchester, Tom Russell, head of New East Manchester, Howard Bernstein, Chief Executive in Manchester, Fionnuala Stringer and Sean McGonigle are much appreciated. We cannot personally name all the staff and residents who gave of their time so generously for reasons of confidentiality, but we hope they know how grateful we are.

Many of the local staff we talked to had worked in housing and in those cities for a long time. Some had grown up there and had a strong attachment to the areas they were working in. Where their experience covered more than one low demand area, we have drawn on their detailed local knowledge extensively.

We would like to thank Max Steinberg at the Housing Corporation, Mike Gahagan at the ODPM, Peter Styche at the Government Office for the North West, staff at the regional development agencies and other government offices for the regions, Merron Simpson at the Chartered Institute of Housing, Ruth Lupton and John Hills at LSE for their helpful suggestions at various stages of the research. Ruth Lupton's detailed national study of 12 of the poorest urban areas in the country has informed our work. Her reports and forthcoming book are listed in the references.

We would like to thank Brenden Nevin and the CURS team at Birmingham University, Glen Bramley and colleagues at Heriot Watt University, Edinburgh, Ivan Turok and colleagues at Glasgow University, the Empty Homes Agency, the Select Committee on Transport, Local Government and the Regions and the Chartered Institute of Housing for providing so much supporting evidence for us to draw on.

We are extremely grateful to Caroline Paskell and Tara Butler who provided valuable research assistance, and to Lucinda Himeur and Jane Dickson who helped greatly in many different ways with the production of the report and organisation of the research. In particular we owe a great debt to Nicola Harrison who worked far out of hours to deliver the report on time and to check the sources.

Finally, we would like to thank the Nuffield Foundation who funded the main fieldwork. This research would not have been possible without their support.

We accept full responsibility for the contents and conclusions of the report. In this fast moving terrain, we apologise for any inaccuracies, having done everything we could to keep up to date.

CWr
26.4.07

···

BOOM OR ABANDONMENT
resolving housing conflicts in cities

BY KATHARINE MUMFORD AND ANNE POWER

···

Chartered Institute of Housing
Policy and Practice Series
in collaboration with the
Housing Studies Association

The Chartered Institute of Housing

The Chartered Institute of Housing is the professional organisation for all people who work in housing. Its purpose is to take a strategic and leading role in encouraging and promoting the provision of good quality affordable housing for all. The Institute has more than 16,500 members working in local authorities, housing associations, the private sector and educational institutions.

Chartered Institute of Housing
Octavia House, Westwood Way
Coventry CV4 8JP
Telephone: 024 7685 1700
Fax: 024 7669 5110

The Housing Studies Association

The Housing Studies Association promotes the study of housing by bringing together housing researchers with others interested in housing research in the housing policy and practitioner communities. It acts as a voice for housing research by organising conferences and seminars, lobbying government and other agencies and providing services to members.

The CIH Housing Policy and Practice Series is published in collaboration with the Housing Studies Association and aims to provide important and valuable material and insights for housing managers, staff, students, trainers and policy makers. Books in the series are designed to promote debate, but the contents do not necessarily reflect the views of the CIH or the HSA. The Editorial Team for the series is currently: General Editors: Dr. Peter Williams, John Perry and Peter Somerville, and Production Editor: Alan Dearling.

Photos supplied by Katharine Mumford and Caroline Paskell.

ISBN: 1-903208-49-1

Boom or abandonment – resolving housing conflicts in cities
By Katharine Mumford and Anne Power

Published by the Chartered Institute of Housing © 2002

Printed by the Charlesworth Group, Huddersfield

CHAPTER 1:
Introduction

In 2002, the vast majority of the population enjoy more space and higher amenities in their homes than ever before. The ratio of mortgage payments to incomes is lower than at any time since 1984 due to low interest rates (Halifax, 2002). But newspapers are 'hyping up' a housing crisis around absurdly high and fast rising house prices. There is strong demand for out-of-city homes across the whole country and a chronic real shortage of homes for sale in the South East, particularly London. People seem to be holding back on selling in the hope of 'making a killing' through the housing boom, creating one kind of snarl-up in the market. Builders are accused of slowing production deliberately in spite of large land banks and high demand in the hope of pushing up even further the already exorbitantly high prices – another distortion of the market (*The Times*, 2002). Meanwhile, private rents are reportedly falling in London as investors snap up properties for letting, restricting people's chance of buying, but expanding the options for renting. The biggest political strife is sparked by the apparent shortage of high quality 'affordable' housing for sale in desirable locations.

Ministers rush to prop up home-buying for key workers – nurses, teachers, policemen, bus drivers – in a desperate game of monopoly, playing for ever higher stakes. Yet the other half of the country – 'The North' – shows acute signs of over-supply, falling prices and actual abandonment in older inner city areas. Many studies have been completed over the last five years, highlighting the seriousness of this imbalance and housing market failure.[1] Demand for properties in large council estates almost everywhere is now low, but in parts of northern cities it has all but collapsed. Glen Bramley's study shows the disproportionate difficulties facing council landlords (Bramley *et al.*, 2000). Many other studies underline the particular problems of low income, large-scale, publicly owned and managed estates.[2] Independent, but government subsidised and regulated housing associations – often referred to by their formal title as Registered Social Landlords or RSLs – are in just as much trouble in many areas, sometimes with no waiting lists and unoccupied, almost new property.[3] It doesn't make sense to the average

---

1   Among the most important are: *Unpopular Housing*, Social Exclusion Unit, 1999; Urban Task Force, 1999; Bramley *et al.*, 2000; Nevin *et al.*, 2001; *Housing Market Renewal bid*, Nevin, 2001; Lord Falconer's statement announcing Housing Market Renewal Fund 2002; John Prescott's announcement following CRS statement, July 2002.

2   These include: *Bringing Britain Together*, Social Exclusion Unit, 1998, plus 18 Policy Action Team reports; Power, 1997; Scottish Partnership reports on Castlemilk and other peripheral estates; Estate Action reports 1985-95; transfer bidding documents, Glasgow, 1998, Birmingham, 1999; Hackney Comprehensive Estates Initiative, 1991; Southwark Five Estates Regeneration Proposal, 1992. There are many similar documents from all over the country and from continental Europe.

3   The financial consequences for RSLs of low demand coupled with the new rent restructuring regime are examined by HACAS Consulting in the CIH report, *Sustaining Success* (CIH, 2000).

house buyer. Neither boom nor abandonment make city neighbourhoods easy places to live in or manage.

The two housing crises are not tied together in the minds of most people and appear to underline the 'poles apart' theory of the north and the south, which the government would like to reject (Cabinet Office, 1999). Yet they are intricately related because gains in the south so often seem to be at the expense of the north. Unlike France, Germany, Spain, Italy or the USA where regional cities are successfully competing for a greater share of national investment, growth and prestige, Britain is overwhelmingly dominated by a seemingly uncontrolled boom in and around London. Even government thinking and projections of housing need are heavily influenced by southern shortages. Higher proportions of housing resources are therefore likely to be dedicated to tackling the affordable housing problems of London and the South East than to making northern inner city neighbourhoods more appealing to better off people.[4] Yet the visibly fragile and spindly shoots of growth in more northern cities are a thin disguise for the full depths of the problem of housing abandonment. And progress to date in reviving city centres and some neighbourhoods needs long-term ongoing investment if it is to take root at all firmly. Edinburgh and some smaller, popular urban areas like Harrogate and Lancaster, are sharp exceptions to this pattern (*The Economist*, 2002c).

Meanwhile, many more affluent people, particularly families, continue to opt out of cities, pushing up house prices in more attractive rural areas, creating an affordability crisis in rural areas as well (Countryside Agency, 2002). Far too little is being done to help core cities outside London build on their strengths and rescue their increasingly depleted, low income, inner neighbourhoods (Lupton, 2001b).

This book, *Boom or Abandonment*, is about the dual housing crisis, underlining a vast economic distance between parts of the urban north and the rest of the country. We examine closely the problems of failing housing in two northern cities, only two and a half to three hours from London (trains permitting), yet in another housing world. Here there is space, infrastructure, easy access to amenities, open countryside, uncongested airports, direct rail links to other parts of the country, attractive homes to a Londoner's eyes and people desperate for work. Yet, the obvious barriers of decades of structural decay, industrial graveyards and unreliable transport deter even brave investors.

If the government wants to straddle the great north-south divide, displayed most visibly in boom and abandonment, then it must see the unaffordability of London homes and the collapse of large areas of inner city housing in northern cities and towns, as linked problems with potentially linked solutions. It must find the key to spreading success in a small island like Britain away from the desperately

---

4   The 2002 Spending Review offers financial support for market restructuring, although at the time of writing no decisions have been made regarding the balance between spending on new housing and on restructuring housing markets.

congested South East to the cities only 100 to 300 miles away. In other developed countries such cities would be near neighbours and by now accelerating success stories. This study tries to understand the great housing contradiction of boom and abandonment from a northern perspective.

We focus on Manchester and Newcastle, two cities that we studied closely in 1997-98 when we gathered widespread evidence of incipient urban abandonment. We revisit the same inner neighbourhoods, then showing many signs of 'slow death' as we called it, some now facing large-scale slum clearance sometimes only a generation after the last attempt to right housing wrongs. Knocking down and rebuilding sometimes seems like playing Legoland games with poor communities since it is often the same places and even the same people who are repeatedly having their lives disrupted. Yet the signs of regrowth are now in places stronger than they were four years ago. We document progress and optimism wherever we find evidence of it.

The Slow Death of Great Cities, our earlier work, coincided with the start of the New Labour government. *Boom or Abandonment* documents four years of quickening problems in large areas of the north while also witnessing growing and often frenetic interventions to turn around the most disadvantaged urban areas. What we saw and heard underlined the sheer drama of the conflict, yet in many ways, solutions are almost within grasp. We examine the scale of the problem nationally, then within the two cities and four poor neighbourhoods at their core. We try to capture the reality of how it is for residents and staff, holding the line against 'desertification' of their much-loved communities. We try to spell out ways to change this imbalance of under and over-development. The government has announced Pathfinder Housing Renewal Initiatives to tackle housing abandonment, targeting the areas we studied, thus underlining the urgency of our message (ODPM, 2002b).

Declining demand for social housing is no longer being hushed-up. As performance targets for publicly funded landlords have sharpened, the sheer lack of demand and scale of empty properties have become more obvious. Urban abandonment is increasingly prominent in all tenures. Meanwhile a new pro-urban agenda is gathering pace as the conflicts between the costs of urban depletion and ever-expanding greenfield development are harder to ignore. The government has officially abandoned a 'predict and provide' approach to building, yet that is precisely how the regions of the North East, North West, Yorkshire and the Humber and West Midlands are setting their housing targets – based on household projections and a requirement on all local authorities to ensure provision to meet those targets. New draft Regional Planning Guidance for the North West (GONW, 2002a) makes a significant shift in favour of more constrained release of greenfield land.

Newcastle and Manchester have been battling with low demand problems for two decades, and have spearheaded attempts to reverse the urban exodus. We wanted to find out how things had moved on in these two cities over the past few years – whether there were developing signs of an urban renaissance, or whether the creeping abandonment we witnessed in 1997-98 had tightened its grip even further. Residents in the worst areas were sometimes quitting the sinking ship, sometimes firmly trapped in a vice of collapsing housing values, and sometimes actively choosing to stay despite deteriorating conditions.

> *Two years ago, I had two empty houses on one side, and now I have five empty on one side. We've got damp in our house because the roof has not been on that house next door for three years* (Manchester resident).

We were struck by the courage of residents battling against conditions that we saw ourselves, giving their all to pulling their neighbourhood back from the brink of collapse and attempting to rebuild their communities. Why were people prepared to invest so much time and energy in the face of such decline? Had the hundreds of efforts and the numerous buds of new growth we witnessed in the late 1990s born fruit, or had the enormity of the problems engulfed attempts to hang on to and revive these urban neighbourhoods?

The experiences of the two cities and the four neighbourhoods within them reflect the dilemmas facing all cities and towns affected by low demand. How do you attract jobs to reverse city population decline, stimulate demand for homes and make depleted areas attractive to earners? How do you encourage workers commuting into city centres to make their homes within the city boundaries and so boost both the population and wealth of the city – adding their human and social resources to the depleted community fabric? Is it possible to turn-around declining neighbourhoods whilst holding on to the existing communities and enhancing the existing physical fabric? Can cities attract 'urban pioneers' into half abandoned areas and will different social groups readily live together in city neighbourhoods? What can city chiefs learn from listening to the residents who, against all the odds, have not given up on their seemingly hopeless neighbourhoods and don't want to leave? How can the problems of social housing in cities – whose popularity has shrunk all round the country – be tackled? Can demolition help, or does it always fuel uncertainty and further population loss? How can the loss of structurally sound housing, sometimes built within the last fifteen years, possibly be justified when there are supposedly acute housing shortages? What alternatives are there? Can local changes in lettings and access rules and other management techniques make any difference to the course of such entrenched decline? And how can cities succeed when greenfield development outside their boundaries continues to offer attractive but subsidised housing options without incorporating the true costs of those choices? It is the infrastructure required to support low density new developments, their sharp dislocation from inner city housing markets which collapse further as a result, their selective incoming population which further polarises our society, along racial as well as social lines (Birmingham, 2002; Rogers and Power, 2000; Turok and Edge, 1999).

We first visited the four neighbourhoods experiencing housing demand problems ('City-Edge' and 'Valleyside' in Manchester and 'Bankside' and 'Riverview' in Newcastle) in 1997 and 1998.[5] We revisited them in 2000, 2001 and 2002, and kept in touch between visits.

In City-Edge, Manchester, a large urban regeneration company called New East Manchester is boosting confidence around the futuristic Commonwealth Games stadium and New Deal for Communities. Many smaller-scale initiatives are sprouting and expanding. Resident activists here are now much more upbeat and hopeful for the future than in 1997 – there is a strong feeling that the neighbourhood is through the worst and that a dedicated rescue attempt, though not without its set-backs, is pulling it further and further away from the edge. A lot has already been demolished but in a neighbourhood already pockmarked with bare land, much of the remaining housing may survive.

In Valleyside, there is no stadium to act as a magnet for investment. Some areas of older low-value private housing have seen tumbling house prices over the past few years, with owner occupiers finding it increasingly hard to sell – the kind of collapse that led to earlier abandonment in East Manchester. Here, and in other parts of North Manchester, some housing association stock is in serious trouble, and parts of the private terraced market have completely collapsed even though plummeting demand for council housing has finally levelled out. How can such a beleaguered community prevent confidence from falling further? New developments of owner occupied housing built in recent years are sometimes struggling to hold their value, yet they form a crucial element in the city's recovery plan. Are they simply moving the same people around?

In Bankside, Newcastle, large-scale demolition of mainly sound and upgraded housing is already underway as part of the council's explicit 'Going for Growth' strategy. The council plans to attract in developers to build an 'urban village' in place of the now blighted council estates, to create a more mixed community including some of the higher earners currently opting to live outside the city boundaries. In the face of strong community protests, one third of the whole area is due to remain, though demolition blight will make it a difficult place to live for some time and may actually drive more people away.

In Riverview, on the other side of Newcastle, smaller-scale demolition is underway and the talk is of an urban village being 'grafted on' to the existing community and in partnership with it. Nonetheless, larger-scale demolition has not been ruled out. Demand for council housing which dominates the area has plummeted to virtually zero.

Older terraced housing in these collapsing neighbourhoods often has no demand but we believe it could become popular in the future as it has in inner London, and

---

5   These neighbourhood names are invented to protect their identity. We do not wish to add to the stigma sometimes attached to the areas.

in popular northern cities like Durham, York, Chester and Lancaster. Places like Leicester, Ipswich, Bristol, Reading also demonstrate the attractions of the older Victorian stock and the charm it can add to potentially monotonous but strong employment centres. The historic street patterns and the variety that older housing adds to 'modern box-like' styles, is a potential asset that more affluent households have put to good use in many parts of the country. Is there a lesson in this housing success story for the troubled northern cities?

There is a chronic time-lag between the emptying of inner neighbourhoods – often exacerbated by demolition, regeneration plans and redevelopment – and repopulation (Power, 1987). Can anyone maintain decent living conditions on the ground for the remaining community while the public and private sectors try to attract urban pioneers into inner cities?

In sharp contrast to the survival struggles of inner neighbourhoods, the efforts to revive the city centres of both Newcastle and Manchester are bearing fruit in lavish style. Refurbishment, conversion and new residential development are boosting city centre populations in parallel with collapse and abandonment a mile or so away. Older, but refurbished properties sell for anything from £200,000 to over £1 million in both cities. Can the clear attractions of urban living be expanded outwards from the city centres and downwards towards middle and lower earners? Local politicians know that their very survival depends on making inner neighbourhoods which are located close to the centre work for people with choice but without a fortune.

> *I don't agree with saying: 'Well what you're faced with is a demographic trend that will mean there's going to be less people in this ring of the doughnut, therefore we should demolish most of the properties'. There has to be a redefinition of what Manchester is, what this community is. Otherwise you'll end up with it just being a series of roads with people travelling in from the posher suburbs to work in the centre...* (Manchester councillor).

To understand the political, organisational and social pressures that abandonment of good housing in the north is causing, we went back in 2000-02 to many of the same sources that had helped us formulate *The Slow Death of Great Cities?* Our main method of gathering new information from Manchester and Newcastle was to spend time in the cities and neighbourhoods, to interview the main actors, including residents, front line staff, city managers, estate agents. We also scoured the local newspapers, collected local reports and other documentary evidence, took photographs, and walked the streets where we had earlier documented empty property to measure how the problems had changed. Throughout the work we draw on our earlier study, on the work of Glen Bramley and colleagues at Herriott Watt University, Brenden Nevin and the CURS team at Birmingham University, Ivan Turok and colleagues at Glasgow University, the Chartered Institute of Housing, the Joseph Rowntree Foundation and government sources. We owe a great deal to their careful research into this problem (Power and Mumford, 1999;

Bramley *et al.*, 2000; Nevin *et al.*, 2001; Nevin, 2001; Holmans and Simpson,1999; Cabinet Office, 1999; Unpopular Housing Action Team, 1999; Social Exclusion Unit, 2001; Select Committee, 2002).

The book is divided into the following sections:

- Chapter 2 examines how the issue of abandonment and low demand has moved forward over the past four years; summarising the most recent evidence of demand trends; discussing causes of low demand and area abandonment; looking at developments in tackling these problems.
- Chapter 3 outlines the histories of four inner neighbourhoods experiencing these problems in acute form and describes their characteristics, based on our original interviews with around 120 staff and residents. We bring the picture up to date in Chapters 4 and 5.
- Chapters 4 and 5 examine the dramatic changes of direction and evolution of abandonment in Manchester and Newcastle.
- Chapter 6 recounts how it appears through the eyes of resident activists and front line staff in the neighbourhoods, using their own words to convey extreme urban decline and deeply committed personal efforts to reverse it.
- Chapter 7 examines the wider forces holding back an urban renaissance, and searches for ways to change the direction of run-down city neighbourhoods.

In spite of the great sensitivity of this issue and the obvious desire of all those directly involved to prevent further loss of confidence, people from different walks of life in both cities seemed anxious to speak out on what seemed an unmanageable problem. 'Talking up' progress to protect all gains, however small, did not stop people from sharing with us what has become a costly and often painful burden. Impoverished inner neighbourhoods in the fourth largest economy in the world are on the brink of collapse, if not in freefall, because of urban abandonment. Surely the seeds of a solution to Britain's imbalanced prosperity and growth lie in this unequal situation? The housing boom in the South East and in many other parts of the country is a long way from the places we describe here.

CHAPTER 2:
The changing picture of low demand and area abandonment

Low demand: a taboo subject

Just a short time ago, in 1997-98, there was little open discussion of low demand. However, media coverage of the problem was beginning to grow. For example, *Inside Housing* highlighted the fact that Newcastle, with a council stock of 38,000, had only 1,000 applicants on the waiting list with 'significant need', yet lost a fifth of its tenants, nearly 8,000, every year (*Inside Housing*, 1997). In 1997, a housing association chief executive went out on a limb by questioning the rationale for continued building, revealing his association's decision to focus investment on its existing housing:

> *Some years ago Bradford & Northern Housing Association took, in my view, a very brave decision under what was then referred to as our policy of prudence, to pull back from the ever escalating cost of underpinning a substantial development programme in favour of investing resources into improving our existing stock for the benefit of tenants. At the same time a major commitment was given to rebuild many of our communities in which we work, including re-creation of job opportunity schemes, and addressing deprivation arising from social decline, drug abuse and similar problems* (Oxley, 1997).

But up until 1998, Gateshead was apparently the only local authority, *'to have been brave enough to say that it will not encourage the development of new homes whilst it has problems of such low demand in its borough'* (Lowe *et al.*, 1998). On the whole, people were talking 'privately and quietly' about these problems, trying to avoid drawing attention to their particular area or organisation (Lowe *et al.*, 1998). One council manager we spoke to explained how, although Newcastle has been publicly raising the issue of low demand for a long time, until recently the council had tried to conceal demand problems in one part of the city:

> *I wouldn't say the East End has got worse – we probably don't try to hide it as much now – we're more open* (Senior manager, Newcastle, 2001).

Councils like Manchester, Liverpool and Newcastle had been battling with difficult-to-let housing since the 1970s (DoE, 1974; 1981). Newcastle predicted in 1976 that it would have a surplus of council housing by 1983 if it kept building (DoE, 1981). It did! In 1975, Gateshead councillors called for a halt to new council building but the recommendation was rejected for fear of being overtaken by neighbouring authorities. Letting problems were already concentrated in the north, but even in London there were empty flats on many large estates and the GLC was advertising vacancies in the *Evening Standard* as 'ready access' and 'hard to let' (DoE, 1981).

Yet the scale of difficulties in the mid 1990s, and the incipient abandonment of whole parts of neighbourhoods in all tenures seemed different from these difficult-to-let experiences of earlier decades. Many housing associations were only just beginning to recognise the problem through worrying increases in turnover of occupants. Reasons for keeping the lid on public discussion of low demand included fears that subsidy might be withdrawn, a housing orthodoxy that focused on unmet need and emphasised new development. There was an historic belief in waiting lists of applicants providing a measure of demand – long since disproved – and concern that vacancies might be blamed on poor housing management (Lowe *et al.*, 1998). Political power was still closely tied into size of stock and for housing associations, rate of growth.

At the same time as housing managers were cautiously expressing concerns about housing markets collapsing, projections of household growth and discussion of housing shortages were taking centre-stage. In our early interviews (in 1997 and 1998), it sometimes felt as though it was a relief for housing managers to tell us about the problems. At the front line there was a feeling of an unstoppable, crazy situation, involving a terrible waste of public money. Housing association officers would watch their own development departments building new properties, whilst knowing that they could not let their existing houses.

> *The constant obsession with building creates the low demand. That's all it is – there's nothing wrong with the [actual] buildings* (Newcastle housing association worker, 1998).

> *Our previous area manager was very development-orientated and he would do anything to stick houses anywhere...Personally, I don't think there's any need for more housing in the area – there's a complete over-supply of housing at the moment. But I couldn't give any cast iron guarantees that our association wouldn't develop there again* (Manchester housing association worker, 1998).

Residents in a Manchester neighbourhood tried to stop one housing association development in the early 1990s, but failed. Some of the properties soon proved unlettable:

> *It isn't that we didn't want the tenants, don't get us wrong, but...we felt the area itself already had enough houses, and we didn't want them. Also, it was taking away that green belt of land. We did actually lobby the town hall...but that was rubber stamped before we got there...Parts of it [are doing OK], but*

a stone's throw away, they can't let them. Nobody wants to go and live over there. You can see that by all the boardings on the windows. There is one single row where nobody wants to go, which is a shame because they're nice houses (Resident, 2000).

Council housing officers would watch new estates being built next door to the properties they managed and then see their tenants move into them, leaving half-empty, destabilised estates behind.

I would say we had our arms tied behind our backs. If housing associations want to poach our tenants then they are free to do so, and there's nothing we can do about it. The worst thing is that they're building the same kind of stuff as we're pulling down (Manchester council housing managers, 1998).

One problem was the inevitable time lag, of two to three years, between new development proposals being allocated funding and actually becoming ready for occupation. Over this time, levels of demand for housing within the areas could change significantly. And there was a belief, albeit easy to criticise with hindsight, that providing modern housing would actually generate demand and give the areas new life:

This was happening at a time when the full extent of the problem was not clear and when it was generally thought that the availability of new housing might stimulate demand and revitalise these areas (Manchester Housing, 2002).

The situation was made worse by government policy in the mid to late 1980s encouraging alternative building by housing associations and focusing grants on the cheapest regions, i.e. those where there was least need. This was ridiculous since the politics of housing is driven by numbers, this would create the biggest *numbers* of units, regardless of whether they were actually wanted.

Lowe *et al.* (1998) concluded:

There is clear evidence that, due largely to economic restructuring, in some parts of the country there is simply too much housing. Housing abandonment in the inner cities and on peripheral housing estates really represents the filtering down of this problem, despite some more localised explanations. The idea of an over-supply of housing cuts against all the orthodoxies in the national models, estimates and projections of housing need.

There is now widespread acknowledgement of the low demand problem at all levels, partly due to the change of government in 1997 which, once established, enabled the 'legitimisation' of low demand as a policy issue (Bramley *et al.*, 2000). As part of the development of its neighbourhood renewal strategy, the government even set up an Unpopular Housing Action Team which reported in 1999:

Unpopular housing and neighbourhood abandonment is increasing in both the public and private sectors...We must solve the problems of unpopular and abandoned housing in order to stabilise communities and stop wasting valuable resources (Unpopular Housing Action Team, 1999).

The incidence of low demand

A majority of local authorities and registered social landlords are experiencing low demand in at least some of their rented stock. Two to three years ago, 12 per cent of the national council stock and 8 per cent of the registered social landlord stock was found to be affected by low demand, compared with under 3 per cent of the private stock (Bramley *et al.*, 2000).[1] All regions are affected at least to some extent, but problems are strongly concentrated in the north and midlands. Problems in London and the south are concentrated in particularly unpopular estates with serious social problems. In these areas, where overall demand is high, most properties can be let although demolition of the least popular estates has helped this. Low demand for private housing is concentrated in northern and midland urban areas. Table 2.1 shows the scale of problems in all tenures and their regional variation.

Table 2.1: Proportion of low demand housing stock by tenure and region (%)

Region	Local authority	Registered social landlord	Private sector
North West	23	19	8.6
North East	22	16	2.8
Yorks & the Humber	13	14	3.8
East Midlands	11	13	2.5
West Midlands	11	8	3.9
South West	4	3	0.7
East of England	4	9	0.9
South East	4	4	0.2
London	6	3	0.4
England	12	8	2.6

Source: Bramley *et al.* (2000) based on a postal survey of LAs & RSLs undertaken in the late 1990s.

There is clearly a stark north-south divide in the incidence of low demand, with the midlands suffering in a way more similar to the northern regions. In the West Midlands, *'planners have earmarked large chunks of the region's cities for massively increased housing investment in a bid to cure creeping low demand'* (*Inside Housing*, 2001a). But they are also planning large-scale demolition of

---

1   More recently, the Department of Transport, Environment and the Regions reported estimates of 880,000 homes in areas of low demand, 59 per cent of which are private and 41 per cent social housing (DTLR, 2002d).

council housing (Birmingham City Council, 2001). Minority ethnic communities in this region, unable to access new, expensive, mostly white suburbs, are often 'trapped' in inner neighbourhoods, *'propping up areas...that would otherwise face collapse and abandonment'* (Bright, 2001). But focus group work with minority ethnic communities in the north and midlands has shown how preferences within these groups are shifting away from smaller terraced neighbourhoods towards more suburban areas (Nevin, 2001). Ironically, minority ethnic communities in areas with low demand for council housing have difficulty getting access to it (Birmingham City Council, 2001; Ratcliffe *et al.*, 2001).

There are also huge variations within regions and even within cities (Cabinet Office, 1999; Holmans and Simpson, 1999) and housing markets have become increasingly polarised (Nevin *et al.*, 2001).

Worsening demand problems

Recent studies have identified the mid 1990s as the visible point of the downturn in demand, and shown that the problem is worsening in the north and midlands. (Holmans and Simpson, 1999; Bramley *et al.*, 2000; Ford and Pawson, 2001.) For example, between 1993-94 and 1997-98 there was an increase in estimated departures from council housing of 29,000 a year in the north whilst there was no real change in the south outside London. And between 1994 and 1998, vacancies in the north rose by 1.2 per cent compared to only 0.1 per cent in the south outside London. The London council vacancy rate in 1998 was actually slightly lower than in 1994 (Holmans and Simpson, 1999).

Over the period 1996-99, the number of housing association homes classed as low demand rose by two thirds, and parts of the East Midlands suffered particularly badly. In Corby, housing associations reported that more than three quarters of their stock (78 per cent) was in low demand (Ford and Pawson, 2001).

The latest figures are shocking – about 10,000 new housing association homes built since 1988 are in low demand. Post-1988 homes account for one in four low demand housing association dwellings in Yorkshire and the Humber, and one in five in the North East (Ford and Pawson, 2002). The now infamous 'Dr Henry Russell Court' affair involved the demolition of 50 brand new housing association homes in Newcastle just three years after they were built, some without ever having been lived in. This scenario may be replayed many times over.

Causes of low demand – what fuels the problems?

Economic and migration trends

The downturn in demand in the mid 1990s occurred at around the same time as an increase in migration from the north and midlands to the south – as the 'attractiveness of the south returned' when its economy recovered after the recession of the early 1990s (Holmans and Simpson, 1999). However, even more significant has been the migration out of cities to their surrounding suburbs of people wanting greenfield homes rather than inner city estates or terraces. Few new private homes were being built within cities. Nearly two thirds of outward migration from the metropolitan areas of the midlands and north between 1991-98 was either to other parts of the same region or to the rest of the north and West Midlands (Bate *et al.*, 2000). While the north-south drift typically amounts to a net flow of around 30,000 people a year, urban-rural movement amounts to a net flow of 90,000 people a year from the six metropolitan counties and London (Cox, 2000). This 'counter-urbanisation cascade' continues all the way down the urban hierarchy – from city to suburb to fringe to town to rural area (Champion, 2000).

There is now far more recognition of the wider causes of low demand; it is not just caused by community factors such as concentrated deprivation in highly stigmatised neighbourhoods. Wider economic and migration trends play a crucial role. Local factors help shape particular neighbourhoods; but the underlying problem of district-wide and regional over-supply has to exist before area abandonment can take root in specific locations. Broadly, the location of low demand reflects economic decline, and associated outward migration trends which have hit northern cities hardest (Power and Mumford, 1999; Unpopular Housing Action Team, 1999). Low demand has long roots, going back many decades (DoE, 1981; Power and Mumford, 1999). The full effects of over-supply may have been masked for over a decade by policy responses (such as changing lettings procedures and advertising vacancies from as early as the 1970s), which eventually could not mop up the surplus any longer (DoE, 1981; Bramley *et al.*, 2000).

Ironically, the North West's recent economic growth appears to be exacerbating the net outward movement from its older towns and cities. The region is experiencing the longest period of economic growth since the war, and there is a very strong relationship between the fall in male unemployment and the fall in social housing waiting lists over the period 1992-97 (Nevin *et al.*, 2001). Regeneration workers we interviewed in both Newcastle and Manchester were worried that, without significant improvements to quality of life in the inner urban areas, new job opportunities could further reduce housing demand as they would enable existing residents to move out. Liverpool has also found that increasing job opportunities and wealth in the city simply lead to more people leaving it.

The overall surplus of housing, and consequent low house prices which make it easier to move into owner occupation outside the cities, fuel this pattern. Both cities are already concerned about the level of inward commuting they are experiencing. Amongst the staff in one Manchester neighbourhood housing office, only the team leader lived locally. The other ten staff all lived right outside Manchester – within a ten mile radius of the city – and commuted into work (Housing team leader, 2001). Nevin *et al.* (2001) found that the local authorities worst affected by low demand were also the authorities experiencing the largest inward commuting; people choosing to live separately from where they work. This has been closely documented in Bradford (Bradford, 2000).

There are still many people moving into cities, at the same time others are moving out.

> *Even in the most extreme case, there were at least seven people moving in for every ten moving out* (Cox, 2000).

But in cities like Birmingham, Liverpool, Manchester and Newcastle, the net outward movement has been large enough to lead to 'sizeable reductions' in population (Cox, 2000). The imbalance has then been reinforced by continued over-building around the cities:

> *We found authorities releasing greenfield land for housing that was in excess of immediate needs...The result is that new housing on some urban edges is increasing more rapidly than demand, and competing with older housing within the city* (Unpopular Housing Action Team, 1999).

> *New building on greenfield sites continues to undermine efforts to renew inner urban areas* (Select Committee, 2002).

Over-building and projections of housing need

The consequences of releasing too much green land are starkly demonstrated by the experience of the North West. In key districts within this region, planned new building vastly exceeds forecast increases in households. When vacancies in the existing stock are also brought into the equation, the surplus of supply over demand is shown to be even greater. Of course, some housing will be removed from the existing stock, but the excess provision is so large that there will be a housing surplus of around 20 properties for every projected new household. Table 2.2 shows this wasteful and self-destructive over-supply of homes, mostly built on greenfields, and directly feeding the abandonment of sound housing in the poorer inner neighbourhoods (Unpopular Housing Action Team, 1999; Rogers and Power, 2000).

Table 2.2: Planned and take-up figures for housing provision – North West

	Forecast annual increase in households	Annual flow of new dwellings	Total outstanding planning permissions (dwellings) at various dates in 98/99	Total vacant dwellings at 01.04.98
East Lancashire	1,110	1,425	8,360	13,700
Salford, Trafford, Manchester, Wigan, Bolton and Bury	2,550	2,550 (excludes replacements)	17,390	30,500
Merseyside (excluding St Helens)	3,070	3,525	11,270	28,200

Source: Unpopular Housing Action Team (1999) based on data supplied by the Government Office for the North West.

Recent figures for Yorkshire and the Humber tell a similar story. The CURS team at Birmingham calculate a net annual increase in the regional housing stock of around 12,300 dwellings per annum, compared to a projected household increase of 12,000. If current trends in dwelling gains and losses and in household formation continue, this annual surplus will continue to build up over time. It will lead to even higher vacancy levels – already standing at 93,100 properties in all tenures in 2000 (Lee *et al.*, 2002). This points to a need to change the way regional housing targets are derived and reviewed.

This illustrates the stark conflict between a 'national projected shortage of hundreds of thousands of homes' and serious over-supply in these regions. Of course, predicted household growth makes more sense when broken down by region: much more of the growth in population and households will be concentrated in the south if recent migration trends continue (Holmans and Simpson, 1999). And there are many uncertainties in the projections – not least the fact that over two thirds of projected households are single. The Urban Task Force suggests that many young single people are likely to want to share, and that two thirds cannot afford even a cheap home of their own (Urban Task Force, 1999). Amongst the 30 to 50 age-group, projected to be the fastest growing group of single person households, accommodation choices will depend on many factors such as supply, cost, family circumstances etc. (Hooper *et al.*, 1998).

There is an apparent paradox in the existence of homelessness alongside low demand. The causes of homelessness have long been connected with rules of eligibility, behaviour and social dislocation rather than actual supply (Cullingworth, 1979). Homelessness is often about much more than the basic need for shelter. As well as the need for support packages, people are often scared to go and live in low demand areas even if their present situation is very unsatisfactory. Fear of physical danger is often coupled with worries about becoming trapped in an unpopular area with no hope of transferring elsewhere (Unpopular Housing Action Team, 1999). This underlines the point that homelessness figures are a poor basis for calculating the need for new housing provision. Waiting lists are not a good indicator either, not least because about 40 per cent of applicants disappear each year through finding other housing solutions, changing plans and circumstances (Prescott-Clark *et al.*, 1994). Bramley *et al.* (2000) propose a more accurate measure of housing need, taking full account of affordability and existing supply in all its forms. Understanding how the whole housing market works is crucial.

Tenure and housing type

Urban population decline affects all tenures. But high concentrations of social housing seem to accelerate the decline of particular areas as 87 per cent of people say they would prefer to buy and therefore do not see social housing as a good choice (Unpopular Housing Action Team, 1999). Social housing in cities concentrates deprivation as often it is only those with no choice who stay or move in to a tenure increasingly seen as a last resort. The ready availability of new and relatively cheap private housing around northern cities makes it easier for people to opt out of social housing and into owner occupation.

One sign of council housing's changing role is increasing turnover, seen even in areas not reporting demand problems, though the increase is steeper in low demand areas (Bramley *et al.*, 2000). The latest figures show that in spite of a net reduction in the overall social housing stock of 21 per cent between 1981 and 1998 due mainly to the right to buy, the number of lettings to new tenants in 1998-99 was 18 per cent higher than in 1980-81. Total lettings to new tenants increased year on year over the 1990s, until 1998-99 when they tailed off slightly. Figure 2.1 shows this. There were still nearly 100,000 more social housing lettings in 1998-99 than ten years earlier, in spite of there being 300,000 *fewer* properties (Wilcox, 2001).

Figure 2.1: Local authority and housing association lettings to new tenants in England (thousands)

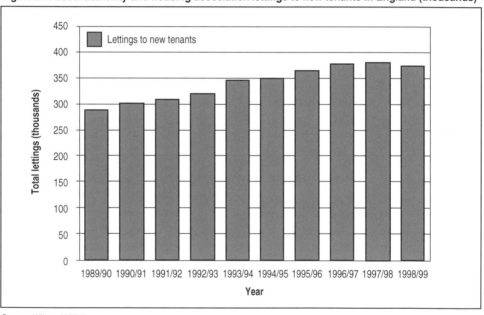

Source: Wilcox (2001).

This growing instability is linked to the changing demographic profile of council housing; it houses both an aging population (subject to higher mortality rates) and a growing number of younger households (who are more mobile) (Nevin *et al.*, 2001). Increasingly, many people see the social rented sector as a temporary move (Holmans and Simpson, 1999). According to a recent Housing Corporation survey, four fifths of young housing association tenants under the age of 25 plan to move out of the sector within the next ten years (Hebden, 2001).

The other major 'problem' type of housing is the pre-1919 terrace in low demand cities. Its value in many major conurbations is collapsing as people opt for plentiful, newly built private housing.

> *Those who can afford [to buy] move out of the rented sector into owner occupation, often leapfrogging the lower priced properties in the process* (Government Office for the North East *et al.*, 2001).

This terraced housing is seen as 'obsolete' because it can fail to meet modern housing standards and aspirations, particularly when present in large quantities (Unpopular Housing Action Team, 1999; Nevin *et al.*, 2001). The terraces used to be the first step on the housing ladder. Now, young families and other first-time buyers can afford to go straight into semi-detached housing which is available relatively cheaply, often outside city boundaries and yet within easy reach of city centres. In this way, inner city terraced housing stock can fall off the bottom of the property ladder in a situation of over-supply.

> *The days of the terraced house are gone! No-one wants 2-up, 2-down, old terraced stock any more* (East Manchester estate agent, 1998).

> *We bought our house for £25,000 five years ago. Now we would be looking at £8,000 – £10,000* (North Manchester resident, 1998).

This is very neighbourhood specific. Whereas many terraced houses of all sizes stand empty in North and East Manchester, in parts of South Manchester such as Didsbury they are snapped up. There is a similar polarisation in demand for terraced housing in Newcastle – terraced homes are highly sought after and selling for high prices in attractive areas of the city, yet are unsaleable and unlettable just a few miles away in parts of the West and East End.

Housing managers we spoke to in low demand neighbourhoods often linked problems in the private terraces to the surrounding deprivation, particularly in large estates of council housing nearby. Past council housing allocation policies targeted the most needy, thereby concentrating deprivation. Full housing benefit, paying all rental costs for families in this situation, can compound rather than solve problems. As well as continuing to 'pull in' the most vulnerable who have nowhere else to go, areas with high concentrations of council housing 'push out' better off and younger residents who aspire to buy. Households with difficult and un-neighbourly behaviour often get caught up in this process as they are evicted from better areas and end up concentrated in areas where few others want to go. The knock-on effects of anti-social behaviour on demand are all embracing. The right to buy is not an attractive option where neighbourhood conditions are in steep decline.

Nearby private terraced housing (traditionally housing working people) is drawn into this polarising process because concentrated deprivation puts extra pressures on services that serve the whole neighbourhood, poor conditions spill over, the whole area gains a bad reputation, and these terraces cannot then maintain their value. A vicious circle is established with renting and owning, council estates and private terraces, newer and older properties all getting caught up in the spiral.

As first-time buyers increasingly avoid the inner city terraces, this housing tends to shift from owner occupation to the private rented sector. For example, the level of private renting in Blackburn has virtually doubled since 1991 (Holmans and Simpson, 1999).

> *There's a lot of negative equity. People can't sell them so they let them to service their debt and live somewhere else. This is perpetuating the change in tenure* (Manchester private sector officer, 1998).

Mainstream working households are wary of buying, and lenders are often reluctant to lend, below a price threshold of £20,000-£30,000 as such low values are taken as a sign of a worsening housing market in which prices are set to fall even further in the future (Bramley *et al.*, 2000). Manchester's demand problems are in part illustrated by the fact that over 17 per cent of houses sold in the city in 1999-00 cost less than £20,000 (Manchester, 2001d), whereas nationally just under 4 per cent of sales are below £20,000 (Bramley *et al.*, 2000).

> *I can't think of a better measure [than house prices] of whether people want to live in a particular neighbourhood or city. The price people are willing to pay in an open market is a superb integrator of all of their different assessments of the locality – the quality of its schools and other public services, the quality of the physical environment, the risk of being a victim of crime* (Schoon, 2001).

Figure 2.2 shows the concentration of low-priced sales by region.

Figure 2.2: Incidence of sales under £20,000 by region

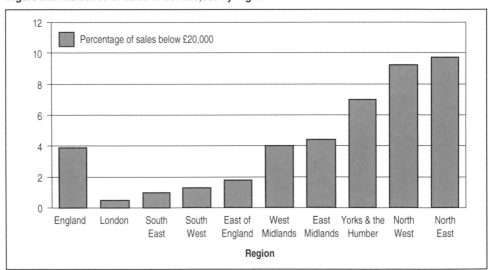

Source: Bramley *et al.* (2000) based on Land Registry data.

For speculative private landlords, in contrast to ordinary buyers, the returns can be sizeable in low demand neighbourhoods. It is possible for a landlord who buys a home for £3,000, to get a gross rate of return of 75-110 per cent per annum compared with a national rate of return of 8-9 per cent (Bramley *et al.*, 2000). Unscrupulous landlords exploit the housing benefit system. For example, in the Liverpool New Deal for Communities area, housing benefit rent could be up to £80 per week, compared to housing association rent of around £42 (Select Committee, 2002). In these areas the private rented sector houses a very high proportion of young men and housing benefit recipients. For many properties in low demand areas, *'...private renting is probably an intermediate step along the road to abandonment'* (Bramley *et al.*, 2000).

The shift from owner occupation to private renting exacerbates instability as private tenants are generally far more mobile than owners. This mobility has increased dramatically since the 1980s. Nationally, the proportion of private tenants who had moved in the previous year increased from 24 per cent in 1984 to 40 per cent in 1994-95 and it was still that high in 1999-00. This compares with 12 per cent of social renters and just 7 per cent of owners moving in the previous year (DTLR, 2001a).

Intra-regional and intra-city variations in demand

Demand for housing often varies considerably within as well as across city boundaries. The paths of popular areas continue to diverge from areas on the edge of abandonment:

> *...in Liverpool and Manchester we are seeing the emergence of thriving niche markets in the city centre with the first £1 million apartment recently being sold in down town Manchester* (Nevin *et al.*, 2001).

In the public sector too, demand varies enormously within cities. There are five year waiting lists for social rented housing in South Manchester, compared with no queues at all for some areas in the north and east of the city (Manchester bid, 2001). Such polarisation is inevitable as area depletion pushes people away, creating demand for different types of housing in different kinds of neighbourhoods (Power, 2000).

The availability of new build housing on the edges of, or outside, city boundaries throws the problems of unpopular inner terraces into even sharper relief. Holmans and Simpson (1999) and Nevin *et al.* (2001) argue that older inner city terraced housing markets are almost entirely disconnected from such outer new build markets. As the affluent suburban market grows, offering more choice and becoming largely self-sustaining, the contrast between this and the inner city terraced market becomes even more stark. Not only is the older market less self-sustaining because its population is older and so there is less 'natural growth', but there is very little inflow to it from elsewhere. This also explains why low-value new private homes built within such older neighbourhoods will often, after a short time delay, increase empty properties locally if clearance doesn't take place at the same time (Nevin *et al.*, 2001). Although the inward flow is almost non-existent, this is not true for the outward flow which continues apace.

Neighbourhood facilities are seen to be much better outside cities than in declining inner urban areas.

> *The major new developments around Britain's towns and cities have been on the urban periphery...Investment in transport, schools and a range of other facilities has tended to follow the growth in population associated with new housing investment. Consequently the quality and range of facilities in those areas has become strikingly different to that in the older urban centres* (Centre for Urban and Regional Studies, Birmingham, in Select Committee, 2002).

Proportionally, the increase in new dwellings started for private owners in 1996, 97 and 98, when the housing market strengthened nationally, was as large in the north as in the south (Holmans and Simpson, 1999). Given that new starts are very sensitive to demand, the authors argue that these figures show that demand for new housing has been retained and that the collapse of local housing markets is not part of a more general slump in demand in the north. However, supply influences demand, making it easier for smaller households to multiply but also, in the end, swamping the market as is now happening around Manchester and Newcastle.

The new house-building starts are in part a hopeful sign, suggesting that there is demand for housing in the north and that clearly the region as a whole is not being abandoned. However, they do raise difficult questions about the future of the very large social rented sector, the inner city privately owned terraces and the current approach to meeting demand. Do you just respond to demand for new dwellings on the edges of cities, and deal with the resulting over-supply by demolishing large swathes of inner city private terraced housing and council housing, much of which is sound and recently improved? This strategy was broadly laid out in Newcastle's *Going for Growth* plan. Or do you develop an 'urban pioneer' approach and try to shift aspirations, making existing housing and older neighbourhoods more attractive through 'choice-based lettings' as the Dutch are doing, through tenure mixing which most people say they prefer, through clever conversions that redesign existing spaces into attractive modern homes, through environmental improvements and so forth? If builders were forced to add the environmental and social costs of greenfield building to the price of new homes, would they still be as keen to spread 'little boxes' over the countryside? More likely, inner city neighbourhoods would quickly regain value.

In Chapters 4 and 5 we examine how the cities of Manchester and Newcastle are grappling with these dilemmas.

Tackling low demand

There is much less consensus about the way forward than there is about the causes of low demand. Demolition is a popular route because the immediate problem is too many homes and too few people. Between 1991 and 1997, government figures indicate that 40,000 council homes were demolished, most in areas with high levels of unpopular housing (Mapstone, 2001). Maintaining empty homes that cannot be let is very costly, and boarded up properties lower the image of an area. Getting rid of the properties seems an obvious solution.

> *There was I, this new person in post, thinking 'nobody wants to live here, we're losing so much money and we're never going to get it back in the foreseeable future – I think we need to demolish – particularly because of the [structural problems]'...All my thoughts and feelings about what I was experiencing in the area told me 'you've just got to cut your losses'...* (Housing association officer, 1998).

Government is concerned that private sector clearance levels have been too low (around 2,000 per year during the 1990s). At this rate, the average house would have to last thousands of years. Cities such as Burnley, Leeds, Salford argue that a new phase of selective inner city clearance is inevitable (Bramley *et al.*, 2000). Strategies to tackle low demand could involve the clearance of 75,000 homes in the North West alone, bringing back images of the large-scale slum clearances of the 1960s, and often provoking intense local opposition (Brauner, 2001).

Many of the people we spoke to in low demand neighbourhoods worried about the disruption of communities and the 'contagious' effects of demolition.

> *It is like a cancer almost...It'll just spread like diseases spread. You've got a little neighbourhood where you've got a lot of empty blocks that are then gutted for demolition...but it's a while before that all starts happening. In the meantime, the effect of them is that they lead to surrounding blocks going into decline. So, because it's a very slow process, it affects other blocks and then it's almost a self-fulfilling prophecy when you say 'well, this area we'll demolish a few' – you end up demolishing quite a lot* (Manchester council housing manager).

The Policy Action Team report on Unpopular Housing, whilst arguing that clearance could form an important part of an area's renewal strategy, stressed that demolition can actually exacerbate problems and sometimes even 'precipitate abandonment':

> *Demolition must be used with care. We found instances where it triggered further decline and broke up communities...Local authorities must make clear the purpose of demolition, to avoid confusing tenants and precipitating abandonment. In Bradford and Newcastle phased demolition strategies*

sometimes encouraged stigmatisation and uncertainty and tenants moved out ahead of schedule (Unpopular Housing Action Team, 1999).

Again, over-supply facilitates this cascading exodus.

Residents, whilst by no means always being anti-demolition, often stress the need for environmental and social improvements (such as reducing crime and unemployment), in contrast to the physical measures like demolition that housing managers often feel are necessary. This came across in Bramley *et al.*'s surveys of residents and housing managers, and in our own interviews. It echoes the slum clearance experience of earlier decades, summed up by the Byker resident who commented that all she had wanted was an inside toilet, but instead they knocked down her house (Konttinen, 1983).

The government's emphasis is on an urban renaissance, reversing 'counter-urbanisation', with strategies and services being co-ordinated around the needs of each neighbourhood. But the neighbourhood renewal strategy is struggling to tackle severe low demand problems and failing housing markets (Select Committee, 2002). The government has set a national target of achieving a turn-around in declining demand by 2010 (Social Exclusion Unit, 2001), but the Housing Corporation is doubtful this target can be met within current resource levels (Evans, 2001a). The recent select committee report on empty homes concluded that low demand would not be turned around by 2010 (Select Committee, 2002).

Managing unpopular housing areas is expensive in people, security measures and higher repair costs resulting from higher turnover. Yet the north's share of housing capital allocations increasingly reflects the region's general over-supply of low-cost housing. The low demand indicator is not used to enhance the allocation of resources to housing associations and there are precious few resources for the more general environmental investments that are necessary to attract firms and jobs into northern cities. Many argue that there should be substantial additional funding for homelessness and projected housing need in order to redirect resources southwards. In addition, southern authorities are calling for an affordability indicator that will concentrate spending on providing more and cheaper homes where people need them, in the south (Martin, 2001, Housing Corporation 2002). This only reinforces the growing 'tilt' of economic growth towards southern regions.

New national planning guidance – such as the introduction of the 'sequential approach' to encourage brownfield development ahead of greenfield – would if vigorously enforced ensure better use of urban land and existing buildings. However, although VAT on brownfield development has been cut it has not been removed altogether, whereas greenfield building carries no VAT at all. The government is under increasing pressure to equalise VAT: *'We recommend that Government reduces VAT to 5 per cent on housing refurbishment projects and raises it to 5 per cent on new build, private greenfield schemes'* (Select Committee, 2002).

There is too little evidence of the sequential approach yet being rigorously applied in practice (Manchester and Newcastle City Councils, 2001; Select Committee, 2002). To make a real difference, it needs to apply between cities and outer local authorities, for example Newcastle, North and South Tyneside, Sunderland, or Manchester, Stockport and the eight other authorities that make up Greater Manchester.

> *There has been little attempt to develop solutions which assess the problems in the context of the wider conurbation and use regional policies to bring together supply and demand...Regional Planning Guidance should develop a sequential test that limits new house building on greenfield sites until the regeneration of the inner urban areas is substantially complete* (Select Committee, 2002).

The government is taking a whole range of action to reduce inequalities at a local level. This action includes area-targeted regeneration initiatives with significant extra funding such as New Deal for Communities and Sure Start (which works with both pre-school children and their parents to ensure that children are 'ready to thrive' when they get to school). It also includes national initiatives such as the New Deal for Employment, and the working families tax credit, aimed at 'making work pay'. Unemployment is already falling faster than the national average in 19 out of the 20 highest unemployment areas (Social Exclusion Unit, 2001). And there are multi-pronged efforts to improve education and health. Schools in the poorest areas are improving their basic literacy and numeracy faster than the average.

There appears to have been some progress in reducing disparity in economic conditions between regions: the difference in unemployment between regions is now half that of the mid 1980s (Cabinet Office, 1999). However, more recent figures suggest that the north-south divide has actually widened on some measures; in the first three years of the Labour government, GDP per head in the North East fell by a point to 23 per cent below the national average, while London was almost 30 per cent above (Hetherington, 2001).

Some research reports broach the subject of 'managed decline', arguing the need to accept that some areas are unsaveable. For example:

> *Taken to its logical conclusion, prioritising investment on sustainability criteria may imply the planned rundown of certain areas where the dynamic of decline is so well-entrenched that commitment of further resources seems unlikely to guarantee positive returns* (Bramley et al., 2000).

It is important to tackle really difficult questions like these. Regeneration funds are far from limitless, and hard decisions have to be made about priorities for spending. But the trouble with descriptions like 'managed decline' is that they are so abstract and far removed from people's daily lives. The practicalities and human implications of such proposals are hard to imagine. For the people living in the areas affected and for housing managers responsible for their condition, it seems an 'unmanageable' way to approach the contradictions of a housing boom and housing collapse, under and over-supply. The approach that offers the best alternative prospect is what Americans call 'smart growth', where the outer boundary of the city is tightly constrained while major efforts are made to improve conditions in the city and attract the investment that would otherwise 'fly to the suburbs' (Katz, 2002). We could call this 'managed regrowth' for inner cities. But we know that it will only work if the tap of greenfield land is firmly turned off in the large hinterland around these cities (Newcastle City Council, 2002; GONW, 2002).

There may be alternatives to large-scale demolition. In a small area of Manchester, as part of a Home Zone initiative, residents are involved in 'area redesign' that thins out the small, densely packed two-up, two-down houses while retaining the residential character of the area. Adjacent terraced houses can be linked together, back yards and alleyways combined to create larger gardens; iron railings restored or installed to create small, protective front areas. There are many other ideas (Bramley *et al.*, 2000; Rogers and Power, 2000; Manchester 2001d). These can make existing homes more desirable and reduce overall supply, whilst at the same time providing the chance to work with and retain people in the existing community who want to stay. In Chapter 4 we show how the building of the commonwealth stadium in East Manchester, combined with a whole range of other investments at the front line such as New Deal for Communities, neighbourhood wardens and 'talking up' the area, is helping to boost confidence in some of Manchester's most deprived neighbourhoods.

In Newcastle, a 'homesteading scheme' in North Benwell attracted a lot of interest. The council acquired a number of unsaleable, unlettable flats in the area from private owners, converted them back into five houses, and sold them for £1 each last year. A condition of sale was that the purchaser must invest at least £12,000 on improvements, and the council would then spend another £25,000 on each home. Despite derision in the national press that homes could be bought so cheaply, more than 100 people applied to buy the houses, and five people were selected. It seems that so far these purchasers are happy with their decision and the local community feels the project has increased confidence within the area. It is too soon to know whether such schemes can eventually stimulate the area's property market and result in higher house prices (Regeneration and Renewal, 2002). The biggest challenge is to scale up the initiatives that work at a micro-level with intense inputs and attention to detail at a more macro level.

Some northern councils and housing associations are encouraging London based tenants to move to low demand areas in the north and midlands. So far, the numbers moving are small; in the hundreds last year. But where people have taken this decision to relocate, it has nearly always worked well. A survey of former Haringey residents who have moved to other parts of the country found that 90 per cent of movers had no regrets following their move, and the remaining 10 per cent did not have plans to return (Select Committee, 2002). Burnley has attracted around 65 Londoners so far, and the council believes that many more could follow if it could find the money to get its properties in the right condition (Cooke, 2002). Of course, linking incomers with jobs, and helping them feel settled in their new area will be crucial to the long-term success of such initiatives. In Rochdale, the council has encouraged groups of families to move from over-crowded parts of the town into low demand areas. These moves have often involved minority ethnic families. With high levels of police and community support, such moves can reduce racial segregation, improve families' housing conditions and boost demand in previously unpopular areas (Select Committee, 2002). Since June 2002, the Housing Corporation and Office for the Deputy Prime Minister have been funding a scheme set up by London councils that aims to help 600 families relocate to empty properties in the north by May 2003. The scheme includes providing advice on training, education and employment opportunities (*Inside Housing*, 2002c).

An exciting, potentially significant national development is in the pipeline in the form of a 'market renewal fund' to 'shore up declining areas before the rot sets in' (Martin, 2002).[2] A group of local authorities and housing organisations in the north and midlands have argued for between £6 billion and £8 billion over the next ten years. Each market renewal area is likely to contain between 40,000 and 150,000 homes, comprising a number of neighbourhoods which will each require an 'area development framework', and co-ordination between local authorities, registered social landlords, private landlords, community groups and individual homeowners (Lipman, 2002).

> *A new approach to housing market renewal must be based on the whole conurbation or sub-region* (Select Committee, 2002).

The market renewal and restructuring proposals highlight the complexities of regenerating multi-tenure neighbourhoods. For example, there are more than 50 housing associations in Birmingham's inner city, each with its own separate business plan. In the absence of confidence or an overall strategic framework, some may pull investment out while others continue to invest (Nevin, 2001). Market renewal partnerships should fill this strategic gap. The government has announced nine pilot areas, including the areas in Manchester and Newcastle that we are involved with.

In England, many northern city centres are experiencing a new lease of life but are surrounded by blighted 'wastelands' (Hetherington, 2001). Will the new life in the city centres be sustained? And will the dynamics that are driving city recovery at the centre spill over into the adjacent neighbourhoods experiencing such sharp decline, helped by the new initiatives we describe?

---

2   The setting up of nine 'pathfinders' and John Prescott's statement on the 2002 Spending Review (ODPM, 2002b) gives a strong indication that significant levels of investment will soon be made available.

The alternative is that our northern cities will consist of a city centre
surrounded by a devastated no man's land encompassed in turn by suburbia
(Select Committee, 2002).

The pressure to revive the inner neighbourhoods is likely to increase as sprawl
problems grow and cutting carbon dioxide emissions to combat global warming
becomes more urgent. People will fight ever harder to protect the remaining
countryside. In reaction to ugly sprawl, Jonathan Dimbleby has proposed a new
National Park covering all remaining green areas of the South East (Riba, 2002).
And the much smaller, often childless households that many of us now live in,
will want a different kind of dwelling, located nearer to the amenities that support
more affluent, younger and older lifestyles. These changes may drive incomers to
reclaim the spaces left empty by radical social and economic shifts. More people
may begin to choose compact city living instead of spread-out, service-deficient,
car-dependent, greenfield homes.

CHAPTER 3:
City extremes

In this chapter we tell the inside story of four urban neighbourhoods experiencing low demand and incipient abandonment – City-Edge and Valleyside in Manchester and Bankside and Riverview in Newcastle. We briefly explain the history of each neighbourhood; we describe their main characteristics and their environment. We trace their development and show the links to today's demand problems. These accounts are based on our original interviews with residents and front line staff in many services – housing, schools, police, community, health and social services. We also talked to senior managers and drew on a wide range of background reports.

In Chapters 4 (Manchester) and 5 (Newcastle) we go on to look in detail at current conditions in the neighbourhoods, and the action being taken to tackle problems.

Neighbourhood characteristics

All four neighbourhoods are dominated by social renting – ranging from just over a half in Bankside to more than four fifths in Riverview, between double and quadruple the national average. All the neighbourhoods have extremely deprived populations – around a half of their working age populations are not in work, study or training, double the national average of 24 per cent.

The four areas are predominantly white – in 1991, 95 per cent or more of their populations were white. This is linked to their long history as working class neighbourhoods, centred on the heavy manufacturing industries of earlier decades. The populations of some of the neighbourhoods are now becoming slightly more mixed, mainly as a result of the dispersal of asylum seekers.

Table 3.1 on the next page summarises different aspects of the neighbourhoods, underlining how far out of line they are with more typical neighbourhoods in terms of their tenure, and levels of unemployment. Figure 3.1 briefly describes their housing stock.

City-Edge, Manchester

City-Edge was a traditional Manchester industrial neighbourhood – housing people who worked in the nearby coal mines, steel industries, engineering and textiles. Mining under the area came to an end in 1969. By the late 1980s, most of

Table 3.1: Characteristics of four low demand neighbourhoods compared with city and national averages

	National average	Manchester			Newcastle		
		Manchester City	City-Edge	Valleyside	Newcastle City	Bankside	Riverview
% social renting[1]	23	45	63	60	40	54	81
% Black & ethnic minority[1]	5.5	13	4	5	4	2	1
% working age population not in work, study or training[1]	24	37	46	48	31	49	50
% terraced housing[2]	28	41	56	59	32	46	53

Sources: 1. 1991 Census. 2. Social Trends (ONS, 1997) and 1991 Census (quoted in Manchester Ward Profiles and Newcastle City Profiles).
Note: The proportion of terraced housing in the neighbourhoods may have changed over the 1990s, mainly as a result of demolition.

Figure 3.1: Description of the type of housing in the neighbourhoods

City-Edge, Manchester

Range of quite self-contained council estates, built in the 1960s right through to the 1990s, comprising houses and low-rise flats. Some new build housing association properties, and a small private sector estate. Pre-1919 terraced houses (most now being demolished).

Valleyside, Manchester

Large number of pre-1919 terraced houses. 1960s and 1970s council estates (one since totally re-modelled). Housing association new build. Some private sector new build.

Bankside, Newcastle

1930s houses (most modernised), pre-1919 terraced houses and Tyneside flats, small amount of housing association new build, small number of high-rise blocks of flats.

Riverview, Newcastle

Inter-war council estates (since modernised) of good quality houses with front and back gardens. Range of post-war developments, including maisonettes and multi-storey blocks. Small amount of housing association new build, and pre-1919 terraced houses and flats.

the other industrial jobs had also been lost. Much of the life-blood of the neighbourhood disappeared along with these industries:

> *The work has gone, so the heart has been knocked out of the community* (Councillor A, 1998).

Clearance and council building

The late nineteenth century terraced houses, built for the workers under strict bye-laws to replace slums with neat hygienic terraces, were largely cleared during the 1960s and 1970s, and replaced with council houses, maisonettes and deck access flats. The flats – known as 'Fort City-Edge' – were deeply unpopular from the outset. They had a life of just fifteen years, before being demolished and replaced by new council houses in the 1990s. These new houses – although high quality, semi-detached, conventionally attractive properties – suffered from the same demand problems. Many are boarded up and the estate is now being considered for demolition – less than fifteen years after it was completed – two rounds of clearance in a generation.

In Lower City-Edge, a small grid of traditional terraced homes survived the original slum clearance process and were improved when it became a Housing Action Area in the 1970s. However, by October 1998, 58 per cent of the 138 privately owned homes were empty, the housing association owned properties in the terraces were also in zero demand, and this area has now been cleared as well. A new build housing association sheltered scheme, built on the edge of this area in the 1990s, was included in the demolition.

Many City-Edge residents went through the original slum clearance of the 1960s and 1970s, and have lived in their new houses since the day they were built. One pointed out how distressing it was to see clearance repeated, 25 years on. Selective demolition of some small blocks of flats within estates has sometimes helped conditions to improve. Grassy patches are spread throughout the neighbourhood – where houses and flats once stood.

Low demand

As the population of the neighbourhood dwindled, and demand fell across the city, only the most vulnerable and those who couldn't get housed elsewhere tended to take up tenancies. New building of housing association properties in the neighbourhood during the 1990s increased supply further, at a time when demand was falling, creating even more empty homes.

In some parts of City-Edge, a vacuum in social control arose – people were overwhelmed by the extent of anti-social behaviour and intimidation, even from very small children, and longer-term residents began to move away. The resources of the police and housing service were stretched, action wasn't taken soon enough and often wasn't effective.

> *The reason that those houses were vandalised and are boarded up today and no-one wants to come onto the estate, is because of the itinerant families who were persecuting people* (Councillor B, 1998).

> *There have been massive problems with neighbour nuisance. The main private landlord [in Lower City-Edge] didn't care who came into his properties – and his part of the terrace was populated by dealers and prostitutes* (Housing association officer, 1998).

> *It's wrecking my health...I was put on valium after the last joyriding incident* (Lower City-Edge resident, 1998).

In these parts of the area, residents who did try to take a stand were attacked:

> *One particularly vocal resident came in for a lot of flak. Their house was being harassed constantly, mainly by the kids and the teenagers who were doing a lot of the damage. So they weren't getting any thanks – if anything they were going through hell trying to do the right thing for the area* (Housing association officer, 1998).

Community spirit

But in many parts of City-Edge, the spirit of the community didn't die, and a striking characteristic of this neighbourhood is the strong community feeling within many of the estates. Estates with strong social organisation have maintained high occupancy. There is a network of active tenants and residents' associations, and determined community leaders – often women.

> *There's a great deal of community spirit, especially amongst the elderly and middle-aged. It's a pleasure to walk onto some of our council estates because you know they're old City-Edge people who used to work in the coal mines and the steel industry* (Councillor B, 1998).

> *We are confident that, with support, [this estate] will be fine...It's pockets of problems – not general – and we're doing something about it* (Resident, 1998).

A local housing report in June 1998 summarised the neighbourhood's demand problems, and the variation that exists within the area:

> *Severe problems exist across City-Edge. Over the last couple of years demand for our housing has plummeted, particularly for one bedroom stock for which there is no current demand. Parts of the area are changing by the week and*

this level and pace of change is very difficult to keep up with. However, there are still areas of City-Edge that are relatively fine (Minutes of City-Edge Housing Forum, 09/06/98).

Since then, the development of the Commonwealth Games stadium on the edge of the neighbourhood is stimulating investment, and New Deal for Communities is underway, linked to a battery of regeneration initiatives that right now are generating considerable optimism. An enthusiastic vision for New East Manchester is gathering support as inward investment fuels new growth.

Valleyside, Manchester

Valleyside in North Manchester is an unusually green inner city neighbourhood, with its large parks, river and canal, open spaces and trees. Open land accounts for 35 per cent of the total land use in North Manchester (Manchester City Council, 1994). Nearly 60 per cent of Valleyside's housing is in terraces – and the rest is mainly flatted council estates built in the 1960s and 1970s. Demand problems became visible in Valleyside later than in City-Edge. Although there had long been council estates with high turnover in Valleyside, it was during the mid 1990s that serious demand problems in both the social and private housing stock became apparent.

Demand problems

As in the other neighbourhoods, demand problems followed job losses. Most major employers had left the area by the late 1980s.

There's very little manufacturing industry left...We haven't got any economic base – no-one's putting money in – it's a spiral of dereliction (Private sector council officer, 1998).

The slack in housing demand across Manchester impacted particularly severely on some of the Valleyside estates which featured a non-traditional, unpopular design.

We've got very little traditional stock – that's the stuff that sells (Housing team leader, 1998).

One estate with few through roads, many cul de sacs and walkways, and poor natural surveillance of public spaces, became infamous for drug dealing during the 1990s. Originally, the council had planned to demolish the entire estate due to the high vacancy rate, but was surprised to find that when the crunch came, many of the surviving residents wanted to stay. Successes were later achieved in repairing relationships with the residents, reducing crime on the estate, and improving its appearance through selective demolition.

Another estate with similar design problems was completely remodelled with Estate Action funding. Ongoing, intensive management, and support from the active residents' association, are helping to protect this capital investment and maintain demand, although it is a hard struggle.

Community instability

New building by housing associations during the 1990s increased local supply, and had the unintended consequence of facilitating local movement, often at the expense of existing council estates:

> It's Peter robbing Paul...They all moved out of [that council estate] into the [housing association homes] (Private sector council officer, 1998).

In the private terraces, anti-social behaviour has been a major problem, particularly as homes have shifted from being owner occupied to being rented out.

> Neighbour nuisance is one of the biggest problems in the private rented sector – some landlords haven't got the ability or experience to deal with it (Private sector council officer, 1998).

The Manchester police believed that people who wanted to make a quick profit by buying houses up at knock-down prices and renting them out to benefit recipients had deliberately engineered decline.

> [Landlords] deliberately put in a bad tenant or let the property run down, so they can buy the property either side for a cut price. I'm sure it goes on quite a lot round here (Police inspector, 1998).

People talked about a 'two-tier community' in Valleyside – a stable core:

> There is quite a large section of the community that has been here a long time, and who are quite committed to the area (Valleyside resident, 1998).

– and a smaller, transient population always on the move:

> To me moving house is a big thing, but to them it's not – it's done very quickly. It's seen as 'life's going to be better when we move house' (Valleyside resident, 1998).

Next steps

Private companies started to build homes for sale in the 1990s, with subsidy from English Partnerships. By encouraging the development of higher quality private housing, the council hopes to create a more mixed population, retaining ambitious workers within the neighbourhoods who would otherwise buy outside the city's boundaries, and attracting new people to live in the city. But in a neighbourhood with too much housing, this is a precarious strategy. Some parts of North Manchester are now hit by falling property values and signs of abandonment. It is possible that whole parts of the area will collapse. It will take a very adventurous and costly strategy to create significant demand. The city council is currently drawing up a detailed strategic regeneration framework for North Manchester, and it is part of the pathfinder project for Housing Market Renewal.

Bankside, Newcastle

Bankside, about two miles west of the city centre, has stunning, south-facing views across the Tyne. There are several connecting bus routes to the centre, but no Metro station. Successive bouts of demolition over the years have left numerous green, grassy spaces.

Bankside was rapidly industrialised between 1851 and 1891, and even before this time it had a long history of industrial activity. Working class housing started to be built on a large scale in the last quarter of the nineteenth century, but much of the workforce lived in slums nearer the city centre.

> *There was no golden age when everyone in the West End lived and worked together in one harmonious community* (Conway and Green, 1996).

Council building and over-supply

Major council house building programmes started after the first world war and continued into the 1930s, by which time local industry was already in decline. There was a revival of industry during the second world war which lasted until the early 1960s, but during the 1970s and 1980s the remaining industrial base crumbled; two major factories closed, and other firms significantly cut their workforce. Both male and female unemployment doubled between 1971 and 1991 (Conway and Green, 1996). This had a devastating impact upon the area, whose entire rationale had been to accommodate workers from the local industries nearby. The population of Bankside fell by 41 per cent between 1971 and 1996, with the loss accelerating into the 1990s.

By the late 1970s, empty council homes were a major problem. A social worker commented that empty properties appeared to suddenly shoot out of control at the beginning of the1990s, but it had *always* been easy for people to obtain housing in Bankside. There was a particularly steep increase in empty council properties between 1989, when there were 40-50 empty homes, and 1991 when the total had risen to around 350. All tenures have been affected – private housing and new build housing association properties as well as council homes. Empty private homes tend to be in the poorest condition – boarded up with odd pieces of wood, often covered in graffiti, with smashed windows. In March 1998, a 'For Sale' sign in one privately owned terrace was advertising a pair of flats for just £3,500.

'Rough' reputation

The neighbourhood has long had a local reputation for toughness, but this whole area of Newcastle became widely infamous following riots in 1991, which were emblazoned across national papers and television screens:

> *The publicity following the riots was horrendous – there was no way you could attract people in after that* (Housing association officer, 1998).

Bankside received major regeneration investment during the 1990s via City Challenge. This significantly improved the physical infrastructure, but did not halt the population exodus.

> *Despite all of our efforts to date, we have not yet succeeded in encouraging people who do not already live in the West End to move there. Extensive marketing of dwellings has been carried out but only a few tenancies have been created as a result. Even then many of these tenants have moved on after only a short period of time. The majority of new tenancies which are let are to existing residents in the West End seeking either to improve their particular circumstances or to 'regroup' around networks of families and friends, mostly to improve their own sense of security* (Report by Director of Housing, 30/01/97).

Attractive, modernised homes with front and back gardens – that would be snapped up in another location – stand empty, boarded up and often vandalised.

> *The West End's problems are not essentially housing problems, and it is a terrible mistake to see them as such* (City Challenge evaluator).

Reported crime in Bankside fell by 50 per cent between 1992 and 1998, helped by an active police presence, witness support, and growing relationships between police, housing and residents. However, unreported crime and fear of crime remain serious problems. High levels of empty, derelict property exacerbate feelings of insecurity. A survey by one tenants' group in 1996 asked residents in a road that was a third empty about the effects of living near so many empty properties. Half said it frightened them and caused worry and depression.

Community activists

There is a long history of resident activism in Bankside, dating back at least to the inter-war period. Yet one activist explained that there is also a culture of defying authority. People who do take on representative roles are often cautious about drawing attention to themselves, or becoming associated with 'authority' figures, for fear of how other residents will react.

Most of the residents we interviewed in 1997-98 said they felt very settled in the area, and stayed because they were part of extended families or community networks there. They were worried that other communities they could move to would be even tougher and they would not want to be the 'newcomer'. Extended family networks are integral to Bankside's character, and can help sustain demand. For example, in one small part of Bankside, the members of one extended family occupy fourteen properties (Bankside Neighbourhood Profile, 2000).

> *For the vast majority of people it's an absolutely OK place to be [because they've got friends and family networks]* (Council officer, 1998).

On the other hand, if one extended family decides to leave, a large number of properties can become vacant in one go, exacerbating letting difficulties. And these close family networks can make it harder for new people to feel part of the area.

> *It wouldn't be easy for outsiders coming in because it is quite a close community, close and possibly closed. The more I work here, the more I realise just how extensive the grapevine is. Most [people] aren't married, there is a multiplicity of surnames, so you don't realise at first the extent of the relationships of a few families within the area...I think some new blood would be very helpful* (Health visitor, 2000).

But large parts of the area have been progressively demolished over the last two decades of plummeting demand, including an almost brand new housing association development offering attractive sheltered homes. Bankside is now at the very heart of Newcastle's *Going for Growth* strategy. A minority of what stands now will survive.

Riverview, Newcastle

Riverview is also situated on the banks of the Tyne, two miles east of the city centre, with far-reaching views over the river and the countryside beyond. Like Bankside, it is linked to the centre by buses but does not have a Metro stop in easy reach. Its homes are almost entirely socially owned – 77 per cent by the council and 4 per cent by housing associations.

Decline of the docks

Riverview was a bustling working class neighbourhood, housing people who worked in the riverside and nearby industries – including iron and chemical works, shipbuilding and related engineering works. This employment base rapidly disappeared during the 1980s, and by the end of the decade had virtually disintegrated. A technology park was developed, but most of the jobs it created were high skill and did not go to local people. Without local jobs for the local population, the area went downhill and demand plummeted. The population fell by 21 per cent between 1981 and 1991.

A lot of people in Lower Riverview don't want to be there – there is no reason for them to be there. Many people don't have an employment link or a family link with the area (Regeneration manager, 1998).

Low demand

Lower Riverview, nearest the river, has experienced the greatest demand difficulties. Its proximity to the riverside and the now defunct heavy industry made it the poorest location. One estate of good quality houses, only built in the 1970s, was almost entirely demolished in 1997 simply because no-one would live in it. Some housing managers suggested to us that the initial demolition gradually spread up the banks as the next layer of homes nearest to the exposed river bank became blighted by the stigma transferred from the lower streets. Demand problems have spread throughout Riverview, where there has been ongoing demolition of unpopular blocks of flats and multi-storeys.

Much of the housing in Riverview comprises high quality inter-war houses with front and back gardens – these are also in very low demand:

It's not the houses' fault! (Renewal officer, 1998).

Social unravelling

Anti-social behaviour problems beset Lower Riverview during much of the 1990s; a few out-of-control families had a devastating impact, out of all proportion to their numbers. Front line staff felt that things had calmed down towards the end of the 1990s. One particularly notorious family was evicted, and a community-run security project, employing local people in a concierge and patrol scheme, helped reduce crime. But there could still be a threatening air within the neighbourhood, and the elderly in particular were often fearful:

It is calmer...it used to seem to be chaos and mayhem the whole time...But the things that go on here – the undercurrent of violence – is still there (Council officer, 1998).

One of the few roads of private terraced housing in the area went downhill very rapidly during 1997. By January 1998, 31 units were vacant out of a total of 99. This decline was attributed to a combination of houses transferring to the private rented sector as elderly owner occupiers died, feuds within the community pushing some owners out, and unscrupulous landlords letting to families evicted by the council for disruptive behaviour. According to a senior police officer, there was evidence that social unrest was actively engineered by a company who wanted to purchase properties at knock-down rates and then let them to housing benefit claimants at a huge profit.

> *[There was] a domino effect – people started leaving in their droves* (Community development officer, 1998).

Several front line staff we spoke to had grown up in Riverview, and sometimes their parents still lived there, but they themselves had moved out although they continued to work in the area. Many of their friends had also moved out into owner occupation as they got jobs. The tenure of the area made staying difficult. They explained what a problem this was for Riverview:

> *If you're successful, you'll move off into more desirable parts...Addressing this is the key to stabilising and improving the area* (Community development officer, 1998).

Community spirit

Despite these problems, there are strong pockets of community spirit, especially amongst the elderly. As in Bankside, this sense of community can be excluding to anyone new to the area, and as demand problems have grown existing residents have become even more suspicious of people who do move in – feeling they must surely be desperate to accept housing in such an unpopular place. On the other hand, the strong sense of community gives some stability to the neighbourhood:

> *The area is not being abandoned by the core population – which is made up of people who've lived here a long time. Many people moved in when Lower Riverview was built in the 1930s, and some even lived here before the estate was built* (Council officer, 1998).

> *We will not shift as we're so happy here* (Resident in the area for over 50 years, 1998).

Riverview residents are now galvanising their remaining energies to prevent a similar fate to Bankside befalling them. They are forming an 'urban village partnership' to help revive the area before it too collapses.

Conclusions

The four neighbourhoods illustrate all the contradictions of current housing policy nationally. It cannot make sense to encourage those that can afford it to move out of cities – enticed by current house-building policies – while simultaneously pouring millions of pounds into trying to stave off neighbourhood collapse resulting from a gross over-supply of homes and a continuing urban exodus – reflected in current regeneration and neighbourhood renewal policy. How cities react to these problems, how they combat neighbourhood collapse and urban exodus is a fine balancing act. With all the accumulated experience of estate and neighbourhood renewal, it is still unclear quite what recipe will work. In Chapter 4 we look at Manchester's strategies for revitalising its inner city, as in the words of the assistant Chief Executive, *'Manchester is one giant, immensely challenging, inner city'.*

CHAPTER 4:
Manchester

Manchester in its heyday was one of the richest, densest, most successful if smokiest cities in the world. Yet for most of the twentieth century the city's population fell. However, in the last few years it has begun to grow again and the city is making huge efforts to build on that growth. This chapter looks closely at current trends across the city and in detail at the progress in two of the most precarious neighbourhoods.

Population trends

The population in 2000 was slightly higher than it was a decade earlier, though was still more than 100,000 below its 1971 level.

> *Manchester's population [loss] has not only halted – but we are now starting to see some consistent signs of growth* (Chief Executive, 2001).

Figure 4.1 shows the fall in Manchester's population since 1971.

Figure 4.1: Manchester's population decline, 1971-2000

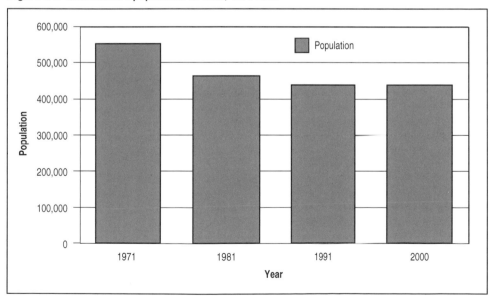

Source: Power and Mumford (1999); Manchester Planning Studies (2001) based on the Registrar General's annual mid year population estimates.

Table 4.1 highlights the slight upturn of recent years:

Table 4.1: Population of the city of Manchester, 1971-2000

	1971	1981	1991	2000
Population	553,600	462,600	438,500	439,549
	1971-81	1981-91	1991-00	
% change	-16	-5	+0.2	

Source: Power and Mumford (1999); and Manchester Planning Studies (2001) based on the Registrar General's annual mid year population estimates.

The other Greater Manchester districts are growing at a higher rate than the city of Manchester, with the exception of Oldham, Salford and Tameside which are still losing population (see Table 4.2). The fortunes of the conurbation as a whole are clearly linked, and Manchester identifies itself as having a key role in the future well-being of the wider region:

The North West's long-term prosperity depends on Manchester remaining a healthy, vibrant city (Manchester, 1999).

Table 4.2: Population change in the Greater Manchester Districts 1991-2000

District	Total population in 2000	% change 1991-2000
Rochdale	210,800	+3.0
Bury	183,000	+2.1
Trafford	220,100	+2.0
Bolton	267,600	+1.8
Stockport	291,100	+1.0
Wigan	312,000	+0.4
Manchester	439,500	+0.2
Tameside	219,300	-0.2
Oldham	218,100	-0.7
Salford	224,300	-2.9
Greater Manchester Total	**2,585,800**	**+0.6**

Source: Manchester Planning Studies (2001) based on information from the Population Estimates Unit, ONS.

Despite a slight upturn in the city's population overall, the two low demand neighbourhoods we tracked over time showed a continuing population loss over the 1990s. City-Edge's population fell by 11 per cent between 1991 and 2000, and Valleyside's by 6 per cent. However, both started to show a slight population increase between 1998 and 2000. This may mark the beginnings of a revival, reflecting overall positive trends in the city.

Figure 4.2: Population change in City-Edge and Valleyside, 1991-2000

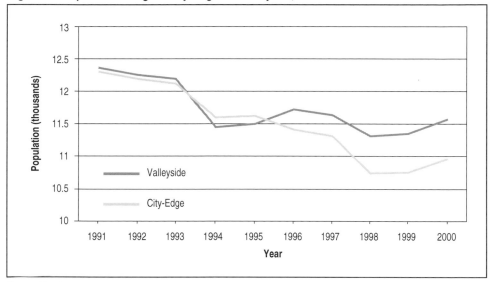

Source: Manchester Planning Studies (2001) based on 1991 Census and mid year estimates.

As the population has fallen, so of course has the population density, already extremely low by European urban standards and less than half the density of inner London (Power and Mumford, 1999). Table 4.3 shows how these inner neighbourhoods have thinned out, albeit with a small upturn in recent years. The population density of the city of Manchester overall was slightly higher in 2000 than in 1991, but it is far below a level that will support important services like frequent, comprehensive buses (Urban Task Force, 1999). This is particularly true for the poorer neighbourhoods.

Table 4.3: Population density in Manchester and two inner neighbourhoods, 1991-2000 (people per hectare)

	Manchester[1]	City-Edge[1]	Valleyside[1]	Inner London[2]
1991	38.0	32.0	35.7	78.1
1992	37.7	31.8	35.4	
1993	37.5	31.6	35.2	
1994	37.4	30.2	33.1	
1995	37.5	30.3	33.2	
1996	37.4	29.7	33.8	
1997	37.1	29.5	33.6	
1998	37.3	28.0	32.7	
1999	37.4	28.0	32.8	
2000	38.1	28.6	33.4	

Sources: 1. Manchester Planning Studies (2001) based on 1991 Census and mid year estimates.
2. Power and Mumford (1999) based on 1991 Census.

City centre developments

The city is concentrating all its resources towards delivering the Urban Task Force vision of renaissance – a compact, mixed use, vibrant city centre, linked by fast public transport to its surrounding neighbourhoods. In the latter half of the 1990s, residential development in the centre took off. A major hotel conversion, *'saw home hunters waiting outside for two days with half of the 110 apartments sold on the first day of release'* (Manchester, 2001c). Many such schemes have resulted in a significant boost to the resident population of the city centre. It remained below 2,000 people from 1981 to 1994, but by 1997 had risen to an estimated 6,000 and is expected to top 10,000 during 2002 (Manchester 1999; 2001c; 2001d).

Following the IRA's devastating terrorist bomb attack in June 1996, a 'city centre task force' was established as a public-private partnership to co-ordinate the rebuilding of the city centre. Large areas of it were re-opened in 1999, with transformed public spaces, 'anchor' department stores and careful restoration of many historic but seriously damaged buildings. The redevelopment is now nearing completion (Manchester, 2001a). Selfridges and Harvey Nichols will soon open stores in the city centre for the first time, and Next will anchor the redevelopment of the Arndale Centre with a four-floor 'flagship superstore' due to open in 2005 (Creasey, 2002).

Piccadilly Gardens, a once desolate area of green space near the train station mainly occupied by an excluded and transient homeless population, is now being reclaimed as the central public garden in a city centre that cries out for more green space. A new office block is being built along one side but the resulting reduction in open space should be compensated for by a more attractive and better used public square (Housing Director, 2001). The ambitious scheme will include walk-through fountains, new lawns and gardens, a tree-lined 'boulevard' and attractive night lighting (Manchester, 2001b).

Piccadilly train station itself, the point of entry for many visitors to Manchester, has also been undergoing a much needed multi-million pound revamp. The city aimed to create a more positive first impression for new visitors, as well as enhancing the environment for its existing residents (Manchester, 2001b). By the time the Commonwealth Games started, this goal had been realised, the station utterly transformed. The West Coast Mainline is improving Manchester's rail connections to the rest of the country and this is part of this complex jigsaw of city centre recovery. By next year, Pendolino trains will be serving Piccadilly, cutting vital journey times to London by at least half an hour in the future.

New hotels and leisure developments have continued to mushroom, and an international concert hall – The Bridgewater Hall – opened in September 1996. Even more important, there is at last an international conference centre in the middle of the city, to rival Birmingham's highly successful centre. Manchester airport's limited hotels will no longer be the venue for major meetings.

Manchester's 'City Pride' vision, launched in 1994, includes the goal that, by 2005, the city will be a 'European regional capital', and a key city on the international scene (Manchester, 2001a).

> *What we've done is diversify our economy: leisure, visitor, corporate / financial, technological, and still a not insignificant manufacturing base... We have deliberately placed sport and culture at the heart of our economic strategy* (Chief Executive, 2001).

The Northern Quarter, between the city centre and Ancoats, is being promoted as *'a vibrant magnet for young people'* (Manchester, 1999). A development of shared ownership homes in the Northern Quarter has been extremely popular – over 300 people applied to buy the 13 available flats (Manchester, 2000a). Interest in this area is growing at such a pace that land values are now beyond the reach of registered social landlords – a *'London problem'* (Housing director, 2001). This was beyond anyone's wildest dreams of just three years ago.

Ancoats, a heritage area at the heart of historic Manchester, housing the very first and most impressive industrial warehouses in the world, is the scene of a developing 'urban village'. Urban Splash – the pioneering and extremely successful property company that made its name in the 1990s for first converting industrial relics in Manchester and Liverpool to attractive mixed uses including apartments, clubs and restaurants – is playing a lead role in this venture. The £20 million scheme includes new shops, restaurants, loft apartments, mews houses and social rented homes (Manchester, 2000). The historic mills and warehouses, and the Ashton Canal, are enticing imaginative developers into a semi-derelict area (New East Manchester, 2001d). The Cardroom Estate within Ancoats is being turned into one of five national Millennium Communities with major government funding. The council is keen to bring families back to live in the city centre, not only young singles and couples. The council is looking to fund a new secondary school nearby; it wants this school to build a reputation for excellence, possibly as a grammar school, to help reverse the pattern of families moving out of the city.

The seeds of success for all these changes have already been sown. The Castlefields area, along the complex canal basin that made Manchester the hub of the first industrial revolution in the world, has been opened up to music, restaurants, bars, clubs, new companies and bijoux housing. However, city centre shops face ongoing competition from the nearby but officially out-of-town Trafford Centre, and will soon face even stiffer competition from the 'city within a city' at Sportcity, East Manchester. There are some unlet retail units in prime positions. One senior manager argued that the city centre probably peaked in 1999 and has just about managed to hold its own since then. There is a constant worry that the centre could lose out. But recent evidence suggests that Manchester's city centre occupies a unique niche with ongoing appeal:

Having seen what has happened in other cities as a consequence of out-of-town 'shopping cities' we are, of course, monitoring the impact of the Trafford Centre. However, initial anxieties appear to be unfounded and periodic comparisons demonstrate that the other attractions within the city centre such as the theatres, historic buildings, library and art gallery mean that people perceive it as more than just another shopping centre but as a place to live and work (Manchester Housing, 2002).

One of the most problematic housing issues for the city as a whole is the shortage of high quality homes within the city boundaries. Manchester is in the strange position of being entirely ringed by nine other separate authorities that make up the Greater Manchester conurbation. It is unusual in having virtually no 'suburban belt' of its own. So higher earners often opt right out of the city in pursuit of executive homes. Manchester, like Newcastle, Glasgow and Birmingham, has a 'commuter problem'. There are around 250,000 people who work in the city but live outside its boundaries (Housing Director, 2001).

Higher-value homes are concentrated on the fringes of the wider conurbation rather than in the city itself...We don't have enough high-quality homes to encourage people who have profited from Manchester's economic upturn to stay in the city, or to attract and retain new residents (Manchester, 1999).

The problem of low quality housing is illustrated by the distribution of council tax bands amongst the city's housing stock. 70 per cent are in the lowest band (A) compared with just 26 per cent nationally. Figure 4.3 shows how poorly Manchester's housing stock is rated:

Figure 4.3: Council tax bands in Manchester and nationally

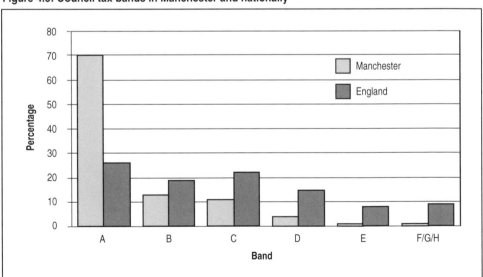

Source: Manchester (1999).

In spite of major obstacles still in its path, the city Chief Executive is firmly upbeat about progress:

Over the last ten years [Manchester's development] has been pretty remarkable. I constantly have to pinch myself!

The city centre still has a somewhat empty feel to it and, on weekday evenings, can seem very quiet, even deserted. Yet the strategy of piecing together reclamation plans, infill building, new uses and quite visionary transformations of a collapsing but imposing industrial infrastructure, has gradually unleashed new life in the city. Deputy Chief Executive Eamonn Boylan, an acute city watcher, notes the critical mass of activity and innovation that continues to drive Manchester's slow and painful regrowth.

Promoting council housing

The number of empty council properties in the neighbourhoods, and in Manchester as a whole, rose steeply from the mid 1990s. But in Valleyside, council vacancies have fallen continually over the past three years. And both City-Edge and Manchester as a whole have seen council vacancies fall within the past year.

Demolition during this time accounts for some of the drop in numbers. In both City-Edge and Valleyside, selective demolition has removed unpopular flats and reduced vacancies. Manchester City Council demolished around 300 council units per year between 1991 and 1997 (Manchester Housing, 1999), and has almost certainly continued to demolish at least as many in recent years.

Table 4.4 shows the trend in council vacancy levels in Manchester and in the two neighbourhoods. Manchester's total stock is currently 63,000 properties, so the overall vacancy level stands at just under 5 per cent.

Table 4.4: Empty council properties in Manchester and two neighbourhoods, 1996-2002

	City-Edge	Valleyside	Manchester
April 1996	45	56	1,577
April 1997	86	147	2,720
April 1998	102	257	3,818
April 1999	85	282	3,671
April 2000	77	237	3,857
April 2001	86	187	3,272
Sept 2001	92	178	3,475
April 2002	64	94	3,104

Source: Manchester Housing weekly void reports (2001) and Manchester Housing (2002). Total city council stock is 63,000 properties.

Manchester's housing department classifies its social housing as being in 'demand', in 'low demand' or in 'no demand', based on housing managers' local knowledge of the actual waiting time new applicants will experience before they can move into a specific property. The demand classification for registered social landlord (RSL) stock is based on both points and waiting times. We summarise these different classifications in Table 4.5, before going on to explore trends in the proportion of properties in 'demand'.

Table 4.5: Manchester's classification of popularity for council and RSL stock

	Council housing definition	**RSL definition**
Demand	Waiting time of 9 months or more	All properties that do not fall into the two categories below.
Low demand	Waiting time of 1-9 months	Waiting period for direct applicants is less than 1 month (or applicants with zero or near-zero points, i.e. little or no housing need can apply), AND the council has had to provide a second set of additional nominations.
No demand	Waiting time of less than 1 month	No direct applicants registered on waiting lists for the property, and council unable to nominate applicants for the property.

Source: Manchester's low demand team (2001).

Up to 2000, demand for social housing continued to fall. There was a 1 per cent fall in the proportion of council and RSL stock in demand across the city between 1999 and 2000. By 2000, only just under two fifths (39 per cent) of council housing across the city was in demand, and only 28 per cent of RSL housing. The year 2000 was the first since the council began recording demand information (in 1996) that the city as a whole did not experience a *significant* further fall in demand for council housing (Manchester Housing Demand Team, 2001a).

Both City-Edge and Valleyside have seen improvements in demand for their council housing over the period 1998-00. However, demand remains very low and in City-Edge is propped up to some extent by people relocating from compulsory clearance areas (Senior LA strategy officer, 2001). In 2000, just 27 per cent of Valleyside's council housing and 32 per cent of City-Edge's was classed as in demand.

Meanwhile, housing associations are often facing critical lettings problems in these neighbourhoods – demand for their homes has plummeted to almost zero. No RSL housing is in demand in City-Edge according to housing association managers, and just 2 per cent in Valleyside.

Figures 4.4 and 4.5 show the trends in each neighbourhood and across the city, compared with the situation in the country as a whole.

Figure 4.4: Proportion of council stock in demand in City-Edge, Valleyside, Manchester and nationally, 1998-2000

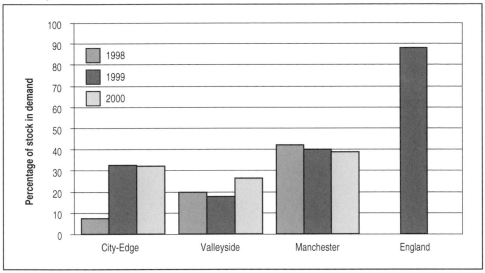

Sources: Manchester Housing Demand Team (2001b, 2002) and Bramley *et al.* (2000).
Notes to Figures 4.4 and 4.5: Bramley's national figure is based on a postal survey conducted in the winter of 1998/99 and represents the proportion of stock that was *not* classified as being in low demand. For the purposes of the survey, the term 'low demand' was applied to areas where any of the following symptoms were apparent: a small or non-existent waiting list, tenancy offers frequently refused, high rates of voids available for letting, high rates of tenancy turnover.

Figure 4.5: Proportion of RSL stock in demand in City-Edge, Valleyside, Manchester and nationally 1998-2000

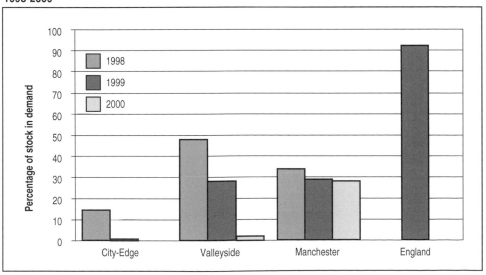

Sources: Manchester Housing Demand Team (2001b; 2002) and Bramley *et al.* (2000).

Manchester has been trying to improve the image of its large stock of council housing across the city, and reach people who until recently were simply not eligible. Its advertising campaigns challenge negative perceptions of council housing. By adopting an estate agent's approach to reasonable housing in areas with a poor reputation, the city has tapped into new markets in a situation where the traditional waiting list no longer attracted enough applicants.

Waiting lists are usually a poor predictor of need and demand, but changes in their size can give an idea of general demand trends. The steep fall in Manchester's general housing waiting list from 1992 was largely a result of the council tidying up the list and ensuring that all registered applicants did want housing. The waiting list has begun to show some slight signs of growth (see Figure 4.6). Although in relation to the size of the council stock and the number of empty homes this growth is small, the council sees it as significant, particularly given the fact that turnover is reducing at the same time. Turnover fell from 18 per cent in 1998-99 to 13 per cent in 2001-02 (Manchester housing demand team, 2002).

Figure 4.6: Numbers on Manchester's general waiting list, 1992-2001

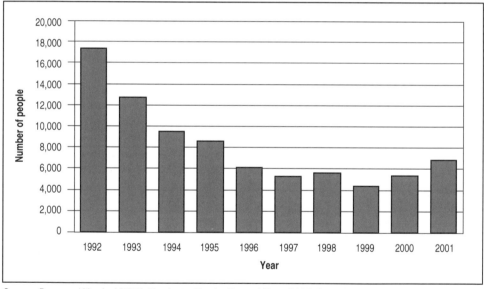

Sources: Power and Mumford (1999); Manchester Housing Demand Team (2001). According to Manchester, the 1992 figure may include transfers although records do not make this clear. All others do not.

More concrete evidence of success can be found in Manchester's special lettings initiatives which focus on open marketing and choice. Its Homes for Rent Hotline, aiming to let low demand properties with no waiting list, took over 40,000 calls in its first three years. These initial inquiries resulted in around 6,000 viewings and 2,700 lets. (Manchester, 2001). Over 80 per cent of people inquiring had never held a Manchester tenancy before, and more than 60 per cent of new tenants were working (Manchester, 2000). This is far higher than the average for council tenants. By 2001, 15 per cent of all new city council lets were attributable to the Hotline, even though it had only been used for low demand areas (Manchester bid, 2001).

Manchester is moving to a 'choice-based lettings' system across the board during 2002; this means that all tenancies will be publicly advertised, not just those in low demand. It has plans to include all housing associations in the scheme, and hopes to work with the other nine Greater Manchester Authorities to develop a conurbation-wide advertising system (Manchester bid, 2001).

Under the new and broader initiative, the Hotline came to an end in December 2001, by which time it had achieved 4,338 lets from 10,316 viewings. Manchester Homefinder, the new choice-based lettings project, has now taken over and expanded the Hotline role. It currently accounts for around 20 per cent of general lettings in Manchester; a figure that will increase as the service continues to expand. It is still the case that nearly two thirds of new Homefinder customers have someone working in their household (Council officer, 2002).

We're bringing empty property back into use after several years [of no demand] (Council officer, 2001).

Other housing management initiatives

The council is also focusing on basic neighbourhood services. Its 'estate management 2000' programme will be implemented across the city from January 2002. The idea is that it will provide rent and repairs services via a call centre, leaving officers on the ground with more time to focus on crime, disorder, property inspections, the environment, and community support. It has introduced a number of neighbourhood warden pilots. Its neighbour nuisance teams work across all tenures. By October 2001, the council had used around 20 Anti Social Behaviour Orders to control the most serious kinds of abusive behaviour. Some estates are now more attractive to new tenants as a direct result of the reduction in nuisance these Orders have brought about. The council also uses a variety of agreements and understandings, which have succeeded in persuading some people to change their behaviour. Because of this, more than nine out of ten serious nuisance cases are resolved without resorting to eviction (Housing Director, 2001).

Within its broad corporate goals and city-wide action to increase the popularity of its housing and improve core services, Manchester's approach to low demand is quite area-specific. Each neighbourhood has distinct strategies, yet is seated within the city as a whole. Local improvements by themselves are not enough.

Making streets attractive in North and East Manchester won't work. We need to restore the functionality and connectivity of place (Housing Director, 2001).

This sense of place is crucial – understanding what quality of life is like in the neighbourhoods, and therefore what is needed to make them more attractive to existing and potential residents. For instance, this is reinforced in the words, *'We're about places [as a whole] not just housing'* (Housing Director, 2001).

In the two neighbourhoods we have followed since 1997 – City-Edge in East Manchester and Valleyside in North Manchester – many extra initiatives are underway to combat the much more intense problems they face compared with other neighbourhoods. Projects in East Manchester include the New Deal for Communities and a wider urban regeneration company (New East Manchester). The Commonwealth Games stadium is driving the regeneration of this area and is expected to bring new prosperity to the poorest part of Manchester. North Manchester has had a series of Single Regeneration Budget – funded projects, and new private sector residential development is being encouraged here. We examine these two areas in more detail in the following sections.

Figure 4.7 summarises the local media view of developments in regeneration, demolition and housing demand issues in Manchester between 1999 and 2001.

Regenerating East Manchester

In 1971, East Manchester supported 34,000 jobs, 63 per cent in manufacturing. By 1985, 20,000 of these jobs had gone (New East Manchester, 2001d). Many derelict former industrial sites resulted from the collapse of manufacturing, as well as high levels of vacant homes as East Manchester's population plummeted.

The divisions and barriers that have progressively been built up, due to latent industrial arteries, contamination, and vacant sites, significantly disrupt and sever local communities from one another, from urban assets such as Philip's Park, and from Manchester as whole (Richard Rogers Partnership).

Key challenges include overcoming the fragmentation within East Manchester, and enhancing links between East Manchester's neighbourhoods and the centre of the city.

We see the area between the City Centre and...the Sportcity site as a wedge of growth that can drive the long-term future of the entire district. Some of the Victorian-era mills and warehouses in this area are breathtaking, but the vacancy, isolation, and hostile security features like barbed wire and huge dogs are simply frightening (Richard Rogers Partnership).

Figure 4.7: Manchester regeneration headlines – summary of key articles from the *Manchester Evening News* 1999-2001

A: City centre developments and wider urban issues

Date	Headline	Sub-heading	Other content details
1999			
2 Feb	The bait for business	Work starts on centre to lure international trade	£21m development of site by GMex for International Convention Centre
3 Feb	Success puts city in top 10 for rent		Manchester one of 10 most expensive cities in the world for office rentals
18 Feb	Quay design to bring in the bargain-hunters	Shopping village hopes to attract the top names	Designer village planned for Salford Quays
21 April	Bigger, better and greener – that's reborn Manchester	Heritage Secretary's tribute to buildings which have returned vision and vitality to a brave city	Heritage awards for buildings and regeneration
28 April	Bold vision is needed		Radical plans to be launched for city centre/ Piccadilly
28 April	Better, by miles	Shops and flats plan to revive canal area	3 miles of canals between Salford Quays and Castlefield
30 April	Town takes to streets over homes		Residents plan to march through Warrington centre in protest at plans for hundreds of new houses to be built on open land at Peel Hall
11 May	All change for bleak Piccadilly	Year 2002 target for massive city centre revamp	
11 May	£100m to put pride back in the old heart of town	Reversing the years of decline that have blighted Piccadilly	
21 May	Canal revamp dream banks £10.8m lifeline		Rochdale Canal wins financial backing from North West Regional Development Agency
15 June	Symbol of our city's rebirth		Regeneration after IRA attack
18 June	Dream city on the waterfront		Regeneration along the canal

Date	Headline	Sub-heading	Other content details
12 Aug	City of the future		Guide to 'new' Manchester
16 Aug	Classic case of creeping decay	Plea for urgent action to save suffering estate	Cardroom estate, Ancoats
19 Aug	Just Manc-tastic!		Guide to 'new' Manchester
1 Sept	Beneath the city dust: a strong heart	Trendy new boulevard symbolises revival after the bomb	Regeneration of the city centre
2000			
24 Feb	Boomtown flats built as property prices just soar ahead	Games and inner city developers help build a brighter future as homebuyers count cost of chasing area's hot-spot homes	*'Even former rundown areas like Hulme...have benefited from demand for homes close to where the action is'*
29 Feb	It's great, Ancoats!	Big-scale bid to revive a city village	
4 Aug	City centre becomes THE place to live as building work booms	People clamouring to buy in Manchester but £100m investment causes heartbreak	Estate agent's report claims Manchester fastest growing city centre, but some people losing out nevertheless
21 Dec	Boom city has jobs for 5,000 people but no-one wants them		Hotel, restaurant and bar jobs unfilled in Manchester as business outstrips employees
2001			
7 Feb	Rail station will be ready for the Games	Piccadilly's £55m new look is making tracks	
8 Feb	Setting the standard Headline	Piccadilly a benchmark for UK	Plans for overhaul of the station
8 March	Village in the city	City centre dwelling is the latest trend in 21st century Manchester	More than 20,000 expected to be living in Manchester city centre by 2005, compared to only 1,000 in 1990
29 March	Estate revival plan	Private firms join rescue of fallen giant...residents learn to face future with confidence	Cardroom estate to be regenerated by Urban Splash and New East Manchester Ltd.
13 June	Green with envy	Why Manchester needs to smarten up its act and take a leaf out of Barcelona's book	Manchester needs green areas

Date	Headline	Sub-heading	Other content details
15 June	Reborn: city that defied IRA blast	Five years on and face of Manchester is still changing	
3 July	£12m to revive first industrial suburb	Housing and business plan for historic Ancoats	Private developer's plans for 92 apartments and 10 business units
12 Sept	The two tales of life in the city	Property sales blow hot and cold as buyers flock into town	City centre apartment sales boom, but property 'deadspots' identified including Hulme

B: Other regeneration, demand problems and demolition

Date	Headline	Sub-heading	Other content details
1999			
4 Feb	Fighting tenants save an estate	Rescued by locals...the problem-plagued Shiredale estate in Harpurhey	Council tenants win 6-month battle to save houses and will join estate management board to get more tenants
26 Feb	We beat the bulldozers!		Shiredale estate saved by locals but they still need to work to improve it
12 March	Crumbling city homes need £1bn	Families abandoning council AND private houses, says secret report	Families moving outside Manchester's boundaries
12 March	Nightmare street	Battling legacy of decay	Community persists despite dereliction
5 May	The exodus holding back city's revival	Empty homes blight on future, say experts	LSE report
11 May	Wrecking crew moves in on flats	Another family quits after dream-home nightmare	£33,000 flats now worth £500 and empty ones being ransacked
13 May	Moss Side calls up 500 new jobs with £9m deal		Call centre and hotel to provide jobs
8 June	Financing a rebirth		Outlying districts (Wythenshawe and Stalybridge) getting regeneration investment
29 June	Time to help our run-down areas		Success and failure in regeneration of Manchester and Salford...whilst there is still much to do, it has worked in Hulme

Date	Headline	Sub-heading	Other content details
30 June	Building on a reborn city's rich heritage	Public plea for help by the man leading Manchester's return to glory	English Heritage report notes local communities must play a role in regeneration…focus on Ancoats
16 July	Sun shines at last on the green grass of Hulme	Trees, sculptures, music…welcome to the Crecents, 1999	
2 Aug	We shall not be moved	Last couple on doomed street hold out for cash	£4.5m scheme to replace 11 Victorian terraces with modern estate is held up by home-owners
2 Sept	Homes that are fit for a Prince	Estate with human touch wins royal approval	Prince Charles tells MPs that Hulme is a model for popular housing
11 Sept	400 jobs connected to new call centre		Detailed plans for call centre on Birley Fields site submitted to council
25 Nov	Passage to a better future		Residents offended by Beswick being branded 'bandit country' which is set to be an improving area
20 Dec	Estate's £90m new dawn	'Pathfinder' scheme ends tenants' decades of despair	Plymouth Grove and Stockport Road estate to be improved
2000			
6 Jan	Blitz no-hope homes!	Families flee the streets beyond redemption/Estates should be bulldozed says report/Suffering locals long for a lasting solution	Centre for Regional Economic and Social Research report, article focused on Salford and Merseybank Estate in Chorlton
20 April	Changing face of Sportcity		Commonwealth Games stadium takes shape
27 May	Arch is symbol of inner-city triumph		Hulme Arch highlights improvements in area
6 June	New look Hulme: *'a haven of hope'* for country's crumbling estates	Manchester's inner-city rebirth showing the way forward, say MPs	
19 July	Bandit country? We're more garden city now	Residents transform area and make homes' boss eat his words	Housing Chief Roger Humber termed parts of East Manchester 'bandit country'…residents cleared area up to great effect

Date	Headline	Sub-heading	Other content details
2001			
26 Jan	Moving with the times	Home experts say Wythenshawe's the place to be / Property prices 'booming' on rundown estate	
28 Feb	Canal is reborn as Gateway to Games	Rundown towpath to be key link to Stadium	Ashton canal
13 March	Gold rush begins	Huge store is first victory for Games	East Manchester to get over 1,000 jobs with UK's biggest supermarket (ASDA) and new district centre
16 March	1,500 jobs in pipeline	New life in old hospital	New science and enterprise centre at Monsall, East Manchester
2 April	Jobs bonus as call firm plans £1.5m growth		Wythenshawe to benefit
7 April	Trams boost for suburbia	'Big Bang' to bring jobs, relief from traffic jams and rise in house prices to South Manchester	
10 April	Golden games plan!	The ultimate sporting prize: sporting spectacle's billions aim to breathe new life into a dying area	The Commonwealth Games in 2002 should be a catalyst for £2bn worth of improvements across East Manchester
25 April	£135m stadium set to rival best in the world		
28 June	£24m plan breathes new life into canal	Transpennine link nears completion	Rochdale canal improvements
2 July	Gold for Games	£100m 'rescue' but council to find £45m	Central government gives more money to ensure success, but city council has to pay more too
30 Aug	City's great Games: on track for gold		Stadium is coming together
6 Oct	2002 Games spectacular proves just the ticket	More than 1,000 a day ringing hotline	
27 Oct	Industrial mill town moves on		Improvements to Ancoats and Rochdale canal

These old industrial buildings have the potential to become one of the area's greatest strengths:

> East Manchester's industrial legacy – of warehouses, mills and canals – can be rehabilitated to create an environment for living and working which has proved highly successful elsewhere (New East Manchester, 2001d).

Many residents applaud the changes.

> We are a spoke in a wheel, the city-centre is the hub. We are a stone's throw out from it. We've got that much regeneration going in, the mills being done up in between. People like us will never be able to afford one of those apartments in the mills, but the point is that [the area] is being used effectively. We need to encourage people that do live in them to spend their money in the area. The city-centre is going to be spot-on! It is lovely (Resident, 2000).

There are now a wealth of regeneration programmes in East Manchester, as Figure 4.8 shows:

Figure 4.8: Regeneration projects in City-Edge and the wider East Manchester area

- New Deal for Communities, worth £52 million over 10 years
- New East Manchester (urban regeneration company), expected to attract £2 billion of public and private funds over 15 years
- Education Action Zone, £4.1 million over 3 years
- Sports Action Zone, £300,000 over 5 years
- Single Regeneration Budget round 5, £25 million
- Sure Start, £2.6 million over 3 years
- Beacons for a Brighter Future initiative, aims to pull together all the initiatives in East Manchester
- Within a Health Action Zone (the whole of Manchester, Salford and Trafford is a designated Health Action Zone)

Source: New Deal, 1999 and New Start, 2001a.

New East Manchester, the urban regeneration company, was launched at the end of 1999. It now provides a strategic overview across the whole of East Manchester, currently an area of 30,000 people, providing a framework for all the other projects to work within. Its key role is to attract large-scale private and public investment within a framework of development that links East Manchester into the city again after decades in incremental decay and loss of rationale.

The Commonwealth Games, which took place in summer 2002, have created an entirely new atmosphere and environment. The international athletics stadium is located in the middle of the developing Sportcity in East Manchester, right on

City-Edge's doorstep. After the Commonwealth Games, the stadium will become the new home of Manchester City Football Club. The council sees it as one of the key ingredients in turning around City-Edge's fortunes – bringing jobs, new facilities and a change of image for the area. There are questions about how much the existing community will benefit, and about whether the huge public spending on this project is justified. A local swimming pool may be closed, despite community opposition. The council says this decision is completely separate from the Games, but it underlines some of the community costs of change. The same thing happened in Cardiff with the Millennium Stadium, where the existing popular swimming pool closed and was not replaced. But that area of Cardiff, right by the centre, is booming. Local athletics organisations are upset that following the Games, the athletics facilities will be immediately converted into a football arena (Brown, 2001). The government and Sport England recently gave more than £100 million to 'bail out' the whole plan as costs over-ran (New Start, 2001a). But for many, it is seen as a vital lifeline for the neighbourhood.

> *It is right here on our doorstep. We are pleased to see that, because it is going to bring life back to this part of the City. We are hoping to benefit from the spin-offs – businesses that are going to come here, a hotel, sports outlet, and supermarkets. We are really hoping that it is going to do well for this area for jobs – that is the next step. There are children at school now – hopefully they will be going into work. That is all people ask for... A decent home to live in, a job to go to, and they will look after the family. We don't want state nanny handouts – we want to be able to do our own – that is traditional in areas like this* (Resident, 2000).

In addition to the stadium and Sportcity, the new town centre adjacent to it will include the national cycling centre, the North West Sports Institute, a tennis centre and new leisure and retail facilities, including a purpose-built ASDA/Walmart. ASDA predicts 50,000 visits per week, and will create in excess of 1,000 jobs. The giant multinational company has been proactive in working to ensure that local people get access to these jobs (New East Manchester, 2001b).

Transport improvements have been agreed. Work on the exciting new metrolink has already begun and will be extended through East Manchester to Ashton-under-Lyne. This new transport artery will generate an entirely different climate of investment in an area that had become cut off from the centre in spite of its proximity. This has fuelled ambitious population targets for East Manchester – doubling the total population from 30,000 to 60,000. The plan is to build up to 12,500 new homes in 10 to 15 years, and improve 7,000 existing homes (New East Manchester, 2001d).

Environmental improvements are being carried out to the area's waterways – two canals and a river valley – and it is hoped that new residential neighbourhoods will be created alongside them. Already developers are renovating some of the warehouses and other abandoned buildings, and new developments are appearing along the canalside on the eastern edge of the city centre. There is now a beautiful direct walking route between the central station and the middle of East Manchester. This forms an extremely innovative, important link between the neighbourhood and the city centre. One new development will be on the canal near the stadium. It is planned to build 300 units there initially; prospective developers were interviewed in October 2001. This development will not receive any subsidy. With its waterside location, close to the stadium, forthcoming light rail metrolink, shops and park, it should be very popular (New East Manchester, 2001b). The whole situation is changing so rapidly it is impossible to keep pace with all the changes.

New East Manchester's absolutely core focus for action is increasing employment opportunities:

> *Unless we restore East Manchester as a centre for employment, nothing is sustainable. I would measure myself in terms of jobs created* (Director, New East Manchester, 2001).

The regeneration plan anticipates nearly 300,000 square metres of new business development, and the creation of up to 8,000 jobs in the area (New East Manchester, 2001d).

East Manchester must also seriously boost the school infrastructure to provide something that might fill the educational gap created by the likes of Manchester Grammar School becoming elite private schools and families leaving the city in search of decent state schools.

> *Unless we offer an educational infrastructure which is better than... surrounding districts, we will continue to see population drift and population instability* (Director, New East Manchester, 2001).

The new, high quality school that the council wants to build to serve Ancoats would also serve City-Edge (there is no secondary school there). This school is just an idea at the moment, but there is quiet determination in the city that it should come to fruition.

Intrinsic to attracting investment is turning around the image of East Manchester:

> *East Manchester conjures up images of an old industrial area that has been in decline for 20 years...To attract investment and jobs, we have to convince people it's an area looking forward not back* (New East Manchester, 2001b).

The Beacons for a Brighter Future Partnership exists to co-ordinate and provide direction for the various regeneration activities taking place in City-Edge and adjoining neighbourhoods, including locally-based projects such as the New

Deal for Communities and SRB programme, as well as initiatives like the Health Action Zone which cover a wider area but impact on these specific neighbourhoods.

The New Deal for Communities (NDC) is specifically focused on City-Edge and an adjoining neighbourhood, with a total population of 11,231 (New Deal, 1999). It is prioritising investment in the physical and social fabric of the neighbourhood – tackling crime, worklessness and environmental conditions – alongside the massive changes to the physical infrastructure being facilitated by New East Manchester. It aims to increase the attractiveness of City-Edge as a place to live so that those who gain employment will not simply move away (New Deal, 1999). Towards the end of 2002, residents will be balloted on a proposed transfer of the rented council stock to a local housing company to enable much needed housing improvements.

Eleven housing associations own stock in the NDC area, illustrating the piecemeal approach of the past. Some are working closely with the council to tackle problems, but many of the housing associations have a much broader area of operation and few have given City-Edge a high priority. Several only have small numbers of properties, so local management is much more difficult and not financially viable; contributing to high levels of empty property (New Deal, 1999). So the council is working with housing associations to consider the future management of the stock. One possible option is that the housing association stock in the area could be managed by the one transfer company, creating a coherent management framework for the area as a whole.

Increasing people's sense of security is a key priority. In 1999, the burglary rate at 81.3 per 1,000 households exceeded the extremely high city-wide rate of 72.6, and was more than three and a half times the national average of 22.7 (New Deal, 1999). And neighbour problems were severe (see Table 4.6).

Table 4.6: Residents experiencing neighbour problems in last two years, 1997-99

Type of neighbour problem	Residents experiencing problem in last two years (%)
Unreasonable noise	40
Abusive language	35
Threats of violence	12
Harassment in the street	10

Source: New Deal (1999) based on Residents' Survey.

The area's population is 95 per cent white (New Deal, 1999), and minority ethnic residents can be particularly vulnerable. Racial harassment drove out a small Somali community in the area. Of eleven Somali families, ten moved out because of racial harassment (Community development worker, 2000). A local research project found that the harassment had included serious verbal and physical abuse of children and adults, and vandalism of the family car and home. Their household survey found that 53 per cent of minority ethnic residents wanted to move away compared with 31 per cent of white respondents (Reid, 2000).

Since New Deal started, significant inroads have already been made on crime – the overall crime rate is down by a quarter (Beacons, 2001). An early project installed one thousand new street lights. Other crime reduction action has included CCTV, 'target hardening' including window locks and door chains provided free to private tenants and owner occupiers and, crucially, extra policing.

> ...funding additional police activity has a massive positive impact on crime figures (Senior regeneration officer, 2000).

An 'alley-gating' programme started in 1999. This means installing locked gates at each end of the alleyways that run along the back of terraces. Residents of the terraced houses backing onto the alleyways all hold a key, and jointly take over responsibility for the alleys from the council. For this reason, alley-gating only works where all residents have become involved and agreed to the change. It requires strong community leadership, even though the council is supportive, and a long-term commitment. Some measure of population stability is therefore crucial and the early alley-gating has been targeted at still stable parts of the area.

By July 2001, 23 alleys had been gated, with a further 214 planned over the next two years (New East Manchester, 2001a). The gated alleys significantly improve security. They have many other benefits as well; gated alleys are much cleaner; they're more attractive, often with tubs of flowering plants; and they encourage more contact between neighbours.

> The alley-way closures have made a big difference. It's been absolutely superb. We went back to people and asked them what they thought. It had reduced the crime, mugging, burglaries, fly-tipping, drug-abuse. They felt more secure (City-Edge resident, 2000).

As well as planting flowers in the newly gated alleyways, hanging baskets thrive in some streets. And the residents of one street, with the support of Groundwork Manchester (a local environmental agency), transformed a derelict patch of land behind their houses into a flourishing community garden.

Table 4.7 shows the quite dramatic reduction in all types of crime, except robbery from the person. The increase in robbery has followed the worrying national trend. The police recorded a 21 per cent rise in robbery across the country during 2000. The initial results of the British Crime Survey found the opposite – recording a national fall in robberies of 22 per cent. The difference is thought to arise because the survey did not interview those aged 16 and under, and much of the rise in robberies is due to thefts of mobile phones from teenagers (Travis, 2001).

The New Deal team is acutely aware of the need to tackle robbery if it is to succeed in helping people feel safer. Amongst other things, it plans to start a 'prolific offenders project', based on the knowledge that a small number of people carry out the bulk of the robberies in the area (New Start, 2001b). A recent survey found that, although fear of attack was still high (55 per cent of respondents), it was significantly lower than in 1999, when 86 per cent of those surveyed feared attack (East Manchester News, 2001).

Table 4.7: Crime in the Beacons area 1999-2001

	Burglary dwellings	Burglary other	Vehicle crime	Robbery from person	Theft	Wounding	Damage	Arson	Total
1999/00	828	467	868	142	73	657	1347	129	4511
2000/01	547	278	640	190	57	569	1008	94	3383
% change	-33.9	-40.5	-26.3	+33.8	-21.9	-13.4	-25.2	-27.1	-25.0

Source: Beacons (2001) based on data supplied by the Greater Manchester Police.

Residents articulated an urgent need for more street supervision. This was particularly acute because of the emptying of the area and its streets, coupled with high crime. Once crime had begun to fall and neighbourhood wardens seemed to stand a chance of success, they were introduced in July 2001. A team of 16 neighbourhood wardens now patrols the area, on foot and bicycle. The scheme runs from 10am until 10pm, 7 days per week. Wardens are not a substitute for street policing and still rely heavily on the police for intervention in case of trouble. But they do provide an essential go-between for the community in brokering many of the links that had disintegrated through ill-use or had simply failed because of the lack of visible front line staff. Figure 4.9 describes the wardens' key tasks.

Figure 4.9: The remit of neighbourhood warden schemes in East Manchester

- To provide a visible presence
- To target areas where residents want reassurance including shopping centres, school routes and post offices
- To be the 'eyes and ears' of the community and report environmental works e.g. litter, faulty lights, vandalism
- To collect information to be passed to the police
- To act as 'good neighbours', carrying out visits to vulnerable residents
- To act as 'hosts/hostesses' of the community, offering help and assistance to visitors and residents

Source: New East Manchester (2001a).

An active Youth Programme is one of many strands of activity aiming to pool and maximise resources. For example, a Beacons' holiday programme, combining the efforts of many different groups, gave 500 young people access to free activities during school holidays over a twelve month period. The activities included music, drama, sport, entertainment (Beacons, 2001).

Residents are being given opportunities to access the Internet. So far, 450 homes have had Internet devices installed, and this will increase to 4,500 via the 'Wired Up Communities' project. As well as giving people the chance to develop computer skills (training is provided), the aim is to increase access to information and give people other ways of interacting with public services. A number of council services are now provided online. It is possible to order a street light repair in this way! (Regeneration manager, 2001b).

Demand for housing

So far, New Deal for Communities' staff feel that all these changes have as yet had little impact on local demand for housing:

> *We have hugely reduced crime but image is still an issue – all the other developments will help that...We have to fundamentally change the housing market; you can't breathe life into a corpse* (Regeneration Manager, 2001b).

But the New Deal, along with the complex array of other developments, may be laying the foundations for a turn-around in the area's fortunes.

City managers believe that only by attracting in new and better off residents can New East Manchester succeed. Yet to do this requires staving off the current major over-supply of new homes in Manchester's hinterland and somehow displacing demand into what was until *very* recently one of Manchester's least successful areas.

Currently, demand in City-Edge is a 'patchwork', varying enormously across the area depending on very locally-specific factors which often aren't related to housing type at all. Semi-detached council houses built within the last fifteen years stand empty awaiting clearance, whilst smaller, less conventionally attractive 1970s council houses are fully occupied.

> *There are some areas where [demand] is healthy, some where it's non-existent... It's not about the stock, the condition, it's about the particular location. Partly it's down to the existing stability of the community. Long-standing, strong residents' associations provide a very solid anchor to an area. Partly [it's explained by anti-social behaviour] – you can lose a community on the back of that* (Regeneration manager, 2001b).

The emphasis in City-Edge – both in the Beacons' approach and the overall strategy of New East Manchester – is very much on working with the people who already live there, and building on the neighbourhood's existing assets:

The Partnership will build on those strengths that already exist and in particular on the strengths of the individual communities. The area comprises a number of small, inter-linked multi-tenure communities where although the strength of community spirit has been weakened, it remains unbroken (New Deal, 1999).

The council has hugely ambitious targets – doubling the population [to 60,000]. It would be wholly counter-productive to try and do all that and displace 30,000 people. Retaining the existing community is fundamental (New East Manchester, 2001b).

Around 2,500 people attended the various consultation events organised by New East Manchester to discuss the East Manchester regeneration framework. They underlined the importance of placing the existing community at the heart of any changes:

The overriding concern, which has been strongly reinforced for NEM by the [consultation] process, is the need to ensure that existing communities are maintained and supported. Whilst the need to re-populate East Manchester is accepted, it is essential that the existing residents choose to stay and continue to provide the backbone upon which a New East Manchester will be built (New East Manchester, 2001c).

This does not mean that demolition is off the agenda. Eventually around 2,500 homes across East Manchester may be demolished (Senior LA strategy officer, 2001). However, so far demolition of council housing has mainly involved very selective removal of small blocks of cottage flats that were causing a nuisance to surrounding houses. The removal of these flats has enhanced the popularity of the houses by avoiding blight over the area as a whole while removing property that had become an eyesore due to abandonment.

One small estate, of semi-detached, high quality homes less than fifteen years old, is due to be demolished. It emptied out as a result of extreme anti-social behaviour. Pressure from developers to create more rational and larger scale development sites may suck in small amounts of relatively stable council housing nearby. But early on it was agreed that most of City-Edge's council estates would survive (with the planned stock transfer to a local housing company bringing in much needed physical investment), and this certainty is helping to give them a new lease of life.

The council classes us as one of the most sustainable estates in the area now, which is lovely! That they aren't even thinking of demolishing us (Resident, 2000).

Meanwhile, some older housing areas in City-Edge have not fared so well. Lower City-Edge has now been cleared. It comprised around 250 terraced houses, just over half of which were privately owned, the rest mainly owned by a housing association. A nearby housing association sheltered scheme built just over ten years ago is also being demolished. The decline of this area is directly attributed to severe levels of crime and anti-social behaviour as more difficult tenants moved in, in the wake of an exodus of traditional residents (New Deal, 1999).

> *The deterioration of physical conditions [in City-Edge] has had a huge negative impact on the community and the human cost of the area's decline should not be under-estimated* (New Deal, 1999).

The council is finding it harder to tackle conditions in the private sector than in its own stock, because it inevitably has less influence over what happens. With a multitude of private landlords and owners, it can be very difficult to co-ordinate action and bring people on board. This applies even more so to the neighbourhoods adjoining City-Edge, which have much larger private sectors. Across the wider East Manchester area, nearly 1,000 private properties are vacant, representing 20 per cent of the stock (Council manager, 2002).

> *The major gap in both the housing strategy and in our ability to manage neighbourhoods is the lack of control over activities in the private rented sector* (New East Manchester, 2001a).

A symptom of City-Edge's continuing problems has been the fall in house prices over the 1990s. This affected not only the traditional terraces (which fell to values of under £10,000 having been selling for up to £30,000 in 1992) but also the small developments of newly built private property in the neighbourhood. For example, new homes which initially sold for £34,000+ were selling for £24,000 just two years later (New Deal, 1999).

One knock-on effect of this drop was a transfer of homes from the owner occupied to the private rented sector. In the New Deal area in 1999, 49 per cent of owner occupiers had plans to leave their current homes. Almost all of these – 94 per cent – wanted to leave the area altogether (New Deal, 1999). Between 1993 and 1999, 61 homes in the New Deal area shifted from owner occupation to private renting (map in New Deal, 1999). This led to higher turnover as private tenants are much more likely to move than owner occupiers (DTLR, 2001).

Sometimes, speculative investors bought up property at very low values, in the expectation that either they would receive compensation through clearance, or that eventually prices would rise again as a result of the regeneration activity. Often they did not let these properties out, but just left them empty, which contributed to the deterioration of the neighbourhood (New Deal, 1999).

The New Deal delivery plan, drawn up in 1999, recognised that until conditions across the area had stabilised, any further attempts to introduce new build housing for sale would be unlikely to be sustained, and would undergo the same shift to private renting experienced on other private estates in the area:

> *The option of supporting new build housing in the short term has been rejected. Evidence has shown that relatively new schemes are already showing a significant drop in value and a drift to private rented accommodation. There is no demand at this stage for new build housing and resources expended would simply be wasted* (New Deal, 1999).

Clearance is one method amongst a wide range of actions that seek to improve conditions in the private stock. Other initiatives include a cross-tenure neighbour nuisance team; a 'bond scheme' in which, once checks have been carried out on the landlord, property and prospective tenant, a bond is provided to the landlord so the tenant can move in without having to find a deposit themselves; demolition of individual properties which are causing concern for local residents; and environmental caretaking schemes (New East Manchester, 2001a).

Property values, particularly for terraced housing, remain extremely low. Traditional two-bed terraced houses in City-Edge, on the market in February 2002, had asking prices ranging from £13,000 to £15,000. A 1970s-style, two-bed terraced house had an asking price of £21,000 (Estate agent website, 2002). Although there are growing concerns about the sustainability of large areas of low-value private housing in adjacent neighbourhoods, confidence in the private market in City-Edge appears to have grown since 1999, when new development of private housing was taken off the agenda until conditions improved. Land contamination that is a residue from centuries of industrial activity makes reclaiming some of the land in East Manchester very expensive. The old mine works which are also causing concern add to those difficulties. Major investors will remain wary of the opportunities that East Manchester clearly offers until a way of tackling these problems has been established. However, the Lower City-Edge clearance site (formerly pre-1900 terraces) is now due to be rebuilt as family-style housing for sale. In all, including the canal-side development, there should be nearly 1,000 units under construction by July 2002 (New East Manchester, 2001b).

> *Sportcity has created a dramatically changed image for East Manchester...it is working* (Chief Executive, 2001).

One road of private sector housing, which had shown the worrying shift from owner occupation to private renting, is now experiencing the reverse. There has recently been a shift back to owner occupation, the road is fully occupied, gardens are well kept. A number of factors helped; a residents' group was formed, a notice board erected in the street to keep people informed, an insecure alleyway was closed off, CCTV installed, and some of the owners from the nearby clearance area bought houses in the road. In February 2002, a semi-detached three-bedroom house was on the market in this road in East Manchester for £30,000 (Estate agent website, 2002).

The atmosphere in East Manchester has shifted from near despair when we first visited to guarded hope as the impacts of many strands of regeneration work their way through the communities that have survived two industrial revolutions.

North Manchester regeneration

The North Manchester Regeneration area covers 7.5 square kilometres, with a population of 20,800 (North Manchester Regeneration, 2001). The Valleyside neighbourhood is situated within this area. It generally has a better quality environment and is more viable than East Manchester, but has recently been experiencing sharp polarisation with some areas doing well, others terribly badly.

Private housing

Until recently, the council was reluctant to talk publicly about the demand problems in parts of North Manchester, particularly in the private sector stock. Understandably, it feared that by highlighting problems it could further reduce confidence in the area and exacerbate the situation. But the council has now gone public on the problems besetting North Manchester's private sector, concluding that parts of the market are not only in trouble but are actually collapsing. Its housing strategy states:

> The recent study of [three areas in North Manchester] has provided clear evidence of localised housing market failure. Falls in house values have led to poor quality and badly managed private renting, a rapid increase in empty homes, many abandoned properties and negative equity (Manchester, 2000).

The private sector vacancy rate nearly doubled between 1997 and 1998, and has continued to grow ever since (see Table 4.8). By October 2001, it was estimated to have reached 20 per cent (Council officer, 2001). Rather than the vacancies being distributed evenly throughout the area (which would still mean that every fifth property lay empty), they tend to be concentrated in particular parts of the area. So some streets are more than half empty, and others are fully occupied.

Table 4.8: Private sector vacancy rate in North Manchester Regeneration area, 1997-2000 (% of stock)

	1997	1998	1999	2000	Oct 2001 (estimate)[1]
Vacancy rate (Total stock: 5,188)	6.2%	12.3%	12.6%	13.0%	20%

Source: Manchester Housing (2001).
Note: 1. Council officer's estimate.

In addition, house prices vary across North Manchester, though they are generally very low. Across fourteen small postcode sectors, the average never rises above £40,000, and is nearly as low as £12,000 in some places. But Figure 4.10 shows that the direction house prices are moving in varies significantly between small areas. Calculations are likely to be based on relatively small numbers of sales but nevertheless suggest that some small pockets are holding their value, some are increasing dramatically, and some are plummeting.

Figure 4.10: Percentage change in average terraced house prices in small postcode sectors of North Manchester, 1995-2001

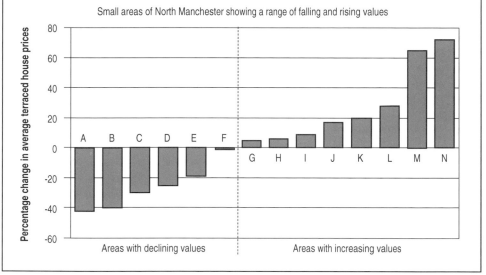

Source: Manchester Housing (2001) based on Land Registry Data. Areas C,G,H and I are situated within Valleyside.

The Chief Executive is blunt about the fact that in places, *'we are grappling with fundamental market failure'* (Chief Executive, 2001).

The council's housing strategy for tackling private housing issues throughout North Manchester is clear:

- it will work to improve neighbourhood conditions through mainstream service delivery;
- it will target capital investment on the areas which appear relatively sustainable;
- it will continue to try to increase the amount of owner occupation in the area, and to extend the choice of properties for sale, particularly at the higher value end of the market;
- it will closely monitor the state of the housing market and use this information to inform future strategy development (Manchester Housing, 2001).

The private sector housing team is undertaking an increasing amount of enforcement action to deal with nuisance dwellings, for example to ensure that refuse is removed and empty properties are made secure. Target hardening initiatives have been underway for some time. There is a rolling programme of environmental schemes, grants to low income owners in areas that are holding on, and consultation about clearance in areas where abandonment has really taken hold.

At the same time as clearing stock where void rates are high, and where they believe it cannot be adapted to meet modern housing aspirations, the council is supporting the parts of the area which are showing signs of life through on-the-ground service improvements. Demolition is the contentious part of the approach, which some residents are actively fighting against. The council is trying to link demolition with the ongoing management initiatives in remaining areas, and is very sensitive about how it is portrayed, being concerned not to reduce confidence further. To the extent that neighbourhood management requires some demolition, it is presented positively as 'getting rid of the nuisance' rather than 'market failure'.

In one group of terraces of about 150 homes, residents were clear that they wanted their area to survive, rejected demolition proposals and launched a 'Hands Off Our Homes' campaign. The council has now declared this a renewal area; the plan is that, in partnership with a registered social landlord, there will be selective demolition combined with environmental improvements and the provision of private gardens (Manchester Housing, 2001). The old houses in this area are large – some are three storey – and several people commented that in more popular areas, like Didsbury, they would be 'worth a fortune':

> They are good solid family houses that are better...than some of the new houses they are putting up. It is well worth keeping some of them I think (Resident).

But 'location, location, location' is a critical problem for places like North Manchester until their reputation as an attractive neighbourhood for most residents can be established. At present, given the extent of problems in the wider area, the council is worried about whether this renewal area will be able to make it.

> I think it's delaying the inevitable. But if the market turns, then maybe this housing type will become viable again. But I think it will take [such a long time]...No matter what investment we put in, it won't work unless we change the [deprivation indices] of the population (Local worker, 2001).

The council has already had its fingers burnt with another renewal area, where demolition of recently improved properties is now being considered. *'Huge, obscene amounts of public money'* – £15 million – was spent on improvements to the terraces, but voids have increased from around 15 per cent to 25 per cent whilst owner occupation has fallen from around 33 per cent to 25 per cent. In one set of terraced houses, only 5 out of 100 houses are occupied. Public efforts in the face of these powerful market forces can feel completely futile. There just aren't enough people to make the improvements work: *'basically the population have just gone'* (Research visit, 2001).

Some people feel that the only option is to reduce the supply of homes, which just aren't meeting people's housing aspirations even when modernised. But other strands of council policy identify the need to re-densify emptying neighbourhoods and to combat outer greenfield building which is ultimately undermining the city's efforts.

Addressing the private housing problems is now the main priority of regeneration:

> *The North Manchester regeneration partnership will now concentrate on longer term restructuring of the market by creating a wider choice of quality homes* (Manchester, 2000).

But it is difficult to see how the housing market can be turned around significantly unless money on a different scale altogether is available to stimulate confidence in the area, in order to create a much healthier mix of housing and reduce the deprivation of the population.

> *In North Manchester, [we] need a funding capacity to demolish, refurbish, replace, make vibrant. There is no national programme which enables such funding. You can [fiddle] around, and we are doing, but you really need a spending capacity of £200 million to £300 million. If you're sincere in talking about sustainable regeneration, you need to be clear about that...We know what to do and how to do it. I have no doubt that the housing market in North Manchester could recover. If we can create the investment capacity, there is no way we can fail. We have shown that you can turn areas around* (Chief Executive, 2001).

A significant development already taking place is the new North Manchester business park – being built on the site of an old hospital. This will comprise over 500,000 square feet of industrial commercial floor space, with the potential for providing at least 1,300 new jobs. In addition, one of the main road corridors is being successfully promoted for business use; approved and pending planning applications have the potential to provide over 200 new jobs (North Manchester Regeneration, 2001).

Local agencies are continuing to try to improve social and economic conditions. The North Manchester Regeneration partnership, with one more year of a 7-year

SRB programme to go, has generated a range of actions. Tangible results have included a GCSE revision club helping a 10 per cent increase in GCSE results in 1998 at the schools where it was organised. A special initiative launched by the police at the end of 2000, to advise people on crime prevention and to target burglars and handlers/sellers of stolen goods, led to 14 arrests and a fall in burglary figures by 21 per cent compared to the same period the year before. A youth café has been launched. A successful community festival was organised in the summer of 2000, with nearly 3,000 people attending. (*North Manchester News*, 2000; North Manchester Regeneration, 2001.) Sure Start is getting underway in part of the area.

An 'Action Team for Jobs' helped over 250 people into work in the space of six months, by providing financial help to cover costs such as clothes, tools, training fees, fares and childcare costs for the first few weeks of a new job, and renewing work-related types of driving licence (such as HGV) (North Manchester News, 2001).

One of North Manchester's key potential assets is its greenery. Parts of this inner city area are like open country. A large park has been the target of a community clean-up day, and is gradually being made more attractive to local people with path improvements, planting events and fishing lessons with a new fishing club for children. Fishing is England's most popular sport, and a local primary head teacher has found that it is becoming quite a high profile sport for some of their boys. Two park wardens are organising a whole range of community activities in the park – including netball for parents, and 'health walks'. A group of local people also came together to look at ways of increasing use of another major park in the area, and new, high quality play equipment has already been installed.

Neighbourhood wardens are now working in an area of around 5,000 properties; including both public and private sector housing. They started work in August 2001 and quickly showed results:

> *Already the streets are cleaner because people are reporting stuff*
> (Senior housing officer, 2001).

New build of homes for sale is continuing. So far, the private homes are at the cheaper end of the owner occupied market. By March 2000, just over 50 per cent of sales in three developments had been to purchasers with a joint income of no more than £15,000 per annum. Private developers in the area were reporting a slow-down in sales, with variable market confidence depending on precise location and circumstances (Manchester, 2000b). As in East Manchester, there is a serious risk of simply undermining existing areas and adding to the surplus, thereby fuelling abandonment.

There are currently concerns about the sustainability of a new estate of around 250 small, relatively low-value family homes. The development is surrounded by increasingly empty terraces, and it is estimated that 10 per cent of the newly purchased houses are already empty. In spite of these worries, over 400 new homes on four sites had been sold by March 2001 (Manchester, 2001d). Flats along arterial routes have been particularly popular (Council officer, 2001). And these developments have been successful in attracting buyers from outside the city; at March 2000, 41 per cent of sales in three developments had been to non-Manchester residents (Manchester, 2000b). Time will tell whether these private developments will be sustainable, and whether it will be possible to begin to sell higher value homes in the area. Certainly the aim is to build: *'at least 1,000 high quality new homes for sale, to offer real housing choice in North Manchester and encourage people with jobs to move into or remain in the area'* (North Manchester Regeneration, 2001).

Social housing

Valleyside's social housing has many low demand problems. Around 60 per cent of the housing in Valleyside is owned by councils or registered social landlords, compared with just 23 per cent nationally. In fact, the large quantity of social housing is thought to contribute to demand problems in the private stock. Increasingly, it is becoming clear that each tenure's fortunes are closely interrelated. There is the fundamental problem of deprivation, associated with the disproportionately high levels of social housing in the area. And population decline makes services less sustainable, which affects all residents. For example, the main secondary school serving Valleyside has recently closed and children are now having to travel out of the area to go to school.

Alongside these whole-area dynamics, are micro-level effects. Often, vacancies in one sector abut vacancies in the other. Equally, stable areas tend to go together too. The council's investment strategy is acting on these links. For example, in order to support future new build housing for sale, they will improve council housing located close to development sites (Senior housing officer, 2001).

Housing associations in North Manchester are experiencing steep increases in low demand problems and have just reached the same low level of demand facing the council; by 2000, more than four fifths of housing association and council housing was in low or no demand (See Figure 4.11). Demand for the council stock has shown a slight improvement in the past year for the first time since 1996. This improvement is too small to judge whether it marks the start of a concrete turn-around. But it is encouraging that, at least for the moment, demand problems in North Manchester's council stock are not getting worse.

Figure 4.11: Social housing demand problems in North Manchester, 1996/98-2000

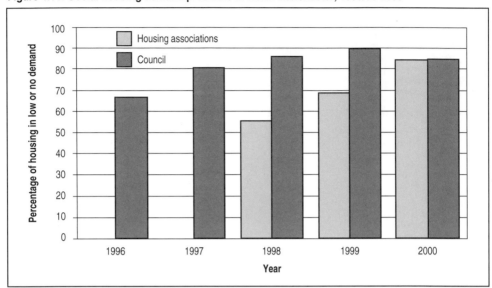

Source: Manchester Housing (2001).

Note: We do not have figures for 1996 and 1997 for housing associations.

Figures 4.4 and 4.5 earlier in this chapter showed how this overall North Manchester pattern has shown up in the Valleyside neighbourhood. Whereas the proportion of Valleyside's housing association stock in demand plummeted from nearly 50 per cent to just 2 per cent in two years, demand for council housing in Valleyside rose from just under 20 per cent in 1998, to nearly 27 per cent by 2000 (Manchester Housing Demand Team, 2001b).

> *Demand hasn't got worse in the council stock. We're very clear now that there are some estates that have a long-term future and are investing in them* (Council officer, 2001).

> *There has been selective demolition of maisonettes; the aspect at the front of that estate looks a lot better. And there is a general feeling of optimism as you go round the estate [compared with 2 years ago]. That does come into school – we feel that in school. And the falling roll has stabilised. In January, it was the first time for a number of years that it was exactly the same number of children as the previous year. We saw that as a real cause for joy* (School governor and local resident, 2000).

The approach to council housing in the area is similar to the private housing strategy; concentrating very limited capital investment on estates which show signs of longer-term sustainability. Estates whose life-span is judged to be shorter don't receive major capital investment (for redesign for example), but they are managed in the same way as the 'sustainable estates', with similarly intensive, on-the-ground initiatives to tackle crime and environmental decay. The council recognises they will not save everything, but they are determined not to make it sound as though they are 'managing decline'. They recognise that estates experiencing low demand at the moment may turn-around in the future.

Some demolition is part of this strategy:

> *To remove blight, we will remove the stock* (Senior housing officer, 2001).

Often this involves reducing the number of properties on an estate, to remove the surplus, rather than clearing an entire estate. So far, at least 15 per cent of the council stock in the regeneration area has been demolished, and there's more demolition to come (Senior housing officer, 2001).

Multi-storeys in part of North Manchester have been marketed to the gay community and this has been quite successful.

> *If we didn't have the gay community in [there] we would have empty multi-storeys!* (Senior housing officer, 2001).

Urban Splash, the successful development company famous for converting industrial relics into bijoux apartments and work spaces in the city centre, is negotiating with the city to transform six empty tower blocks in North Manchester. Urban Splash is confident of changing 'the public's perception of the tower block'. The plan is for the blocks to be refurbished, and 360 flats to be sold, some through shared ownership (*Inside Housing*, 2002b).

One of the council estates in the area was extensively remodelled several years ago. The physical redesign has made a huge difference to residents' quality of life – by removing intimidating walk-ways and cul de sacs, creating proper roads, reversing houses so they face the streets, demolishing maisonettes or converting them into rows of houses.

> *It has always been a very, very friendly estate, even at its poorest time. Now with the redesign of the estate, we have natural surveillance. A classic example is where I live. Since our houses were reversed, I've seen more of my neighbour in the four years since the estate action than I did in 28 years previous. We are in and out of one another's gardens. It is just amazing. When you are walking around the estate, people are sitting out with their parasols and their hanging baskets. It is really, really nice. Although this has always been a friendly estate, we are more friendly now because we see each other more often...My quality of life has improved 1,000 per cent, 22,000 per cent...just because of our homes!* (Resident, 2000).

On the whole, occupancy is being maintained and turnover remains relatively low. Dedicated inputs from staff and residents are helping.

The good thing about [this estate] is the way that the commitment has been sustained over several years now by both the residents and the officers... Maintaining something that is good and keeping it good, and not letting it slip back to where it was, and protecting all the financial and human investment that has gone in there. I think that is special (Senior housing officer, 2000).

Crime has reduced substantially, yet neighbour nuisance is a constant battle, demanding the intensive efforts of resident activists and locally-based staff. A bus service now runs through the estate, but within two weeks of it starting, the evening service was withdrawn because of stone-throwing at the bus. A group of boys have been unsettling residents, and they seem unreachable:

They were bored off their heads and pinching cars, going out thieving, it's a buzz for them. We can't compete with that, the youth service can't compete with that (Resident, 2001).

There have also been successes. One family who had been severely disturbing their neighbours, has completely changed its behaviour. Residents didn't want to drive them away; they just wanted them to modify their behaviour. It took a long time, and the intervention of a whole range of different agencies:

All the necessary agencies have worked together and there's been a 100 per cent improvement (Resident, 2001).

This resident activist explained the long time-scale needed to turn things around, *'With the [residents'] forum I think we can keep on top of it. It took about 10 years for the estate to go down the toilet (1975 to 1985) but it's going to take 30 years to change people's attitudes.'*

Alongside changes in the area's physical and economic infrastructure – like the remodelling of this estate and the developing business park – support and confidence building among individual residents has helped to hold things together. Person-to-person contact is fundamental to front line work in public and voluntary services, and to resident activism. Many staff and residents we spoke to explained how crucial these personal relationships and efforts are. For example, a primary school in the area runs a 'nurture group', to take care of children who have missed out in some way, who often have very difficult home circumstances and whose behaviour can disrupt ordinary classes. Sometimes children attend the group for a very short time as a result of a specific problem; sometimes all the children from a family attend the group on a long-term basis. The children's time is divided between the group and the normal classroom; it is a very flexible arrangement. The nurture group focuses on anger management, sharing, playing together. The staff to pupil ratio is high; there can be as many as two staff to five children. Children love attending it, and the head is in no doubt that when they return to the classroom having been in the nurture group, their behaviour shows a marked improvement.

North Manchester could become a highly attractive, low-cost and therefore very useful source of solid housing for the city. But conversion of the stock to modern standards is not enough. Restoring the vitality of the whole area as part of the city renaissance is crucial.

Conclusion

All the signs indicate that Manchester may have turned a corner. Its increasingly diverse economy is strengthening – encompassing leisure, tourism, corporate, technological and manufacturing sectors. The city's total population grew by 0.2 per cent over the 1990s, halting the relentless fall it had been experiencing for decades. Will this growth be sustained?

Manchester has a 'commuter problem', associated with a lack of high quality homes within the city to accommodate higher earners, who settle outside the city boundaries instead. Its city centre is meeting some of the demand for high quality homes. But the prices of city centre apartments are beyond the reach of many, who therefore choose to live outside the city rather than buy in an area where house values are extremely low and may be set to fall further. Will the demand for homes in the city centre continue, and eventually push values up in the low demand neighbourhoods radiating out from the centre? Or will there be ever increasing polarisation within the city?

So far, and perhaps inevitably, the city's initial population turn-around has not been uniform across the city. The two low demand neighbourhoods of Valleyside and City-Edge continued to lose population over the 1990s, though they too are now experiencing a slight upturn.

The total council vacancy rate has recently fallen, partly as a result of ongoing demolition. The decline in demand for council housing across the city has slowed. It is encouraging that council housing demand problems appear to no longer be in freefall, but from such a low point enormous efforts are required to actually hold and build on improvements. Worryingly, housing associations appear to be overtaking the council in their experience of low demand. And there are serious concerns that more and more of the city's private terraced stock is becoming vulnerable, and some pockets are failing altogether. Growing employment within the city may actually exacerbate demand problems in all tenures, as more people have the financial means to move out (Nevin et al., 2001).

Alongside its city-wide initiatives – such as moving to a choice-based lettings scheme for all council properties (eventually to include housing associations as well) – Manchester is developing different approaches in different areas. It has succeeded in attracting large-scale investment to East Manchester. But what of North Manchester without a major sports stadium to help change its image? Many of its remaining council estates appear to be just about holding on with dedicated management inputs (sometimes following partial clearance or major redevelopment), though housing association stock often seems increasingly precarious. New build private developments have had mixed success. As well as improvements to conditions and services in the neighbourhoods in which developments are located, increasing their value surely requires the 'policy and planning scales' to be firmly tipped towards urban living and away from development outside city boundaries.

> *In the North West and similar regions no new planning permissions should be granted for greenfield sites* (Select Committee, 2002).

Both East and North Manchester are struggling with vacancy levels in private housing of 20 per cent. But these areas are now part of the housing market renewal pathfinder project and a detailed regeneration framework for North Manchester is currently being drawn up.

It is on North Manchester's large quantity of private terraced housing that concern is particularly and increasingly focused, and where it is hoped market renewal funding will bring about the greatest benefits. This housing can be extremely vulnerable, with the market collapsing completely in some areas. Investing in small pockets is very risky when it is unlikely the properties will hold their value; in some cases it has felt like flushing literally millions of pounds down the drain. Intensive management inputs are harder to make work when there are so many different landlords, but can have positive results, as the new neighbourhood warden scheme in Valleyside is showing. However, small-scale efforts are often swamped by wider, more devastating market forces. These concentrated inputs need to be multiplied across many adjacent areas in order to hold conditions and attract private investment.

Sometimes the only option seems to be clearance. But clearance could also represent the waste of a valuable resource – the houses themselves – doubly so when costly improvements have already been carried out. Terraced houses are not necessarily unpopular, as so many areas demonstrate, even within Manchester and Newcastle. Even within North Manchester, some small areas have experienced significant house prices rises over the past six years. Terraced houses can be highly prized, and can be adapted to become successful ultra modern homes, as Urban Splash is currently arguing in Salford. Some local managers feel that the problem is not the property type as such, but the sheer over-supply of identical, small houses, and just too few people living in the city. They point out that one of the reasons terraced houses in Didsbury are popular is because they are mixed in with a variety of different housing types.

Imaginative conversions and environmental improvements could help – by reducing overall supply without wholesale clearance, and creating more variety. Manchester City Council stresses that, although it envisages a lot more demolition being necessary, it does want to retain and improve existing housing where possible:

> *While it is my belief that significant rationalisation of the existing stock is necessary, that will be pursued in the context of our aim to increase population over a period of time and will utilise, wherever possible, existing stock that can be improved to enable it to play a role within the new housing market, thus ensuring that there is a mix of types and values that can secure demand in the long term* (Deputy Chief Executive).

Ultimately, of course, it is the position of a neighbourhood in the 'area popularity hierarchy' that is key to understanding property values. This hierarchy extends way beyond city boundaries. Neighbourhood conditions both help to determine, and in turn are affected by, the position of the neighbourhood in the hierarchy. So how can 'neighbourhood values' be made more equal – how can the hierarchy begin to flatten out?

Development controls, applied across the city region, are clearly part of the answer. Making streets and houses more attractive, improving local services, facilities and transport links, are another important part. But what happens to residents living in half-empty streets whilst we wait for the hoped-for revival of these neighbourhoods? What will be the catalyst in the process of increasing their value, reducing deprivation, stopping economically active residents being pushed out, creating a more mixed population? It is in areas like North and East Manchester that the market renewal fund is needed most, and could really come into its own, but only if linked to cutting new build in outer local authorities. As we have found all over Newcastle and Manchester, there are always existing residents who don't want to go, who fight clearance passionately, and who want to help form the foundations of renewal. Significant funds are needed to underpin this commitment; build up confidence in the neighbourhoods amongst employers, businesses, existing and potential residents; reduce the risk involved in becoming a home owner; and thus set further investment in train as risks genuinely fall.

CHAPTER 5:
Newcastle

The main development in Newcastle's urban policy in the past two years has been the council's controversial 'Going for Growth' strategy, facing the problem of urban population decline head-on. Their Green Paper was published in January 2000. Going for Growth is a highly ambitious 20 year vision – with an overall aim of reinvigorating Newcastle, halting the outflow of population, and attracting people back to live within the city boundaries, particularly the higher earners who tend to choose executive homes in the surrounding countryside. The city hopes to 'recapture' this important segment of the population in part by building large homes in Newcastle Great Park – a recently annexed greenbelt area in the northern part of the city. But Newcastle strongly denies that it wants to build an executive enclave. Instead, it will encourage high density, high quality, mixed use, mixed tenure, more urban, more modern developments.

The Going for Growth strategy describes the West End of the city and parts of the East End as being deeply entrenched in a downward spiral of decline that large amounts of regeneration investment have so far failed to reverse. It is rooted in the belief that only a radical 'restructuring' of the most badly affected communities, such as Bankside, will bring about real change for the better. This led to controversial proposals for large-scale demolition, mainly within the West End, involving 6,600 homes (Newcastle City Council, 2000a, b, c and d).

Employment within the city is increasing, and the city's unemployment rate is falling; it is now half its 1997 level. Unemployment in our two low demand neighbourhoods – Bankside and Riverview – has also been falling significantly (see Table 5.1). The absolute fall in unemployment in these neighbourhoods is extremely important; down by nearly 8 percentage points in both neighbourhoods compared to around 4 points in the UK as a whole. But the neighbourhoods started with a much lower employment base, and their proportional change has not been as great as for the city overall, or the average for the UK. In this sense, unemployment has actually become a relatively more significant problem within these areas (Hills, 2002). This is partly due to the restructuring in the type of employment available; manufacturing and engineering industries still exist, but they have repositioned themselves in specialist niche markets requiring high skills and a minimal workforce. Overall, there are fewer low skill manual jobs within the city. There have been increases in retail, clerical (call centre) and leisure jobs, but these are often low paid and students compete successfully for them. Women also seem to do better in these sectors. For many men in the inner neighbourhoods, the city's labour market appears to have little to offer (Lupton, 2001a). However, there are serious shortages in some manual occupations such as building trades. There are also new opportunities in offshore marine development (Newcastle City Council, 2002).

Table 5.1: Unemployment rates for two neighbourhoods, Newcastle, Tyne & Wear, the North East and the UK, January 1997 – June 2001

	Jan97 (%)	Jan98 (%)	Jan99 (%)	Jan00 (%)	Jan01 (%)	June01 (%)	Absolute change 97-01 (% points)	Proportional change 97-01 (%)
Bankside	18.8	15.4	13.1	13.2	11.5	10.9	- 7.9	- 42
Riverview	19.6	19.1	17.8	16.5	13.6	12.1	- 7.5	- 38
Newcastle	10.7	9.2	8.0	7.7	6.6	5.6	- 5.1	- 48
Tyne & Wear	9.7	8.5	7.9	7.4	6.5	5.6	- 4.1	- 42
NE Region	8.9	7.9	7.9	7.4	6.6	5.3	- 3.6	- 40
UK	6.8	5.3	4.8	4.3	3.7	3.1	- 3.7	- 54

Source: Newcastle City Council website, based on data from the Office of National Statistics.

Alongside the city's overall employment gains there is significant growth in commuter traffic, indicating that surrounding areas are benefiting by having the new workers choosing to live in them, at Newcastle's expense (Community and Housing Director, 2001). Unlike Manchester, Newcastle is still losing population. Having slowed down in the early 1990s, there are concerns that the loss has actually quickened recently:

> *2,000 plus people a year are leaving now. It used to be 1500. So the flight is increasing* (Senior manager, 2001).

Mid year population estimates suggest that Newcastle is currently losing population more quickly than any other English city. Figure 5.1 shows this pattern, and also highlights Manchester's encouraging recent growth. However, the picture is likely to become clearer when the 2001 Census is published, as mid year population estimates are, of course, only estimates with some inevitable inaccuracies.

Figure 5.1: Core cities population comparisons, 1998-1999 and 1999-2000

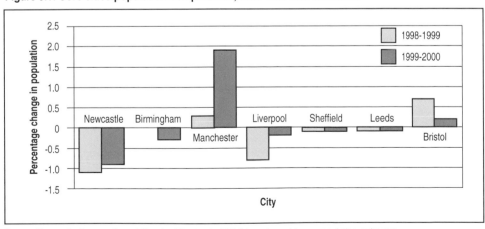

Source: Newcastle Community and Housing Directorate (2001) based on mid year population estimates.

The Going for Growth Green Paper set out clear targets to be achieved by 2020: an increase in the city's population of 15,500; 30,000 new jobs created; 20,000 new houses built; and, most controversially, 6,600 existing houses demolished (Newcastle City Council, 2000a; 2000b). This means a net addition of 13,400 new homes for 15,500 people. This is presumably based on the growth in single person households, but it raises serious questions about the projections of housing need and demand in the city. Most single people will not be able to afford, and some may not want, a self-contained home. Recent evidence suggests that many young single people choose to share and that real household growth is slower than projections have suggested (DTLR, 2002). Nonetheless, household growth far outstrips population growth, and in cities like Newcastle this can lead to greater demand for housing than population figures would suggest (Maclennan, 2002).

Of the new homes, up to 10,000 will be built in the West End and up to 5,900 in the East End (Newcastle City Council, 2001a). However, the government has yet to agree the new build figures that Newcastle has submitted (Newcastle City Council, 2001h). Community protests have resulted in downward revisions of the demolition plans, though wide-scale clearance is still planned for Bankside and is proceeding quite rapidly.

There is a target of 30,000 new jobs, of which 13,000 are planned to be in the West End, and 4,200 in the East End (Newcastle City Council, 2001a). Specific education aims within the strategy include raising educational attainment, helping to reverse the trend of families moving out of the city.

Figure 5.2 summarises local newspaper headlines to give a snapshot of how the Going for Growth strategy has been perceived and has developed between 1999 and 2001. Figure 5.3 gives an overview of city centre developments and other regeneration activities.

City-wide developments

Gateshead is a stone's throw away from Newcastle on the other side of the Tyne. The two cities have long been rivals, with Newcastle holding the status of regional capital and Gateshead trying to galvanise resources that will put it on the national map. Now both are working closely together to form one strong urban centre. They are jointly bidding to be European Capital of Culture in 2008 (*Housing*, 2001).

The two councils have launched a 'Gateshead Newcastle Buzzin campaign' to celebrate distinctive local traditions and attractions such as the Angel of the North, as the first phase in a marketing initiative to attract both visitors and businesses to the area. The aim is to stimulate local people's pride in their city and to consolidate this new image, before spreading the message way beyond the city boundaries. The new 'brand image' will celebrate the area as being: '...*passionate, resilient, inventive, welcoming, with a sense of carnival and zest for life*' (Newcastle Gateshead Initiative, 2001).

Figure 5.2: Going for Growth – summary of key articles from the *Newcastle Evening Chronicle* 1999-2001

Date	Headline	Sub-heading	Other content details
1999			
14 Jan	Housing plan gets a green light	New town *v* country row won't stop massive development near airport	Housing scheme within Northern Development Area
16 April	£80,000 bill as housing row goes on	New inquiry set to decide if homes and factories development goes ahead	Public inquiry likely into plan for 2,500 houses and business park in Northern Development Area
3 June	Homes plan for the West End	Council plans major revamp to halt district's decline	
17 June	Brave new world built along Tyne	Multi-million pound plans to give Newcastle housing for the future	Slogan 'Go for Growth' mentioned
5 Aug	We're pulling down your lovely homes	House proud tenants get shock news that their street will be bulldozed	Scotswood street to be demolished
10 Aug	You can help shape future of your city	Council launches consultation drive to halt Newcastle's decline	Surveys sent to 124,000 homes and businesses
17 Aug	Barrier to new city houses is set to fall	Council set to lift objection to huge scheme but public inquiry is ahead	North Tyneside Council no longer opposed to Northern Development Area scheme
2000			
9 May	City renaissance is to be unveiled		Residents in the dark over Going for Growth and don't know which streets earmarked for demolition
1 June	Green light	Prescott to say 'yes' to £100m scheme which will provide 8,000 jobs and 2,500 new homes	Newcastle Great Park/ Northern Development Area
6 June	Major changes set for a city of growth	City council to unveil new proposals to create two new riverside villages	
8 June	The battle for Scotswood	Residents pledge to fight plans for revamp	Shock and anger about scale of demolition proposals leads to protests

Date	Headline	Sub-heading	Other content details
9 June	Deliver us from this demolition	Vicar's anger as church looks likely to fall victim to revitalisation plans	Church undergoing £600,000 refurbishment may be demolished, and in any case vicar worried community won't be there to use it
10 June	Architect confronts critics over plans to demolish homes		Richard Rogers insists that there needs consultation before decide on demolition
13 June	Tell us: where do we go from here?	Homeowners fear for their futures	West End
14 June	Furious families hit back at architect	West End residents claim they are being made to look like fools and idiots	
21 June	Families stage homes protest	We've been locked out of demolition debate – residents	
23 June	Scrap West End plan say church		Going for Growth will not help the area or its people say Anglican churches
1 July	City plan causes home heartbreak	Couple fear dream house will be demolished in city regeneration	
10 July	Massive survey puts city growth plan to the test	Researchers quiz residents over multi-million pound scheme	
17 July	Is plan right way ahead?	Opinions divided over blueprint for revamping run-down communities	
27 July	Row rages as crisis grips plan to bulldoze thousands of homes	Leaders under fire	Criticism of Going for Growth consultation process by residents, Lib Dem and some Labour councillors
2 Aug	Council goes to war	Labour city chiefs facing threat of split	Backbench rebellion over Going for Growth demolition plans, and Richard Rogers distances himself from the council's proposals
3 Aug	Council backs plan for growth	Councillors abstain in stormy meeting over city regeneration strategy	

Date	Headline	Sub-heading	Other content details
4 Aug	We'll change Growth scheme		More consultation to adapt plans for Going for Growth
22 Aug	Your say on the £100m city reshaping plan	Homes and jobs scheme is going out for Tyneside public's scrutiny	Newcastle Great Park/ Northern Development Area
12 Sept	Growth plan chiefs rapped	Residents back vote of no confidence in demolition scheme	
14 Sept	Demolition plan is not our idea	Architect distances himself from controversial targets	Richard Rogers
15 Sept	Going for views	Survey of businesses	West End
21 Sept	Homes demolition plan scaled down	Bulldozers put on hold as council chiefs take heed of outcry from residents	
4 Oct	Council promise talks on estates	Residents to have a say in growth plan	
5 Oct	Storm after protest group is snubbed	Council refuses to meet alliance fighting huge homes rebuilding scheme	Council claims Newcastle Community Alliance politically motivated and says it prefers to work with individual groups
12 Oct	Residents battle to keep the bulldozers at bay	Generations of families facing the threat of eviction to allow demolition of their homes, come up with alternative vision for their area	Cruddas Park
14 Oct	Worries of going for broke	Small firms are concerned about future in West End	Going for Growth might undermine trade as people move out
18 Oct	Project plans set to boost city blackspot	Investment and new jobs proposed for East End by regeneration scheme	
7 Nov	Residents split over demolition plans	West End and East End clash over proposals set out in housing project	
9 Nov	Families celebrating as homes are saved	Council agrees to revise its controversial scheme to bulldoze houses	

Date	Headline	Sub-heading	Other content details
22 Nov	Gannin' alang the road together	Scotswood residents determined to have a say in the future	Residents arrange meetings for consultation
27 Nov	Fury as Council deny climbdown	Chiefs accused of bowing to pressure over demolition plan	Accusation by Lib Dems, but Labour answers that it's reacting to consultation
6 Dec	Demolition blow	Leading architect walks out on Newcastle Council's controversial regeneration project	Lord Rogers leaves
6 Dec	Delays put our shops in danger	Shopkeepers slam bosses over wait for regeneration work	Byker ward
2001			
19 Jan	A rosy future ahead for city homes	Benwell booster	Council lifts the threat of demolition from Benwell streets
7 March	We are Going to be friends	Truce declared in city's new look war as sides agree to work together	Scotswood
9 April	Strategy continues with demolitions	Empty houses are to be pulled down as part of Going for Growth plan	Byker
25 April	Demolition job in swing	Bulldozers move in to set in motion the innovative Going for Growth scheme	Byker 'eyesores'
12 May	Mapping a future for the West End	Pledge to Scotswood residents, you won't be forced out of the area	
16 May	Survey looks at future of homes	Talks are latest step in the regeneration of the West End	
17 May	Bitter blow for estate residents	Council approval for demolition to start in Lower Scotswood	
18 June	Going to learn	Swedish officials visit city to find out about regeneration plan	

Date	Headline	Sub-heading	Other content details
27 June	Seven fight for facelift project	Residents will pick firm to revamp the riverside	7 'big name players' shortlisted for regeneration of Walker Riverside
27 June	Regeneration plans revealed		Latest blueprints for West and East End Going for Growth
29 June	We'll help families forced out	Team set up to ease regeneration	Relocation team still not actually in place by Dec 2001
6 July	£1bn needed to finance schemes		More than £1bn needed for Going for Growth and other city schemes
16 July	Working together	Residents and council unite to shape inner-city's future	Latest Going for Growth proposals kick-start consultation exercise in affected areas
20 July	Demolition to begin on East End homes	Families agree with council scheme to regenerate areas of Tyneside	Majority of residents surveyed back plans to pull down 209 properties in Walker
4 Aug	Go ahead for housing plan	Tenants on the move in Going for Growth scheme	Massive operation to shift 3,000 tenants is expected to start in 2002
16 Aug	You can't bulldoze our dream house	Couple's desperate plea to council following fears of estate demolition	Couple who've spent thousands of pounds on improvements fear their East End home may be demolished
16 Aug	Going was a major mistake		Family is unhappy at being forced to move by Going for Growth
28 Sept	Building for a better future	Councillors back West End housing regeneration scheme	Cabinet meeting backs demolition of housing in Scotswood
27 Oct	Decision due on city revamp		Council to decide whether to demolish Area 8 in Scotswood

Figure 5.3: Other regeneration developments in Newcastle – summary of key articles from the *Newcastle Evening Chronicle* **1999-2001**

A: City centre and city-wide developments

Date	Headline	Sub-heading	Other content details
1999			
15 Jan	Homes plan on the 100 mark	Grainger Town project builds its 100th flat	
18 Feb	Name that Toon		Gateshead's population set to fall significantly
22 Feb	Empty homes scandal		Scale of empty homes in Newcastle
15 March	A new lease of life	Five year action plan to blend history with the modern world of business	Council launches Grainger Town Plan for regeneration of city centre
21 April	Looking ahead	Sketch unveils multi-million facelift for neglected city centre streets	
27 May	First class lifestyle	Luxury apartments planned for 19th century post office could set you back £390,000	English Partnerships support
30 June	Building on a new vision		Implications of the Urban Task Force report for the North East
21 July	Scandal of our ruined history	How the heritage of Tyneside is crumbling	Focus on Roman history
27 July	Plan unveiled to take city into the future	Millennium blueprint for Newcastle includes expanded shopping heartland and public squares	Launch of City Centre Action Plan
30 July	Super North plan is heading for lift-off	Families will benefit from ambitious strategy to thrust area into 21st century	One North East sends economic strategy leaflets to homes
13 Aug	Thousands set to leave North	Geordies turn their backs on low paid region and head south	Office for National Statistics report predicts population decline
17 Aug	Property boom in city centre		
19 Aug	House prices are on the up		Northern Rock report shows prices at most active in 10 years

Date	Headline	Sub-heading	Other content details
8 Sept	Village reborn	Ambitious project to breathe new life into former powerhouse valley	Ouseburn
2000			
6 Jan	City's Euro lifeline	Grants from the EU totalling millions of pounds fly in the face of damning urban report	EU money comes just hours after publication of Housing Corporation that *'says run-down communities should be left to die'*
2 June	Business park will provide 5,000 jobs	Second big boost for Tyneside as Prescott launches new industrial site	Newburn Riverside Park
16 June	World class	Revival is hailed a huge success	Grainger Town Project given national recognition
15 Sept	Summit to meet on city's future	Delegates to debate how Newcastle's centre should be shaped	
1 Nov	D-Day for massive city change	Councillors will decide on £80m scheme to improve Grainger Town	
10 Nov	Tyneside's doing the business!	Industry chiefs line up in £1m bid to attract new investment to North East	Newcastle Gateshead initiative to launch £1m marketing campaign
4 Dec	World seeks our Quay to river revival	International visitors pour into Tyneside to learn our city revamp secrets	
2001			
2 May	Homeowners to cash in as prices rocket	Housing boom is predicted in the North East	
3 May	We are buzzin'...that's official	Newcastle and Gateshead team up to bid for European Capital of Culture 2008	
8 June	Reborn city thriving	Scaffolding is a sign of the renaissance of an area which has big housing and entertainment ideas for its people	Grainger Town
14 June	Streets ahead for success	Grainger Town's regeneration has gone into overdrive – with £63m in private finance boosting rebirth of historic heart of Tyneside	

Date	Headline	Sub-heading	Other content details
5 July	There's a Village coming to Toon!	Massive development schemes at Newcastle's heart costing millions of pounds are set to be approved by city council, despite protest	City centre schemes
26 July	Plan to change face of the city	Massive chunk of old Newcastle is earmarked for multi-million-pound redevelopment	
14 Aug	Tuning into jobs boom	Labour chief's delight at Quayside work success	John Prescott visits, and commends changes along Quayside
30 Aug	40,000 new jobs in vision for region	Development agency hopes scheme will create 4,000 new businesses	One North East introduces 3 year Regional Action Plan
25 Sept	Scandal of the North's homeless	Families live in B&Bs as thousands of homes stand empty	
12 Oct	£1m That's the price these days of a Tyneside flat…	….And here's what you'll get for all of 50p	Comparing cost of Quayside apartments with 50p homes in Benwell homesteading scheme
19 Oct	It's the right Tyne to pick us	Newcastle Gateshead bid for Capital of Culture	

B: Other regeneration and demolition

Date	Headline	Sub-heading	Other content details
1999			
15 Jan	Good riddance		Families celebrate demolition of vandalised homes in North Benwell
4 Feb	A £50 million shot in the arm		Newcastle City Council's bid for New Deal for Communities for Inner West
13 Feb	Working flat out for a better life		Council gives go ahead for first phase of clearance in Benwell
15 Feb	Wrecked flats will face the bulldozer		Elderly people's flats to go (Dr Henry Russell Court, Scotswood)
16 Feb	Let them stand		Objection to demolition of Scotswood flats

Date	Headline	Sub-heading	Other content details
17 Feb	Chance in a million to improve the city		West End regeneration money is pledged from central government
2 March	Facelift for old towers		3 East End tower blocks to be renovated
11 March	Fightback breeds a new spirit		Byker past and present
18 March	Cash means better times are in store	West End shops to get £1m facelift as part of 5 year regeneration scheme	Adelaide Terrace to be renovated as part of Benwell regeneration
7 April	Looking to a brighter new future	West End residents plan major revamp	Residents might get £7m for jobs and training from SRB
3 May	Our streets fit for a princess		Regenerated Benwell receives visit from Princess Anne
5 May	Houses are flattened after just 3 years	£2 million development in crime-plagued West End is bulldozed	Dr Henry Russell Court, Scotswood
21 May	Bulldozers pull down homes no-one wants	Campaign ends in victory as vandal-hit houses are demolished by council	Tenants cheer demolition of 15 'difficult-to-let' council houses in Daisy Hill, East End
29 June	Revamps plan for inner cities	Millions on the way to improve rundown communities	Urban Task Force report, including proposals for a Renaissance Fund
17 July	Regeneration cash injection		£119.5m from SRB for Newcastle
27 July	This area is too good to leave	Determination pays off with move to purpose-built flat	Focus on residents who stayed in Benwell despite bad national press following plans for 50p house sales
6 Aug	150 are left in race for the 50p houses	Sale of the century latest	Shortlist of 150; 5 to be chosen 'to turn the derelict properties into the home of their dreams' in Benwell
13 Aug	Project aiming for jobs boom	Consortium seeks go-ahead for redevelopment to breathe new life into area	South Benwell Regeneration Consortium in £25m project including building 2 call centres
18 Aug	House outrage	Father's fury over being left with huge debts as nearby flats go in 50p deal	North Benwell resident left with large mortgage still to pay after compulsory purchase

Date	Headline	Sub-heading	Other content details
25 Aug	£5m spent to improve area		Reviving the Heart of the West End has spent more than £5m in 3 years since it was set up
28 Aug	New life for old housing estate		SRB finance of £635,000 for 98 homes in Heaton
4 Sept	Eyesore estate is razed to the ground	Demolition starts of decaying houses to make way for gardens	Benwell terraces partially demolished
10 Sept	Shops area revamp agreed		One North East agrees £1.5m upgrade of Shields Road shopping area at heart of Byker
15 Nov	Work on target at pool project	Councillors pay a flying visit to check out flagship scheme	Pool and library complex in East End
9 Dec	Aid to recovery	Community leaders in the West End want government minister to witness revival	North Benwell wants Mo Mowlam to visit
15 Dec	£60m plan to revamp Byker	Shops and businesses scheme may bring 1,000 jobs	Fossway area, plans submitted by private developers together with East End Partnership
2000			
4 Feb	Euro cash gives estate a boost	Funding bonus means landscaping can go ahead	North Benwell and ERDF money
12 April	£49m boost for West End		New Deal for Communities money
11 Aug	Hellhole estate cleans up its act	Residents reclaim streets from gangs	Blaydon
8 Dec	Massive cash boost to aid North estates	Government announces multi-million-pound package to help the region's council housing	£8.3m under the government's housing investment strategy
2001			
20 Feb	Community aims to boost profile	Project leaders seek ways to improve the image of their area	West End groups, including Reviving the Heart
13 April	Spend faster, team is told	Community cash worth £49m could be lost to group holding regeneration purse strings	New Deal for Communities, West End

The stunning Gateshead Millennium Bridge, reminiscent of the now famous Bilbao pedestrian bridge but with its own unique 'opening eye', was completed in September 2001. The nearby Baltic Flour Mills (on the Gateshead bank of the Tyne), an imposing early building, has become a huge arts centre; *'our version of the Tate Modern'* (Senior council manager, 2001). Other developments on Gateshead Quays include plans for building 1,225 new homes and creating 1,500 new jobs for the region (Buzzin Supplement, 2001). Some of this is already happening. A scheme is being developed to improve public transport serving the Tyneside Quays, and to link them both to Newcastle city centre and to Gateshead town centre (Nexus, 2001). The Newcastle banks of the Tyne are already thriving, with new upmarket hotels and conference facilities, popular high density riverside flats and houses, new high tech industries and an attractive riverside walk.

Newcastle council has had some success in rejuvenating tower blocks, particularly those near the city centre – for example on the edge of the West End. The multi-storey flats have become relatively easy to let thanks to major improvements in security, caretaking and social support, and are in much greater demand than nearby council houses, which are often left standing empty. Council managers believe that this is because tower blocks are often more adaptable than houses: they can be made to feel secure more easily than a spread-out streetscape, for example with round the clock concierge, and they can be targeted at specific groups such as older people or young people as long as there is careful supervision. An extra incentive for such modifications is that tower blocks are much more expensive to demolish than houses.

City centre: Grainger Town

The regeneration of Grainger Town in the heart of the city began in 1997, taking its inspiration from European cities such as Barcelona and Prague whose historic core areas are thriving. A 1991 study found a third of the area's floor space was vacant, and there were significant problems of decay amongst the buildings which date back to the 1830s and 1840s. Grainger Town is supposed to be one of the most complete and certainly one of the most beautiful city centres in the country. Its gracious Georgian buildings include a theatre, shops and elaborate apartments. In recent times, not many people lived in this part of the city, and one of the main aims of the regeneration project has been to reintroduce a resident population. So far, nearly 300 flats have been created or are under construction, many as part of a major Living Over the Shop (LOTS) scheme (Grainger Townlife, 2001).

> *Developments are standing on their own now – there's no issue of subsidy. There's developer confidence* (Community and Housing Director, 2001).

Since 1997, 211 new businesses have been set up, and 574 jobs have been created. Neglected, run-down buildings have been restored to their former beauty and rejuvenated with completely new uses (such as wine bars, pubs, luxury offices).

Big name shops have been established in what is becoming the 'Bond Street of the North'! (Citylife, 2001).

These developments in the City Centre help Newcastle secure its role as a Cosmopolitan Capital (Newcastle City Council, 2001b).

By the end of 2001, around £85 million had been invested in Grainger Town, including nearly £70 million from the private sector (Citylife, 2001).

Quayside

Below the city centre, within a short walk, residential developments alongside the central Quayside are expanding rapidly. A new Wimpey development is selling well. The council wants to encourage high density, brownfield, residential development for families, not only for single people. At a new development site on the riverside just inside the West End (Elswick Riverside), the council will provide appropriate primary schooling to support this end (Community and Housing Director, 2001).

Regeneration of the eastern riverside began with the St Peter's Basin private residential development in the late 1980s (near the Byker estate). House prices there are stable rather than rising, there is significant turnover and it is a somewhat isolated development which needs to become more integrated within the East End as well as with the flourishing Quayside (Newcastle City Council, 2000c). There are plans to improve pedestrian links between St Peter's Basin, Byker Estate and the main Shields Road (Newcastle City Council, 2001b).

Ouseburn

The Ouseburn area, a dramatically steep valley on the edge of the centre, running down to the Tyne, has numerous old industrial buildings left over from its place at the heart of the Industrial Revolution. With the support of Single Regeneration Budget funding, the Ouseburn Partnership is stimulating the development of an urban village. Flat conversions are underway, and live-work units are selling to small new enterprises, adding to the economic diversity of this area which already contains more than 200 small businesses. A business association is developing. Educational visits are popular, an indoor equestrian centre will open in 2002, and a riverside walkway is linking the Valley with the Quayside. A large Victorian warehouse is being converted into the 'Centre for the Children's Book', a project celebrating children's literature. A living heritage project provides local people with the chance to share memories and experiences of living and working in the area. In the 1930s and 1950s nearly all the old terraces in the lower valley were demolished, but many people were rehoused in nearby areas and many still feel a strong connection to the Ouseburn. Over 200 people and 30 community groups are members of the heritage project, which has compiled a detailed social history of this valley (Ouseburn Partnership, 2000; 2001).

Byker

Byker is an internationally renowned large council estate, built in the late 1970s to replace a traditional settled community of terraced streets, on the eastern edge of the city centre. Byker was an old and large slum clearance area, where the old terraced houses were condemned and cleared for lack of basic amenities, rather than structural or social problems. The architects worked closely with the community and helped as many people as they could move straight into the new Byker. The new estate was constructed within the Byker Wall – built to shield homes from a planned new inner ring road that never happened. Byker is now struggling with mounting disrepair, lack of reinvestment and disconnection in spite of its proximity to the city centre. Some people are hopeful that closer links between Byker and the private Quayside developments will have a positive knock-on effect on Byker.

> *I've actually heard quite a lot of positive things said about it. Some people have said 'Aye well, when they start building further along the quayside they'll be more bloody worried about what gans on [in Byker] because they won't want this place to look like a shit-hole when they've got £100,000 flats, £250,000 houses sitting just across the other side of the road'* (Local manager, 2000).

Regular maintenance is seriously inadequate, and there has been almost no major improvement or renewal since it was built.

> *The whole estate is now around 25 years old. And it needs investment. If you look around Byker, there hasn't been a lot done. And everything is starting to deteriorate. There's so much detail in Byker, so many features. And it's the detail that's going to deteriorate...on the footpaths, the edging is going, all the cobbled areas are starting to come apart. There is a need for really big investment* (Housing manager, 2000).

Byker has pockets of very high vacancy rates and just over 6 per cent of all properties were empty at June 2001 (Newcastle City Council, 2001g). There are also parts of Byker in strong demand. The number of empty properties continues to fluctuate. The council in 1998 proposed demolishing a small corner of the estate that had fallen into disuse, provoking intense opposition. A number of articulate residents strongly fought against demolition, winning support from Lord Richard Rogers and Ralph Erskine, the original architect. English Heritage is now considering whether to grant Byker Listed Building Status. Rather than demolition, the new emphasis is on the development of a Byker Action Plan for the whole estate – to increase stability, tackle crime, insecurity and anti-social behaviour, improve the local environment and increase accessibility (Newcastle City Council, 2001b). Basic repairs to the fabric are being carried out again.

> *Byker still does [have sustainability] although we've got these problems...It is saveable. I think, first and foremost, there's still a very, very large core of*

people who want Byker to be the Byker that it was when it was built...It is a very, very special housing estate (Housing manager, 2000).

Residents identify tackling crime and improving community safety as the highest priorities. Rates of crime far exceed city-wide averages. For example, recent figures show a theft rate of 101 per 1,000 households in Byker, compared with 68 per 1,000 households city-wide (Newcastle City Council, 2001f).

[Byker] is now a shadow of its former self and it appears as an estate under siege. Urgent action is needed to save the estate from further decay and dereliction...The 'listing' of the Byker estate needs to be seen as the catalyst for the comprehensive regeneration of this remarkable dwelling environment (Byker residents, 2001).

Young people are often responsible for the estate's disorder problems. But most respond to targeted initiatives, and a youth project over the summer of 2001 significantly reduced crime. Around 20 'hard-core' trouble-makers are very difficult to reach. But joint working rooted in good relations between the housing department, police and the youth offender team is resulting in individually tailored responses to these most persistent young offenders. These include support from the youth service, acceptable behaviour contracts, and occasionally Anti Social Behaviour Orders.

Important advances in the estate's security have already been made. Street wardens are now operating in Byker. The installation of a door entry system in the Wall makes it possible for the families living in flats there to control the comings and goings, creating a much more secure atmosphere. Residents led a successful bid for CCTV on the estate, and are now involved in the design of the CCTV system. The Home Office is providing the capital funding, the council will fund the revenue requirements to back it up. The longer-term aim is to have a concierge system.

A Conservation Plan is also being developed, involving residents, maintenance teams, architects and others, aimed at preserving the positive aspects of the estate and tackling the negatives (Newcastle City Council, 2001d). The small area that had been proposed for demolition because of its high vacancy rates, is now likely to be converted to 'live-and-work' units for artists. Student artists shown around the site have already expressed enthusiasm for the idea (Project North East, 2001).

The involvement of English Heritage in protecting Byker from demolition is so far proving to be a double-edged sword; on the one hand it is hoped that it will help to lever in much-needed funding as it raises the estate's profile; on the other, it may slow down the action needed as everything is checked in minute detail. So far it has done more of the latter than the former. At the moment the estate is in a kind of limbo, whilst English Heritage considers whether to list it – this process has already been ongoing for more than eighteen months, and it could take nearly as long again before a final decision is made. This seems tragic in the light of

Newcastle's willingness to think again and come up with the careful physical overhaul that the estate requires, which will mean significant capital resources.

At the same time, basic maintenance, environmental care, and continuing security improvements together could make a big difference to the look and feel of Byker. The many residents with a strong attachment to Byker, partly through being rehoused there in the first place from the original old Byker, are an important anchor for the city as it tries to hold onto its ever more depleted population base.

It's depressing to see such an opportunity as Byker going downhill. However, I still have not seen anywhere else as good as my flat, so I will be sticking around for a while! (Byker resident, 2001).

Rescuing and restoring Byker, now the declared aim of the city, could give a powerful signal to other low income communities that things can get better.

Increasing ethnic diversity

The city is becoming more ethnically diverse as the city council agreed to be part of the government's asylum dispersal scheme. In both the East End and the West End, local agencies and residents' groups have worked to assist with the arrival of asylum seekers.

Because of flagging demand for Byker, the estate has become one of the centres for housing asylum seekers under the dispersal policy. Asylum seekers made up 2 per cent of Byker's population in 2000-01, compared with 0.8 per cent in 1995-96 (Neighbourhood Manager, 2001). Some asylum seekers have experienced harassment, including physical attacks (Byker Asylum Seekers Support Group, 2001). Such incidents are thought to be rare (Newcastle City Council, 2002). Alarms given to vulnerable asylum seekers (12 in total in the area) have very rarely needed to be activated, and reported incidents of harassment in Byker fell from 56 in 2000-01 to 19 in 2001-02 (Newcastle City Council, 2002). The Byker Asylum Seekers Support Group, tenants' associations, and a large number of individuals, provide important support to asylum seekers in this almost exclusively white area.

The council recognises the need to support refugees and prepare the receiving communities. Its policy is to assist with the national dispersal programme, but to ensure that people are not isolated. It has been stressed that it should not be about just using up empty properties (Community and Housing Director, 2001).

A greater cultural mix is seen as an important part of the revitalisation of individual neighbourhoods as well as Newcastle as a whole.

We hope those who stay will settle into the local community and add to its diversity and vitality (Reviving the Heart of the West End, 2000).

The council chose Elswick in the West End for its New Deal for Communities area in part because it is multi-ethnic, lively, and entrepreneurial. It is seen to have more chance of recovery partly as a result of its ethnic diversity.

Bankside (West End), Riverview (East End) and Going for Growth

Extreme problems in the neighbourhoods

Bankside is presented in the Going for Growth strategy as a neighbourhood that has received huge investment in both physical improvements and intensive housing management, yet has growing numbers of empty properties in all tenures and a *'depressed misfunctioning property market'*, with extremely low house prices of under £10,000. Shifts from owner occupation to private renting, actual abandonment by some owner occupiers, as well as virtually zero demand for social renting, create a continuing need for demolition (Newcastle City Council, 2000d). The cost of decline in Bankside and other parts of the West End is a huge drain on the council's resources – calculated as an additional £10 million a year. And, in some cases, estates which have had millions of pounds worth of investment because they were so unpopular have higher void rates than those which have had no investment (Newcastle City Council, 2000b).

Local staff and residents confirm the scale of problems.

> *Bankside [suffered] the highest loss of population in the city. Between 1971 and 1998 the population has fallen by 43 per cent...Which is a phenomenal amount when you are trying to maintain levels for schools, doctors surgeries, shops...It's desperate really. It's a very hard area to try to turn around...We haven't, in spite of all sorts of marketing tricks, been able to attract new people into Bankside. The population continues to drift away* (Senior housing manager, 2000).

The council identified two thirds of Bankside's council housing as unlettable or difficult-to-let in 2000 (see Table 5.2).

Table 5.2: Demand for council properties in Bankside at September 2000

Demand category (based on staff views)	Proportion of council housing
Unlettable	34%
Difficult-to-let	32%
Lettable	34%

Source: Newcastle City Council (2000d).

Riverview also has high vacancy rates, particularly in the riverside area (Lower Riverview). By 2000, local managers could see few signs of demand: *'Demand [in Lower Riverview] is now virtually nil. That's spreading throughout the wider Riverview area'* (Housing manager, 2000). A year and a half later, the Lower Riverview housing manager could not see any improvement: *'There's little demand for anything. It's not getting better, that's for sure'* (Housing manager, 2001).

A whole section of private property on the main road is completely derelict – houses are empty, vandalised and burnt out. The council has issued compulsory purchase orders and these properties will eventually be demolished. Their decline is partly attributed to the council evicting anti-social tenants who then moved very locally into these private sector tenancies:

> *People we evict end up in the private [sector]...Now those are being demolished – where do they go [next]?* (Housing manager, 2001).

Despite very specific voids targets across the city, and top priority being given to letting empty properties, housing managers have been up against forces often well beyond their control.

> *Our approach needs to be radical, we must accept that in certain areas the urban structure is broken and cannot be mended* (Newcastle City Council, 2000b).

The number of empty properties has continued to creep up despite ongoing demolition (Newcastle City Council, 1999).

> *We have drawn lines on maps before...[thinking] let's draw a line on the map and let's not do any more demolition beyond that. We've done this exercise countless times now...And then we've had to go back [to residents] and say 'oh, we're sorry, we were wrong again, the population has continued to drift away...'* (Senior housing manager, 2000).

Table 5.3 shows the pattern of rising vacancy rates in the two neighbourhoods, and city-wide, despite ongoing demolition. Sometimes reductions in vacancies have been the result of targeted marketing initiatives, but often they are explained by demolition, following which the proportion of empty properties begins to rise again. Bankside was between 30 per cent and 40 per cent empty at the beginning of October 2001 (Housing manager, 2001). The major clearance already underway was having a very grave impact on community conditions.

From 1991 to July 2000, Bankside's council stock reduced by 40 per cent as a result of demolition. 52 new build housing association properties were also demolished, some without ever having been lived in (Newcastle City Council, 2000d).

Table 5.3: Local authority voids – Newcastle and 2 neighbourhoods (percentage of stock empty each year)

Year	Bankside	Lower Riverview	Newcastle
1988	2.7	6.4	3.6
1989	5.3	6.3	4.3
1990	9.4	9.5	5.6
1992	19.5[1]	9.9	3.8
1993	9.5	6.4	2.9
1995	11.4	8.4	4.2
1996	14.7	12.4	4.4
1997	14.7	13.1	4.4
1998	13.3	17.5	4.2
1999	13.0	20.0	4.5
2000	16.0	8.0	4.2
2001	21.0[2]	11.0[2]	5.0[2]

Notes: All figures are for March each year. Figures from 1997 and earlier are from Newcastle Housing Annual Reports. Bankside figures from 1995 and earlier represent a combination of two housing areas that were then counted separately. Figures for 1998-2000 were supplied by the housing department (2001).
1. This steep increase in voids coincided with an increase in the amount of crime committed by young men against their own community (Power and Mumford, 1999). The sharp fall after 1992 is mainly accounted for by the demolition of 407 council properties in 92-93 (Newcastle Housing, 1998).
2. Housing Business Plan, 2001.

Figure 5.4 shows the pattern of empty council properties in five Bankside streets that have experienced a steep increase in vacancies from 1997 to 2001. Only road 4 is due to be retained. Demolition is already underway in road 2 which is why its void figure has reached a high of 56. Road 3 had already been partially demolished by summer 2000 and will now be fully demolished. The other roads are due to undergo either total or partial demolition in the coming months.

Figure 5.4: Pattern of empty council property in five roads in Bankside, 1997-2001

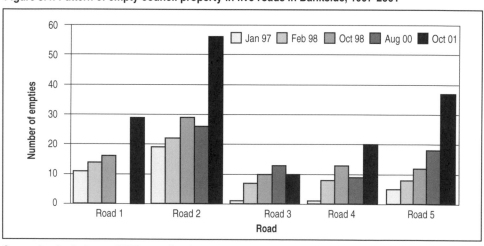

Sources: Local authority map (1997), estate housing management committee reports (1998), Bankside neighbourhood profile (2000), information supplied by housing department (2001). Data was not available for road 1 in 2000.

Lower Riverview has not experienced quite such dramatic changes as Bankside, but some of its streets have been demolished, or are about to be demolished. We followed the fortunes of five roads and one block of flats between 1998 and 2001. Their trajectories over this period fall into three main types:

(i)   relatively stable with few or no voids (roads 2 and 3);

(ii)   a worrying increase in voids over the period which may signal ongoing abandonment but still with a chance to be halted (block 4 and road 6);

(iii)   already high vacancy levels in 1998 turning into significant abandonment by 2001 (road 1 is due to be partially demolished, and road 5 will now be completely demolished having already undergone some selective demolition since 1998). Figure 5.5 shows these different patterns.

Figure 5.5: Different patterns of empty council property in Lower Riverview streets, 1998-2001 (%)

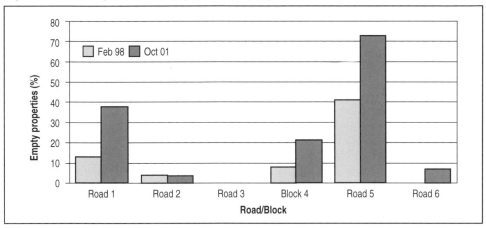

Sources: Local authority administrative records (1998) and information supplied by housing department (2001).
Note: Road 3 was a court in a block of flats and the other courts were in roads.

Going for Growth in action

According to the city council, 90 per cent of respondents to the Going for Growth green paper supported the overall policy direction (Newcastle City Council, 2000b). But the demolition proposals have caused widespread angst and the proposal to build on former greenbelt land while demolishing many sound and modernised homes has provoked serious questioning of Newcastle's original strategy. These homes often seem attractive in the eyes of visitors to the city and, particularly for southerners from high demand areas, the complete lack of appeal is hard to understand. Chair of the Urban Task Force, Richard Rogers, was involved in the initial stages of advising on a 'masterplan' for the West End, but he was dismayed by the scale and insensitivity of the demolition proposals. He moved quickly to distance himself from the original Going for Growth plans.

> *When I walked along the beautiful streets of Bankside and was told that this must be demolished, my heart filled with questions...We must build around anything with a flicker of life* (Richard Rogers quoted in *The Guardian*, 2000).

A Bankside resident whose street is due to be demolished said:

I used to love this area...It's so sad – it's so beautiful when you look across [the Tyne]. You can see all the way along the river (Bankside resident, 2001).

The council has sought to reassure residents that it will provide choice in their rehousing and will seek to minimise disruption (Newcastle City Council, 2000b), but fear and uncertainty are inevitable when such a large amount of demolition is planned. Although the maps in the council's draft plans always carried a caveat in the text that they were subject to consultation, the identification of areas to be 'restructured' left little room for doubt about the council's ultimate intentions. Few believed that targeted 'problem areas' would survive intact. The council had lost confidence in their ability to restore the neighbourhoods we were following, as is apparent in their statement: *'It is clear that some areas such as within Bankside and Lower Riverview are beyond resuscitation'* (Newcastle City Council, 2000c).

As well as the belief that some housing is unsaveable, a key part of the council's rationale for significant demolition in these neighbourhoods is the idea that the cleared sites must be large enough to give private developers the confidence to build anew.

The sites must be of a scale that will not be 'pulled down' in quality and desirability by adjacent declining areas (Newcastle City Council, 2000c).

The kind of small-scale demolition of single streets or parts of streets that has happened until recently does not result in attractive development sites. The following map shows Bankside in 1999 – already scarred by demolition but with bare land dotted between remaining, often still unpopular homes:

Figure 5.6: Schematic map of Bankside showing demolition sites in 1999

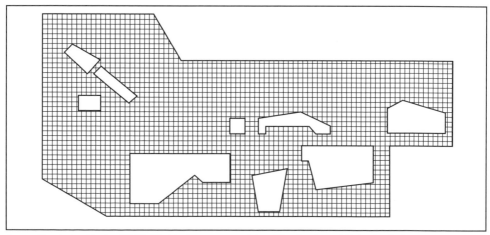

Source: Mumford and Lupton (1999). The blank areas represent demolition sites from which local authority owned housing has been cleared and not replaced.

Alongside housing redevelopment, Going for Growth proposes a new district transport system for the West End involving street-running trams, an improved public transport system for the East End, and new cross-Tyne links. The target is to open a tram-line through the West End in 2007. The trams are planned to integrate with the existing Newcastle Metro network (Community and Housing Director, 2001). New developments at moderately high density are being planned around the proposed public transport links. The Metro network already links to the Metro Centre and will provide some of the basic infrastructure. Whether the ambitious tramway plans will come off, or on what time-scale, is unclear. The exact route is currently being debated and funding has not yet been agreed. With much of the population removed and a critical density of new homes still a long way off, it is hard to see the government funding this tramway first. The whole strategy is premised on enhanced local employment opportunities although there are few specific plans compared with Sportcity in East Manchester. Improved public spaces and parks are supposed to make the area more attractive (Newcastle City Council, 2000c; 2001a).

At the moment with population still falling, it is unclear how a new community of residents with money to spend, workers employed in the inner areas and new enterprises will be kick-started. Getting rid of property and rehousing people away are relatively easy in a situation of serious over-supply. But turning this into inward flows of people and private investment is slower and more challenging.

The debate surrounding Going for Growth continued to rage throughout 2001. The West End and East End regeneration plans were published in June 2001. These are generally a continuation of the plans proposed at earlier stages, but modified as a result of the shocked reactions of local communities and of further consultation.

> [The first plans were] technically very good, but in human terms a disaster. You can't impose a blueprint for a city like that. Telling people they would be taking out houses [across the West End] and replacing them with bijou residences...But now consultation is much better (Senior manager, 2001).

> [Residents] feel that Going for Growth is something that's up there, when really we need to be starting down here and going up that way (Neighbourhood manager, 2000).

> You can't socially engineer an area like this. Would policy-makers like someone going to their area and saying 'right, abandon your home because there's too many of you here, and there's some empty properties there, so we'll just move you into there, and that's it, sorted'? It's disrespectful... Economically it makes a load of sense just to level the area to the ground and start again. But that doesn't take into account the human cost and the social cost. (Bankside resident, 2000).

Many people commented that the original plans were presented as a fait accompli, and seriously damaged relations between the council and the inner city communities, for instance, *'We all lost a lot of the confidence of people through the way Going for Growth was originally thrown [at them]'* (Neighbourhood manager, 2001).

People opposed blanket demolition and the complete destruction of communities it implied (Newcastle City Council, 2001c).

> *There were pockets of housing that were relatively good and still occupied by quite stable communities. They were aghast at the proposals [when] they saw themselves in areas of demolition* (Neighbourhood manager, 2001).

These reactions prompted a 'huge rethink' by the council. Some demolition plans have been withdrawn, others have been significantly scaled down. In some cases, the threat of demolition seemed to result in the community gaining strength by coming together to fight, and a new lease of life for the estate. For example, on one East End estate:

> *[It's] now a scalpel sort of scheme rather than a bulldozer flattening...The good thing is that it did galvanise that community. They came up with a very good scheme to save half the estate and provide space for new social housing* (Neighbourhood manager, 2001).

> *The [residents in Lower Riverview] have got themselves organised better than they have ever been here before...a number of groups have sprung up...There are residents involved that probably years ago you would never get them up* (Housing manager, 2001).

In another part of the East End, the council proposed demolishing one street where nearly a quarter of properties vacant. This street was dominated by four or five extended families who, through their closed family network, were making newcomers feel unwelcome so they would quickly move out. The threat of demolition prompted these extended families to talk to housing managers and to realise they had to start welcoming people into their street. The vacancy level is now under 2 per cent, and the demolition plans have been withdrawn (Lupton, 2001).

Bankside has always had active and organised residents. After much anguish, a joint working group was formed between Bankside residents and the council to oversee Going for Growth in the area. Both parties expressed the belief that the existing community should form the foundations of the 'new Bankside', whilst agreeing the need to attract new people into the area (Bankside and City Council Going for Growth Partnership, 2001). There still is a core population in Bankside with strong attachments to the area but in order to save their shrinking community they have had to accept a more open view of 'community'.

I think people who now live in Bankside are the community who have very strong links with Bankside. They've lived there a long time, and I think they're very keen to see it survive. They've got a very strong attachment to the area. (Senior housing manager, 2000).

However, where conditions are particularly precarious, talk of demolition can spark further decline as the future of a neighbourhood comes into question. A question mark has been hanging over Bankside for a long time – first as a result of the 'creeping demolition' that the council is now determined to prevent (Community and Housing Director, 2001), and then as a result of the Going for Growth proposals which have inevitably involved a lengthy decision-making process. One aim of Going for Growth is to have a bold regeneration plan that sets out a clear future for neighbourhoods and does not let them just fade away gradually. But the process involved in making such radical changes can itself blight whole areas. Going for Growth has in practice knocked the stuffing out of areas that were 'hanging on'.

In some respects [Bankside] is now blighted by all the talk and rumour about demolition...It must be hard to be a family living in Bankside at the moment. When people are wondering 'should I decorate or should I not?', 'should I buy a carpet or should I not?' (Senior housing manager, 2000).

The clearance of Bankside

Social housing lettings in Bankside essentially came to an end as clearance decisions were awaited. Some residents saw this halt to lettings as the council 'demolishing by stealth' (Housing manager, 2001).

In theory, the revised Going for Growth plans placed a much greater emphasis on community, and expressed the right of existing residents to remain living in their neighbourhoods after redevelopment. This was reflected in statements such as: *'In areas of declining population neighbourhoods and their local services are being threatened. A key challenge is to support the residents affected, maintain their social support networks and provide a continued focus for community activity'* (Newcastle, City Council, 2001b).

This talk of preserving community and scaling down the demolition plans represented a significant shift in language from the initial 'wipe the slate clean' impression given in the green paper. However, only a minority of Bankside will be left standing. During the autumn of 2001, the council conducted household surveys in possible clearance areas. Of the eight parts of Bankside surveyed, five agreed with the council's assessment that the area in question was considered unviable. But support for demolition in these areas was by no means unanimous. The proportion in favour of demolition ranged from 56 to 65 per cent. In the three remaining areas, 75 to 90 per cent opposed demolition (*Inside Housing*, 2001b). Organised residents' protests are the only thing holding back the bulldozers from some parts of the five areas targeted for demolition – and clearance is already underway in others. As one housing official put it, *'If it wasn't for the residents, there'd be nothing left'* (Housing manager, 2001).

We tracked the fate of some of the streets that had quite high occupancy when we visited in 1998. In February 1998, 13 streets of council properties in Bankside had between one and four empty properties. Just over three and a half years later, in October 2001, eight of these streets still had fewer than five voids. Of the others, one had been completely demolished, another no longer contained any council houses, and the other three had 29 voids between them. Of the eight streets that have maintained a high and constant occupancy from 1998 to 2001, two are due to be demolished shortly, and a further two are due to be partly demolished. Thus, the rapid changes being made to Bankside's landscape are actually drawing in streets that in terms of their occupancy rates are amongst the more stable. This is inevitable with a large-scale demolition plan that, with the best will in the world, offers a blunt instrument 'sweeping away all in its path'.

It must be questionable whether the remaining fraction of housing in Bankside will be sustainable as everything around it is cleared away. It is not one block of housing – rather, it represents separate areas in different parts of the neighbourhood, begging the question: *'Is it just a softly, softly approach [to total clearance]?'* (Housing manager, 2001).

Several local staff believed that the whole area was doomed to be flattened and they faced this prospect with deep regret, but the council emphasises that one third of the whole area will remain (Newcastle City Council, 2002).

A resident raised with us the scenario that must worry and deter many developers – the residents of ill repute who may yet remain in the area. *'Where are the 'pioneers' who will live near [our anti-social neighbours]? So I really think the top part of the estate will come down as well'* (Bankside resident, 2001).

Some people described a sense of frustration and outrage at the knowledge that sound housing was being demolished for social reasons. Was a management solution possible?

> *There's uncertainty and there's sheer frustration...We had an area of housing for elderly people – the sheer frustration at the cost of that and the fact that because of kids the whole thing had to come down...Some imaginative and innovative youth work could make quite a lot of difference. A lot of their trouble is misplaced energy* (Health visitor, 2000).

> *Anti-social people have brought the area to where it's at now...I feel very bitter and resentful that because of some people's anti-social lives, the area's gone downhill and it's given the council the ability to demolish the area. But they're not doing anything about their anti-social behaviour – they'll just move them and they'll rot another area* (Bankside resident, 2001).

Demolition plans are forcing the resettlement of difficult families out of demolition neighbourhoods and into other areas – where their anti-social behaviour continues and destabilises the new area. This is already showing up as a problem and is set to get worse as demolition bites further. This problem is well documented in other demolition areas (Islington, 2001).

Going for Growth dominates the life of the neighbourhood, with even young children knowing which of the eight designated areas they live in (Locally-based researcher, 2001). To residents and locally-based staff, the planners and strategists appear far removed from the reality of living through clearance. This process is terribly hard for the people living and working in the area:

> It's easier when you're not meeting people every day to say 'this should go here and that should go there'. The effect on people is devastating...people who've lived in the same house for 20, 30 years and they just don't want to go...[One] road is fully let on one side, but it's going (Housing manager, 2001).

> One negative effect of the housing coming down is vermin. One of my mums has had awful trouble with rats, since the houses below her were demolished. That had huge implications for her mental health, which was fragile to start with... (Health visitor, 2000).

One family described how anti-social behaviour had escalated. Their street is increasingly empty, vandalised and burnt out. The daughter said,

> There's all the graffiti and smashed up houses and kids' faces with looks that could kill...It's quite embarrassing. You live here and they probably think you're part of that, but you're not (12 year old girl, Bankside, 2001).

Their street and other nearby, mixed tenure terraces will be demolished. In the meantime, conditions in this small area have severely deteriorated, and residents live with deep uncertainty about what the future holds, when they will move, and where they will move to. This puts a huge strain on people.

> [I have] borderline depression...So many meetings where people have burst into tears because of the pressure and uncertainty (Bankside resident, 2001).

The uncertainty is unsettling younger residents too. There are worries that these feelings may eventually bubble over into larger-scale disorder. During the summer, fires were lit in empty properties along the main road. To put it mildly, 'Young people are feeling very unsettled' (Locally-based researcher, 2001).

Most residents now seem resigned to demolition, whatever their initial views, with a minority very keen on it, and a minority still actively contesting the demolition of one of the areas in particular, which had never been expected to fall under the bulldozer. Those who are staying are concerned about living in the middle of a demolition site, and worry about the lack of detailed plans for the 'new Bankside'. This may yet undermine the survival of even small parts of the area.

> ...people want reassurance that the remaining Bankside will be more than a set of streets with few services and much disruption (Locally-based researcher, 2001).

In the same way as developers need sites offering a critical mass, so do communities if they are to survive. That is why the demolition proposals are having such an unintentionally negative impact.

For those whose homes are being demolished, the rehousing process is fraught with difficulty. The promised relocation team was not in place by autumn 2001, even though clearance was already underway. At 1st December 2001 only the manager had been appointed with a staff team still to be assembled. The local housing office is having to field enquiries from people desperate to know what their future holds, and local voluntary groups are providing advice and support where possible.

Whether people will have a 'right to return' seems unclear. As part of the household survey in proposed clearance areas, people were told:

> If [your road] was declared as an area for redevelopment you would be given priority under the council's lettings policy to move to another home of your choice. This could be in Bankside or any other area (subject to appropriate accommodation being available) (Newcastle City Council, household survey, 2001).

Often people who have so far been rehoused outside the neighbourhood are seeing these moves as temporary, and are expecting to move back into the remodelled Bankside in the future. Some residents think that there will not be enough rented housing in the new Bankside and they will not be able to afford the new properties that are built for sale. Others feel that once people have moved away, they are likely to settle into their new area and not want to uproot again and return to Bankside anyway. Empty properties in the remaining parts of the area are now being refurbished and brought back into use, and the housing office anticipates that from now on those wanting to remain in the area will be able to be accommodated in these properties, but for those who have already left, a typical view is that, 'People seem really confused about the time-scale for moving back in. There is no relocation team in place yet' (Locally-based researcher, 2001).

Because of the housing surplus in Newcastle over a long period (20 years in the West End), people have been able to 'under-occupy' houses; for example single people in a two-bed property instead of the usual one-bed flat. They will not be entitled to the same size property when they are rehoused. Similarly, some people were allocated houses (including 'double houses' i.e. two knocked into one) to match the size of their family when they had children living at home, but these children have now grown up and moved away. They are very unlikely to be able to move to a house of a similar size. These are the kinds of detailed rehousing issues that add to the uncertainty, anxiety and delays, and also the costs of redevelopment. Rehousing large groups of people gives everyone the chance to stake a claim that is not always realisable.

The process of clearance is obviously reducing the population quite dramatically, as many are rehoused outside the neighbourhood and some people move away ahead of demolition. This is also having a negative impact on already fragile services.

> *[Through Going for Growth] more schools are becoming fragile...[The main secondary serving the West End has recently stabilised its school roll] but I'm not confident it will remain stable as Going for Growth bites in* (Senior council manager, 2001).

> *All the shops are shutting up and clearing off* (Housing manager, Bankside, 2001).

Difficult and controversial decisions are being taken about whether to keep certain schools open; the population drain has left a big surplus of school places and prompted school closures. By September 2003, 3,911 Newcastle school places will have been removed since September 2000 (Newcastle Education and Libraries Directorate, 2001). One Bankside primary was recently closed.

> *[This closure] created a great deal of anger. But for the receiving schools, it gave them a lifeline – pupils, finance, stability. One school went down but three others have seriously benefited from the influx of pupils* (Senior manager, 2001).

The main goal of Going for Growth is to bring about repopulation after the clearance, and there is a desire to maintain a core framework of services throughout the process. For example, the aim is to *'keep alive the schools we need for the future'*. One idea is 'full service schools' – where a variety of agencies share school premises, using up surplus space and so preventing school closure. Of course, there are many complications and risks to sharing schools with other services, particularly in a very depleted area with major security problems. Any different uses must not compromise the safety of pupils (School organisation plan, 2001-2006). The idea of keeping 'phantom' schools going while the city awaits population regrowth is expensive and vulnerable to problems such as in retaining staff as well as children. It is the price of demolition that not only homes go, but the service infrastructure of the area. This takes a great deal of public money to recreate. Currently it is not on offer because forecasts of regrowth are so uncertain and time-scales so far into the future.

Yet the intensity of the problems in the West End makes people question whether there is any alternative to Going for Growth in spite of all these worries.

> *I know it's painful for a lot of people, but I don't see what the alternative is. We've had a lot of big-hitting professionals in [the West End] and together we've made no difference. The depth of problems is so great...we have got to try something new* (Senior council manager, 2001).

Riverview – a new urban village?

In Lower Riverview, the demolition plan is on a smaller-scale, currently involving a small number of streets and parts of streets. But the council is monitoring how stable the remainder of the streets in the neighbourhood stay, open to the possibility of further demolition. Thus a question mark also hovers above this neighbourhood:

> *It does create a sense of unease, it really does...Do you decorate for Christmas?...The future's uncertain...because there isn't a demand for these type of houses. [Yet] they're good, solid build* (Housing manager, 2001).

There are worries about the inevitable time lags between the Going for Growth proposals, clearance, repopulation, and major infrastructure improvement (such as transport). A typical view is that if, *'The whole plan if it was all done at once would be good'* (Housing manager, 2001).

But it can't be all done at once, and in the meantime a generation of children are living through the upheaval. It is likely that the process will take at least 20 years (Nevin, 2001).

The council wants to carry out significant redevelopment in Lower Riverview to create a new urban village. It has established a 'Riverside Regeneration Partnership' including residents, developers, the local authority, voluntary organisations and others.

> *Visually, if you take everything out it's a fantastic site...but you have to work with the community...Hopefully things will pick up once the partnership is established early in [2002]* (Housing manager, 2001).

Going for Growth plans include investment in the more stable and popular estates across the East End. Diversifying tenure is a key objective, as is tackling unemployment (Newcastle City Council, 2001b). The Newcastle Offshore Supply Base is located close to Lower Riverview and, together with local marine industry, should have the capacity to create 1,500 new jobs in the next ten years – in manufacturing, design and engineering (Newcastle City Council, 2000c). Morrisons (a large supermarket chain) will come on stream in July 2002.

They have made a commitment to local employment so the council is already meeting with them to develop a scheme for putting local people forward for jobs and training courses (Lupton, 2001). New construction jobs should arise as a result of the redevelopment of Lower Riverview, and the council plans to establish local agreements with developers to ensure that local people have opportunities for training and employment (Newcastle City Council, 2001b).

Riverview has been included in a Sure Start programme since mid 2000, and in an area-based SRB programme since 1996. Projects funded by SRB include the revitalisation of a nearby shopping centre, adult education and training initiatives, safety and security projects, and housing improvements (Lupton, 2000).

> *External works have picked up the area. For the people living there, having money spent on them, it's a boost* (Housing manager, 2001).

If Newcastle can stop the drift away from the city and limit how much it allows to be built until population recovery shows up in real demand, then maybe Riverview will survive in most parts. It is hard to be dispassionate in hoping for this outcome.

Conclusion

There is no doubt that Newcastle has grabbed the low demand bull by the horns. Abandonment is no longer whispered about in dark corridors – it is being tackled head on. But is yet another bout of large-scale demolition, after the mass clearance of earlier decades, really the answer? Shouldn't the destruction of communities this inevitably brings, so well documented in 'Family and Kinship' and other studies, make us more cautious? (Young and Wilmott, 1957).

The council is right that 'creeping demolition' during the 1990s was helping to slowly kill low demand neighbourhoods like Bankside as it steeped them in permanent uncertainty. No road was safe – as soon as a few vacancies appeared, people knew that their street might be the next to fall under the bulldozer.

Management inputs, dedicated help from residents and significant capital investment in the physical fabric were having limited impact in the face of the much wider downward pulls on inner neighbourhoods of outward migration and concentrated deprivation. Modernised houses and flats remained empty. But can the mass demolition of sound housing be justified – housing which would be considered desirable in another location if the social and environmental conditions could be tackled? The existing community is very divided in its views.

Is there a win-win scenario? Does increasing the number of people living within the city's boundaries, reducing commuting, and creating a more economically active population inevitably mean displacing existing communities? Do urban communities like Bankside inevitably lose out?

The government sets a net rather than a gross limit on new house-building for each authority; any amount of demolished housing can be replaced, home for home. So, the more Newcastle City Council demolishes, the more it can build anew and supply a different kind of product. This may be directly driving Newcastle's plans for large-scale demolition, in addition to the pressure to create large enough sites to attract developers. However, the council stresses that its objective is not to replace existing housing with executive style homes, but rather to create imaginative, mixed use, mixed tenure, thriving urban communities.

But it may be possible for Newcastle to meet its population growth objectives and turn-around declining neighbourhoods – which are such a drain on the city's resources and provide such a hostile living environment – in partnership with existing communities rather than in conflict with them. In fact, it may be impossible without them, as they provide the anchor for existing services and can provide the foundations on which new services and population growth can be built. The proposed partnership approach to establishing an 'urban village' in Lower Riverview could prove to be a workable model for a more negotiated way forward throughout the city. It is already probably too late in Bankside.

Time will tell what the outcomes of these different approaches will be. In the meantime, the human cost of the clearance in the West End is rising – in anxiety, disrupted community networks, displaced families, service closure. We should be in no doubt that bulldozer solutions to the problems of entrenched poverty and urban decline are far from quick or painless, anymore than the slow decline and piecemeal demolition of the last 20 years. Even in Bankside, there may still be much to play for as residents in some parts of the area continue to oppose demolition plans. Even within the council there is not unanimous agreement with the current approach. Such a controversial and high profile strategy is almost bound to generate different and conflicting reactions.

Newcastle council is trying to make far-reaching changes to its urban structure and population; it is trying to create a unique opportunity to turn-around the city's fortunes. It realises that radical action is essential. The inclusion of existing communities in its plans for a renaissance will not only affect how its achievements are judged in the future, but could be pivotal to its success.

In the next chapter, we look at the experiences of resident activists and front line staff in both Newcastle and Manchester. We explore why, in the face of overwhelming difficulties, people are prepared to invest so much time and energy in rescuing communities in trouble, often taking real risks to make these devastated areas work again.

CHAPTER 6:
Resident activists and front line staff in low demand neighbourhoods

When we walk down the street, it's really upsetting. The top part of the street for some reason is more stable and people look after their gardens. Then you get mid-way and there are empty houses where the properties have been boarded up and the gardens have rubbish thrown in. And then from half-way down to the bottom of the street, especially on one side, all the houses are empty...and vandalised (Maria).

We've got damp in our house because the roof has not been on that house next door for three years...We're not going anywhere...There are people like us who want to see those terraced houses kept (Jane).

So many people would be happier if they knew the streets were safer; that there weren't drugs around; if they knew their kids weren't going to get into trouble when they go out to play; if they knew their houses weren't going to get burgled. But those things are happening (Newcastle health visitor).

People who were thinking of moving are staying put. At least three people I know are putting in right to buy papers because they can see a future for their children. Some of the youngsters that moved out are coming back now because they've got elderly parents. That is the type of community I like - just like it used to be (Tina).

In the midst of dereliction and population flight, we met residents determined to stay and prepared to give their all to improving conditions. They often made the difference between the success and failure of regeneration attempts. In City-Edge, local housing managers attributed some of the variation in demand across the neighbourhood to the action of residents' groups to help areas survive. Where groups were active, they greatly strengthened the local community.

It seems to be wherever there is a resident's association, people want to move in (Tina).

Women play a particularly important role in community affairs, all round the world (UNCHS, 1996; 2000). Manchester and Newcastle are no exceptions. The seven resident activists, all from different groups, whose experience this chapter reflects, are all women. Family, home and community are dominant arenas in women's lives. Their stake in what happens is not so much higher than men's, but more weighted. The burden of community and neighbourhood responsibility falls more heavily on their shoulders because of their role as primary family and community organisers, as well as increasingly part or full breadwinners too.

The strength of their views is often not reflected in the machinery and decisions of government, both local and central, nor by the financial and organisational structures that shape neighbourhood developments, far removed from the level of actual neighbourhoods. Because women operate most often at a highly local scale, they are seriously disenfranchised in shaping the destiny of their neighbourhoods which is mainly decided 'higher up'. Meanwhile, people operating at city level or beyond see neighbourhoods and resident activists as small elements in a much bigger game. It is therefore not surprising that the resident perspective and the 'higher authority' perspective so often fail to meet.

In this chapter, we try to reflect the nature of this problem, first relaying the views expressed to us by resident activists, then by local workers whose job it is both to implement higher level decisions and to listen and respond to residents. These very local perspectives are at the heart of understanding the problems of neighbourhood renewal.

Among the resident activists, some had stopped their involvement during the course of the research. One family had been forced to flee because the anti-social behaviour directed at them had got so severe. One had stopped because of family commitments, though was still involved informally. Another resident stopped when she started a degree course, and she was also prompted to leave because the 'local politics' had got too much. Table 6.1 summarises the action of the seven activists whose experiences we draw on in this chapter.

Why people get involved in trying to improve neighbourhood conditions

Resident action is often prompted by the direct threat of demolition – people come together in a bid to save their homes. And very often, people get involved as a result of seeing a neighbourhood they are very attached to begin to decline. Where others choose to move away, these activists either don't have that option or, more often amongst the residents we spoke to, don't want to be pushed out.

> *Personally, I'm at home here. I feel my roots are here...This is where we wish to stay – it's our chosen place to stay* (Clare).

Neither do they want to live amongst continually deteriorating conditions. They want to change things, restore their area's character, and force the council to sit up and take notice.

Table 6.1: A summary of action undertaken by seven resident activists

Name	Gender	Age	Length of residence in area	Organisation	Example of specific activities undertaken	Still involved in 2002?
Clare	Female	Over 55	Whole life	Tenants' and residents' association	Local lettings, chasing council repairs and environmental services, lobbying the council for home improvements	Stepped down as chair due to family commitments, still involved informally
Ann	Female	40 - 55	33 years	Residents' association and community forum	Involvement in estate redevelopment and neighbourhood management, community declaration, tackling anti-social behaviour, activities for children and young people	Yes
Sandra	Female	40 - 55	24 years	Tenants' and residents' association	Local lettings, alley-gating, traffic calmers, security lighting, lobbying council repairs and street cleaning services	Yes
Tina	Female	Over 55	Whole life	Homewatch and area-wide regeneration forum	Local lettings, liaison between residents and police, practical security improvements, lobbying council	Yes
Maria	Female	40-55	21 years	Community project and credit union	Grant giving programme, community development work, area planning, chasing up council services	No. Stopped for a variety of reasons and has since moved away
Lisa	Female	Under 40	11 years	Residents' association	Attempts to bring local people together and challenge anti-social behaviour	Moved away as a result of extreme harassment
Jane	Female	40 - 55	10 years	School governor	Many different school-based activities	Yes

Note: 1. These names are invented to preserve people's anonymity.

Ann has lived on her estate for 33 years, and has always been involved in anything concerning children's play. She helped re-establish a residents' association in 1985, by which time there were already lots of empty properties and problems with drugs on her estate. She sums up her reasons for getting involved: *'It is all about having an interest in where you live. The classic quote I always think of is Kennedy's, and I say the same here...It isn't what the estate can do for you, but what you can do for your estate.'*

Similarly, Sandra has lived in her area for 24 years and it's where she wants to stay. But from 1990, she noticed a gradual decline.

> *It didn't happen all of a sudden. The facilities were slowly going and not being replaced. Different buildings didn't get utilised – they got knocked down. Nuisance neighbours made a big change. It seemed that local people were moving out of the area, leaving it free for people who weren't bothered...Overall, the decline was that people were frightened to live here. It really had a bad name.*

Six years ago, she and two other residents decided that they had to do something to reverse this deterioration:

> *It was a lovely day. We sat there and looked at the state of the streets and thought 'what's happening here?' I love my house where I live – I brought my children up here and a lot of my family live here. Everybody used to be friendly and would do things for each other, and that wasn't happening.*

Sandra identified the need for structured action to combat the erosion of local social links and of basic conditions: *'When we decided to have the TRA, the main thing was that we wanted the community spirit back. We knew that we had it, because of the length of time that the neighbours had lived there. But because it was such a mess, nobody seemed to be bothering.'*

Tina has lived in her house since it was built 25 years ago. Like Ann and Sandra, she feels a strong attachment to her area and was prompted to get involved because she wanted a return to the stable neighbourhood that had existed when she first moved in. Whole streets of people moved in to her estate when it was first built from nearby slum clearance areas; many had been neighbours before. But they gradually moved away, as a result of death, marriage, or 'bettering themselves' by getting a mortgage further out, and things began to change. She couldn't bear to see conditions deteriorate and at the beginning of the 1990s realised that if she didn't do something, no-one else would:

> *If you don't do it, who will? I live here, and I want to live in a nice place...When we started we all said 'no, we don't want to live like that, so we will do something to change it'.*

Sometimes, people's involvement in their local communities has even longer roots. Clare lives on a 1970s estate; she and her husband have also been there since it was built. They moved there from a clearance area, just a stone's throw away. It was during the clearance process that Clare first took action – to challenge the council over their rehousing plans. Once living on the new estate, she remained known to people as a kind of unofficial community activist and they would go to her with any problems. Then when conditions on her estate started going seriously downhill in the mid 1990s, she instigated action. She canvassed the whole estate, and was given whole hearted endorsement to set up a tenants and residents association.

The striking fact is that these neighbourhoods are where these residents want to be. They have often lived there all their lives, some have become owner occupiers through the right to buy, and they don't want to move away. So they choose to get involved to restore the quality of life they used to enjoy on their estates.

For Maria, becoming involved in her local community project was triggered by casual information exchange. She joined a local group within a year of moving to the neighbourhood (in 1980), when she was a young mother. A chance meeting with another woman on the bus, and a chat about how there had to be more to life than housework, prompted her to go to the local playgroup. And then a doctor encouraged her to get involved in a local forum, partly to help combat the postnatal depression she was experiencing. One thing led to another, and a real turning point was getting involved in the women's group. Maria said, *'It was one of those big events in your life where suddenly I wasn't a mother or a daughter or a sister, I was me...'*

As an activist, Maria drew great strength from working alongside other determined women:

> *There was a strength in local people, incredibly strong people, people who are dealing with loads of social issues...I was driven by the social issues I was dealing with, and driven by a need just to be acknowledged as a decent person, because I wasn't getting that at home.*

Jane's starting point was a desire to contribute something to her local community, having just moved into the area. She became a school governor at her local primary school, encouraged by her local church. Then, once her children became pupils there, she had a vested interest in continuing.

> *It was a way of actually giving back to the community. It was a way of using what I'd done at work in something very close to home...The local church sees the school as a very important place. They see it as very much something the church should be reaching into to support.*

Local churches can play an important supportive role within these neighbourhoods; in organising direct action (such as working with schools, taking part in and even spearheading regeneration activity, organising local events) as well as being places where informal social links between residents are made as they attend services and other church-based activities. Sometimes there is far more social than strictly religious content to this community linkage.

Practical action taken by residents' groups

Sometimes the groups have taken forward specific projects on their own. For example, Sandra's group led a pioneering project to get alleyways closed off along the back of terraces. They first sought the opinions of the 300 households in their group of terraces, and received a huge vote of support:

> *We sent a flier round and got every single one back! Every single one in favour...They wanted the TRA to really work for the alleyway closure.*

The council helped the TRA get started on this project, by giving them £1,000 towards legal costs – the ownership of the alleys has to be formally reassigned from the council to the residents themselves. Then the TRA successfully applied for additional funding from many other sources: New Deal for Communities; Single Regeneration Budget; the local housing association; Britain in Bloom; Shell. Sandra has noticed huge improvements since the gates have been in place.

Often, the groups' main focus is monitoring the council's service provision, reporting repairs, chasing them up, lobbying for improvements.

Sometimes they have got involved with more dramatic redesign projects. Ann's estate was completely remodelled during the late 1990s, with government regeneration funding and Housing Association Grant. She says, *'The estate has been completely and utterly transformed.'*

Before its transformation, in the words of one council officer:

> *This was the worst council estate in this part of the city. It had the most punishing design and layout you can possibly imagine. It had rates of crime and drug-related activity that just went through the roof. It had massive void problems.*

Residents have played a vital role in the estate's renewal; helping to develop new management approaches and generating community support. A 'joint-landlord agreement' ensures that the council and the three housing associations that now own property on the estate follow similar policies so that all tenants get the same treatment. In March 1998, residents launched a 'community declaration':

The community declaration is putting into words what everybody expects of each other. To be nice to each other, live alongside each other...It all makes for a better community...It is all about 'I will try to do my best to be a good neighbour, good tenant and good citizen'.

Ann believes the majority of people do behave in a neighbourly way in any case, whether or not they sign a declaration. But it seems the declaration is helping to bolster a sense of community on the estate, and give people a more formal stake in it. It also forces residents to articulate their social requirements, thereby bonding people together in a way that had been eroded by all the changes and pressures we have outlined. A minority sign the declaration because they think they have to in order to move into the estate, then once they've got their tenancy they behave anti-socially despite having signed up. But the declaration gives landlords a firm base from which to exercise control over property conditions, ensuring their tenants' right to 'peaceful enjoyment of their home'.

As new tenants arrive to live on the estate, the housing officers still invite them to sign the declaration. Three and a half years on, Ann is keen to update the declaration and get people to re-commit to it. The estate is constantly changing, and new challenges are arising all the time. Anti-social behaviour is an ever-present problem, a constant battle, but the resident activists and locally-based staff never stop trying to combat it and think up new ways of bringing people on board. The declaration is a useful baseline against which residents and staff can measure progress or back-sliding in standards. It is a way of holding people to some common values and standards driven by residents who want better.

Because of the systems that have been set up – the community declaration and the landlords joint estate agreement – we can identify far quicker areas of concern...Now people are more willing to report...The [residents] are more concerned about the estate.

However, it's a day in, day out struggle.

Vandalism is showing its ugly head again. Children...congregate round [the flats], go round the back, kick the fences in, even set fire to the bins...We have attempted to target them. Sometimes they come to senior youth club. It's all about: how do we replace that buzz they're getting [from anti-social activities]? You've always got different generations coming up.

Residents' efforts to tackle social conditions on the estate are helping to protect the physical improvements. They are very clear that they would be nowhere without sympathetic front line staff. The intense co-operation and the willingness to act galvanises everyone's efforts.

The forum organise all to do with the sustainability of the estate...The police come, the landlords, youth service, teachers, local councillor tries to come...

It all stems from here locally and it is all about...identifying a problem or a hot-spot. Housing officers play a vital role in co-ordinating all this...We do get 99 per cent support from them.

Other groups have tackled financial problems in the community. Maria's community action has included setting up the first credit union in the North East. She says, *'[The credit union is] still going strong. We've had so many hundreds of thousands of pounds stay within the community. That was brilliant – a collective achievement.'*

This resident has such a strong commitment to her neighbourhood and the residents she works with that she set up a trust fund, with a prize awarded to her for her community activity. She could have kept the money for herself and as she was on income support it would have made a huge difference to her and her family, *'...but I knew in my heart it was in recognition of the collective action that we'd all done. So I used the money to set up a trust fund. And we make awards of between £2,000 and £2,500 a year to groups who are working to make the area a better place to live in...they are continuing to carry that spirit of community on.'*

A key motivation for Tina in setting up a Homewatch group in her neighbourhood was increasing people's sense of security. She works closely with both the police and the housing department. At first people called her a grass and threatened her, but gradually they got used to the work she was doing. As people grew to trust the confidentiality of the scheme, they began to give her information that would curb crime and make their streets and homes safer. In the two years between 1998 and 2000 she felt conditions had definitely improved, as a result of a whole combination of action by residents, police and housing:

The fall in crime in our area has been dramatic...Touch wood, we've not had a burglary in a hell of a long time...We can't actually attribute it to one thing. We've had extra policing and the nuisance team has come on-line. People realise now that you live 'with' a community. If you do things against them, then they won't keep you. That has made a change to people's attitudes. The majority of people are finding that there is a calmness in the area, a confidence.

Increasing confidence in the area is sometimes an explicit goal of these groups, and is nearly always implicit in their work: *'We tell people: Stop knocking where you live – don't say the name of this area like you've trodden in something!'*

Local lettings

All the residents live in areas of low demand, where social landlords are desperate to allocate empty houses. Often only those in acute need, with least choice, will accept offers in these areas, and so the concentration of vulnerable people grows.

We're in limbo – the homeless persons unit is putting people into the estate – it's like a dumping ground.

Where the community is already fragile, this can spell disaster, leading to more empty properties and eventual demolition. The problem comes when the majority of people are unable to enforce basic standards of behaviour amongst particular individuals in the face of intense decline. People are scared of retaliation, community resources are depleted because of selective out-migration, local services are under pressure, and a minority increasingly feels able to publicly flout the rules and behave extremely destructively (Richardson and Mumford, 2002). Local lettings schemes can help bolster community controls in conditions of social breakdown and high levels of empty property. In areas like the ones we visited, they can help to attract new tenants who have more positive links with the community and so assist in the prevention of further destabilisation.

Given local authorities' legal responsibilities in areas like homelessness and equal opportunities, local lettings schemes can be controversial, particularly in areas of high housing demand or ethnic diversity. They could also be seen to work against the growing emphasis on transparent, choice-based lettings schemes. However, both Newcastle and Manchester have a clear surplus of social housing, particularly in the four neighbourhoods we focus on, and this housing needs to be actively marketed to enable estates to survive.

Choice-based lettings are a very innovative way of putting social housing on an equal footing with other tenures, by treating tenants as people of value who should be able to make their own choices. And open marketing of social housing challenges its image as being solely for people in crisis, making it clear that a much wider section of the community can access it. There is a great deal of evidence that rehousing homeless families on a one-offer only basis generates more empty properties because it generates more refusals, appeals, and bureaucratic delays (Power and Tunstall, 1995; Birmingham City Council, 2002). Unlike in other countries, where homelessness policy is to protect households in the most extreme circumstances, in this country it is a major access route to social housing, which is why it can go so badly wrong. There is now broad agreement amongst social landlords that ghettoising the poorest people just doesn't work.

Local lettings initiatives, prompted by low demand and social disorder problems, need not be incompatible with choice-based lettings (Cole *et al.*, 2001). In fact, local lettings schemes can be a creative way of introducing choice-based lettings, as well as rebuilding community relations in situations where they have been so badly damaged that estates have become unlettable.

Some of the residents' groups we spoke to had negotiated 'nominations agreements' and local lettings with the council, so that they could recommend people to move into their estate. These special nomination and local lettings schemes depend heavily on the local housing officer being willing to broker local needs, residents' priority for a peaceful, stable estate and central bureaucratic rules. In these examples, the residents' groups build up their own lists of people – recommended by existing residents, most of whom are themselves on very low incomes. They in turn recommend these people to the council. This local system has in many cases helped generate unexpected demand. Without these recommendations, some estates would be much less stable and some properties would remain empty altogether, facing demolition. Financially and socially, local lettings can be very useful in a situation of extreme low demand.

> As soon as [a house] comes empty, we have a nominee list. There is a lady moving out on Monday, and we have already got a lady that wants that property. That works. Out of all the people that the TRA have nominated to the council, every single one of them has stayed. The ones that the council have put in, if we've not had anyone on the list, have never stayed.

By getting involved with the housing nominations process as well as with local community relations, residents want to ensure that people who come to live on the estate value it. They want them to actively choose to live there, and be good neighbours. There is clearly a danger of people being unfairly excluded and of an estate becoming a 'clique'. However, in all the examples we saw, the housing department retained the final decision on nominations, so people in emergency situations had a way in. The impression conveyed by residents was that they were genuinely trying to rebuild their communities rather than 'pick and choose' new residents. They wanted to set out expected standards of behaviour, taken for granted in most areas but in a state of collapse in these fragile areas, and create a sense of individual responsibility for enforcing them. They wanted proof from the in-movers of commitment to the basic improvements they had worked so hard to achieve, so that their work to save and restore the community would survive.

Because it is existing residents who make the recommendation, the expectation is that they will feel a sense of responsibility for the new resident's behaviour. This acts as an informal control on conditions, helping bind people into shared standards of behaviour.

> I've said to everybody who recommends someone: if there is any sign of trouble, you will be the first person that I come to to complain. And this has never happened.

In high demand areas, 'community lettings' schemes are set up to try to ensure that the families of existing residents and those with a local connection are not excluded altogether by the pressure for housing. In low demand areas, these schemes have an even more urgent agenda of preventing wholesale abandonment. In this situation, local lettings agreements can help the estate's value to rise in people's eyes. The estate is no longer the place at the bottom of the pile where you go when you can't find anything else; it is somewhere you have to make an effort to get into.

[I was talking to a surveyor and] he said: 'Just a minute, I know about you. A client of mine was living [in a street due to be demolished]. When I asked her where she was going to live, she said she had a lovely council house, in the area, on a lovely estate and she said you can only get in by recommendation. She said she was more than happy.'

There is wider evidence to support the view that local lettings help reduce empty property, increase community stability, generate housing income and improve conditions (Power and Tunstall, 1995).

Reaching excluded young people

Resident activists described ways in which they tried to reach out to the most needy members of the community, often young boys who spent a lot of time on the street. Ann had spoken to the boys on her estate who had formed a gang and regularly stole cars. She hadn't managed to win them over, but she had decided it was important to understand what they needed.

A group of youths were rampaging through the estate and I couldn't get through to them in any shape or form. I tried – saying 'what is it you want exactly'?

Tina believes in speaking to anyone, however scared she might feel, whatever they might have said to her in the past. It's a way of trying to keep some cohesion in a close but divided community.

Sometimes your knees can be knocking while you are speaking to someone, but you can't show it.

Maria has managed to overcome her fear of young people out on the streets, often up to no good:

I use my fear to go to them first...I've ended up having some really interesting conversations, always making sure that I keep my back-yard wall between me and them. One young lad, who I've seen loads of times, and he's one of those lads who's got a really lined face, he looks as if he must be on drugs, and yet I've always made a point of saying, 'hi, are you alright, how are you doing?' and he always looks and smiles...Time and time again, the same people I find scary have responded so positively to being spoken to positively. And they're actually lovely.

This belief in trying to bind people together through social contact makes it possible for these women to carry on in the face of often extreme behaviour and intense decay. In the end their efforts only work as long as the wider society supports the enforcement of basic, liveable conditions in the poorest areas.

Desperate moments and disillusionment

We described how Tina was called a 'grass' and received nasty threats when she first took on a community leadership role. But over time, she became accepted and security on the estate has improved significantly. Lisa had an altogether different experience. She lived on an estate where anti-social behaviour was out of control. She knew people who had moved into the estate and off in one day, because the gangs of children targeted newcomers. They were making people's lives impossible, and gradually nearly all of the original residents moved away.

> *It is difficult to describe the experience of living next to these people. Old people are afraid to leave their homes – they are trapped by fear of intimidation. They never know what will happen next* (Policy officer).

Still Lisa kept going. She and her family loved their council home (which was less than ten years old) and really wanted to stay. She tried to get the anti-social families on board, even inviting them to join the tenants' association, but they would not get involved.

Lisa later co-operated with the housing and police services in taking action through the courts. She and her family had to have a 24-hour guard outside their home for two weeks following the court case against the key troublemakers, because of the seriousness of the threats they received. The process of legal action was very lengthy, and even after the troublemakers were evicted, they kept harassing Lisa and her family, despite injunctions. Living with this level of harassment and nuisance intruded constantly upon the family's life:

> *You can't settle, you can't rest...you don't know what they're up to...it's a chore to live there.*

Lisa felt there was nothing more she could do – she had put herself and her family at risk by co-operating with the council and the police, but still the trouble continued. She didn't want to move away, but by 1998 could see no alternative, and said, *'If I felt for a moment I could make a difference I would stay.'*

By summer 2000, Lisa and her family had moved away from the area. She even changed her job so she could not be found. She moved very reluctantly – she was attached to the area and loved her house – but the harassment just kept continuing. Lisa felt that moving was the right thing to do, and she is very happy in her new area. But she was upset that it had to come to that, saying, *'It's wrong that innocent people are moving. I was sorry to leave. You feel as though you've lost, as though you've let them win.'*

Residents often reached low-points because of their lack of control over how local services operated. At one point, Clare was feeling terribly despondent both because the local lettings agreement had lapsed and because minor repairs just weren't getting done. She felt abandoned:

We've all grown old together on this estate. The majority of us are still here – at our age where do we move to now? We have brought our families up here – this is where we want to stay. That's what's making us so disgusted – we've already got a community, which we can see is falling apart. We need some help...

In 2001, as well as describing some hugely positive changes brought about by the area's regeneration programme, she still felt let down by some public services. She had asked for some very overgrown trees to be thinned out, but her experience was that, *'[It took 3 months before they did it] and they made a big mess of it. You just feel 'what's the point?' Before it was the residents letting us down, now it's the services.'*

And Tina commented:

One thing that infuriates me is grounds maintenance. It hasn't changed in 2½ years – still the same problems...People don't even know who owns what land. There are arguments over who actually maintains it. It's not good enough...A piece of derelict land pulls down the rest of the area. Someone's got to take responsibility. It's them kind of issues that really get on your nerves because they're still the same issues that we had at the beginning.

Maria has found that since she stopped being so actively involved, she has felt less and less attached to the area and increasingly overwhelmed by the surrounding deprivation.

When I was involved as an activist...every living, breathing moment apart from the children, everything was about being an activist in the community. And I felt a sense of pride and commitment. I felt driven to be always challenging the inequalities and the oppression that I saw, where people misjudged people in the area. Now that I'm not actively involved, I can't see why I would have an investment.

It's not to say that it's all bleak and horrible...but there isn't anything pleasant. It's not like living in an area where people might be more friendly and say hello in the street. [Now I'm not part of the community project] I don't have that intense sense of belonging and being part of the collective...

What I dislike is things like...the filth, the mess, the people who feel it's OK to shriek and shout and swear in the street...The fact that some people I know just put the dog shit in the back lane.

And I think one of the saddest things for me is seeing children, and again not all of them, but children who have faces like old men. They've got lined faces. They look as if they've seen something that an adult shouldn't have seen. And it's really distressing, it really is...So many times I see children either playing out or on the way to school and it's almost as if they're enraged. They wouldn't walk along the street but they would kick a brick, or they would pick up a stone and throw it or they'd try to smash a fence, or they'd smash glass...You've got kids who are shaking the bus stop, kicking the bus stop, shouting, jumping in and off of the road, jumping on the wall, bumping into adults...they don't seem to have any social boundaries where they would consider it discourteous to bump into someone, let alone say 'sorry'.

So these are all minor things in some ways, but they build-up to a picture where I feel sometimes besieged.

Maria knew she was going to have to move away because her street was coming down. She really lost heart as she saw all the things she had fought so hard for gradually falling apart. In the end there would be nothing after years of effort.

Ann, like most of the active residents, is something of an optimist. She remains very actively involved, but the constant struggle against vandalism and anti-social behaviour can get her down too. Ann said, *'I'm always optimistic because I live here and that's my nature. But it's like when this [builder's] compound was being robbed on the first day...You do get despondent and think 'I should move'.'*

Usually, action falls to just a few people, who can end up shouldering a heavy burden.

I wish that there were more residents that would come to the meetings, but I don't know whether it is meant to flatter me when I say, 'come to the meetings' and they say, 'we'll leave it to you and you'll let us know what is happening'. I think sometimes people are put off meetings – thinking it's very above their heads. I don't think they realise they can speak like I do. I say 'hang on, I'm not sure what you mean there, can you say it in simple language'...But I think sometimes [the other residents] have got a lot of trust in me, and I just wonder whether I'm up to it. I hope I'm not going to disappoint anybody (Clare).

These activists can become a focus for everyone's worries. Being a community leader can put you between the grass roots and officialdom. Activists may develop an understanding of why some problems can't be tackled in the way residents want, leaving the community representatives empty handed and in danger of appearing to change sides.

The back-biting does annoy me. It can be fine while you're doing something for them, but the minute you turn round and say, 'no, I don't think you can expect the council to do that', it's 'she doesn't help you, she works for the council' (Tina).

The representative roles themselves can get more onerous – as both public bodies and other residents expect these representatives to take on more responsibilities.

Their very commitment, ability and willingness makes them 'sitting ducks'. Ann feels disheartened when parents expect her to keep the community centre open longer hours for their children, but aren't willing to help run activities themselves. Jane is concerned that the role of school governors is continually expanding (for example now including assessment of the head teacher's salary) and their burden is getting heavier:

> *There aren't that many people who have the time to do that sort of thing and to do it to the level that is expected of them. [Schools] are going to find it increasingly difficult to keep [governors] I think if the load...just keeps growing.*

Because of multiple pressures like these, resident leadership often goes in waves. As one person steps down, another person wants to or feels they should take on the role, and so the groups and informal networks are sustained. But many of the activists we spoke to in these low demand neighbourhoods had been involved for an extremely long time, and there wasn't always someone willing to take over. In low demand areas, it is the younger generation that tends to move away, leaving older residents to struggle on. For example, Clare stepped down as chair of the tenants' association in 2001 because of personal commitments, but no-one wanted to take it over, and the association has now folded. Clare has continued to help get things sorted out on the estate in the absence of anyone willing to fill her shoes, because she cares about the area, and because people come to her just as they always have done.

> *I can't bear to see it go down, so I will always be involved to some extent...We have to live with the mistakes – no-one else.*

Ann has accepted that people's willingness to be involved will wax and wane, and she is prepared to be the person who stays constant throughout, the identifiable community representative.

> *People will only take an interest in something when it affects them – then they will come on mass – and then it will dwindle off. If we're here to serve those needs, all good and well.*

Looking to the future

By winter 2001, Maria's area had been declared for compulsory clearance. Maria was coping with constantly deteriorating living conditions and just wanted to get away. Anti-social behaviour was escalating, people were lighting fires nearly every night, and she was very conscious of the presence of shotguns and air rifles. But she almost felt 'pushed out'; conditions had got so bad in her street that even before the clearance order was issued she felt she had to go. By the time the decision was announced, she reluctantly felt demolition had become the only option because the problems hadn't been managed properly earlier on. So eventually she felt, '*I would want to go and live somewhere else now...Truthfully, they can't pull this place down fast enough.'*

Maria has recently moved right out of the area into a house she loves. She and her family are thrilled to be living in a calm place, where they feel secure. A huge weight has been lifted from her shoulders and she feels a great sense of relief that the agony is over.

Residents in some other areas feel the opposite way, and have begun to see concrete signs of an upturn in their area's fortunes:

> *We always knew that it would work out...but we didn't realise how successful it would be! It has been a lot of hard work – but well worth it. And it's not just my area – as a whole, the area has all been improved. It is more comfortable to walk around. Things are beginning to develop that people can see. They get fed up of all the talk that things will get better...but now you can see it visually.*

Residents saw regeneration investment as a vote of confidence:

> *It's much more hopeful now. We are beginning to see a future. Since you were last here we've got the New Deal for Communities' money. We all felt very strong when we knew the New Deal money was coming our way – that was a real lift. It was a big reward.*

Residents who believed their area could be rescued, saw the revival of their neighbourhoods as a medium to long-term project.

> *You can't do it all overnight – it's going to take at least another 5 years [to get where we want to be].*

Tina felt it would take twenty years before the area completely turned around, so did not expect to see the culmination of all the regeneration efforts in her lifetime. She explained her motivation for working towards something that she might not see through herself,

> *I know there are going to be big changes in 3 years, even more in 5 years, and a lot of changes by 10 years. I think before this project is finished, you will be talking 20 years. I honestly believe it will take that long. It will be worth it. I said to my husband, 'we'll not see half of this, we'll be dead and done!' We still do it, and we think sometimes 'what the hell am I doing?' I say to the kids 'this is for your future', and they look at you as if to say 'what do you care?' I say 'I do' and then they realise that I'm not so bad after all!*

Older residents are often holding onto an ideal of community that they feel 'makes life worth living'. All residents who are activists are motivated by the idea of giving back to the community some of what they have received and of protecting what they see as a communal entitlement to decent basic conditions. Their generosity in offering all the energy they have in preventing social disintegration is something that local staff find deeply motivating. It is probably one of the biggest rewards of working in a declining neighbourhood.

Local services and front line staff: 'Mr Regeneration'

Locally-based staff have a direct impact on neighbourhood conditions in all sorts of ways – including the confidence they can generate amongst residents.

> *[The New Deal manager] is a lovely man. He's so committed. The reason we got involved was him as a person. His staff adore him. You don't hear a wrong word against him. He's got lovely management skills. He puts in as much, if not more, than anyone else. It's a 24 hour thing with [him]...He is, as far as we're concerned, 'Mr Regeneration'. Without him, I doubt if any of us would have stayed as long as we have* (Manchester resident).

We met many dedicated workers, some of whom had grown up in these neighbourhoods themselves, with a passionate desire to make things work and a strong belief in local people. Of course, the efforts of staff are affected by much wider changes, which sometimes feel utterly overwhelming.

Residents were sometimes deeply frustrated by service failures – for example they talked about no-one taking responsibility for derelict land, and lapses in local lettings agreements. Residents were acutely aware of how trapped local staff often were by the bureaucracy which governed their working practices. Staff were neither free to identify with local problems and find local solutions, but nor were they valued by the bigger official system. One resident described how she hoped the whole culture of the housing department would change when the stock transfer planned for her area went through:

> *You get this problem in the middle – it seems to be built on bullying. [Housing officers] are threatened with discipline if they don't follow a certain procedure. [The stock transfer steering group is saying] staff will not be able to bring their existing work practices with them...They will have to be debriefed and retrained...They will have to be a lot more flexible, otherwise it will not work. We need a change in the way of managing* (Manchester resident).

Staff were sometimes so alienated by the conditions that they could not bear to respond to any further demands or problems. One resident told us about a staff member she felt had let her down badly. This resident was trying to help prevent damage, and felt terribly hurt when the estate manager asked who she thought she was to be complaining.

> *On one occasion I rang the housing trust and said 'look there's people been going in next door, and I've called the police as well. They've been using the*

place to do drugs and been trying to set fires...' I've got the kids in here, and I don't want this property set alight. And I was asked by the estate manager, 'And who are you?' And I thought this is absolutely incredible...When they become vacant, the tenants don't tell them they've left, I would let them know. I would tell them when a property was vandalised, I would tell them before it was vandalised. And they could still treat me with such contempt and disrespect (Newcastle resident).

In general, the residents we spoke to were quick to praise helpful staff and express their high opinion of workers they felt were making a real difference.

[Our housing officer] has worked hard and he should get recognition. If we had a hundred of him in the city, we wouldn't have half the problems (Manchester resident).

The two community workers...when I first was involved...[were] absolutely inspiring people (Newcastle resident).

Managing unpopular neighbourhoods – staff 'chasing their tails'

The problems of managing unpopular inner city neighbourhoods have been documented over and over again (Urban Task Force, 1999; SEU, 1998). The poverty, instability and declining population within low demand areas all impact on local services, and increase pressures on staff. Housing officers face a constant battle to let properties:

I do feel for my staff. They often feel like rats trapped in a wheel – constantly chasing their tails, trying to find tenants...It can be a strain. You struggle to find someone from a non-existent waiting list...You'll get them into your property and it is terrific if they stop, but if a tenancy survives 12 weeks or 16 weeks you've gone to a lot of effort for very little return. You've probably spent a lot of money bringing the house up to a lettable standard, only for you to have it re-secured or for it to be vandalised (Newcastle senior housing manager).

A local police officer explained how depopulation undermines community controls:

If there's nobody in the houses, there's no-one to complain if kids or criminals start hanging around the area and driving stolen cars around...There'll be nobody around when criminals kick in the back door and steal the boiler. In a populated area, there are less opportunities for crime. Most crime is opportunistic. If there are people around, you know there's more chance that someone will tell the police and you'll get caught (Manchester police inspector).

A Manchester housing officer explained how staffing levels were a problem for his team:

> *We are under-manned and reacting constantly to political pressure [to deal with these acute problems]* (Manchester housing manager).

Sometimes there are very sensitive issues to be brokered – particularly demolition. Staff can find themselves with a delicate balancing act to perform; representing their organisation on the one hand (whilst not always feeling fully informed), and at the same time trying to do their best for the communities they serve.

> *It is not clear what [Going for Growth] will mean in practice locally. Have only had snippets of suggestions. The centralised staff of policy-makers need to talk to people on the ground* (Newcastle neighbourhood manager).

> *In the housing office they appear to be poorly informed. And what they are informed of makes them aware it's a badly run project* (Locally-based researcher, Newcastle).

Front line staff see the problems being played out every day, see people suffering, see areas in crisis. But they are often far removed from, and feel powerless to influence, the broader housing agenda. Their organisations invariably position themselves with a view to their own survival – aware of their standing on the national stage, and the resource implications of any stand they take:

> *We don't plan, we react to population. We haven't got the tools to deal with downsizing – especially when [until recently] it was all about bed-spaces, a huge growth programme, the working class 60s, 70s housing agenda* (Manchester housing manager).

The result is that front line staff are often left 'carrying the can' for decisions taken in a different era, with everyone wanting to cover their back. Staff exposed in this way can become defensive, cagey and unresponsive to legitimate complaints. In the worst cases, they see resident activists as nuisances. Most local staff did not seem to take this view however.

Teachers really struggle with conditions

Schools can suffer falling rolls. This not only has a direct impact on the funding they receive, meaning they have to reduce the number of teachers, but it also means they come under pressure to accept pupils excluded from other schools.

> *As the roll's dropped, so the money's dropped. This has meant that as teachers have left, we've not been able to replace them. You haven't got a balance of curriculum expertise anymore. The staff is becoming top-heavy*

and age-heavy as well, because you're not able to bring in any new blood (Newcastle primary school head).

High pupil turnover can make it much more difficult for staff and children alike. The constant loss of pupils and short stays by many recent incomers impacts on the performance of all children, and makes continuity of teaching much more difficult. The results often reflect these problems.

> *It has a big impact on attainment. Most of the children moving at Year 6 [final year] tend to be children who've been moved round a lot. Their attainment just isn't as it should be, because they've just not been in school. So we get them at Year 6 and they immediately affect our results* (Manchester primary school head).

The same social problems that affect lettings of houses affect school intakes. High levels of deprivation often mean children come to school with extra needs.

> *There really is a problem in areas of high social deprivation. People can't make excuses about it – and I don't want to – but we're actually climbing a steeper mountain than schools in other areas* (Newcastle secondary school head).

Teachers are often coping with the consequences of poor home conditions. Keeping control in the classroom can itself be a tremendous challenge where many pupils are out of their depth because they have only joined the school recently, and others don't want to be there because of home pressures or emotional problems.

> *If people went and worked in these schools for a month or so, they would value how much these schools are doing with very difficult children...We do have parents that don't value education and are aggressive* (Newcastle senior manager).

> *I do get down. There are things going on in the children's lives and out on the estate that depress me and make me glad I don't live here* (Manchester primary school head).

Lack of parental control can lead to serious behavioural difficulties. Many children spend a lot of their spare time unsupervised on the streets.

> *The majority of children I see from around 18 months upwards have either got or are heading for behavioural problems...more than half, definitely. An awful lot of it is to do with management by the parents, often the fact that there is only one parent, and a variety of males in the house, coming and going...The worse thing...is seeing these children when they grow, between 8 and 11, boys...A lot of these lads are without fathers or have very little contact with*

their fathers. They are incredibly vulnerable. They roam the streets. They get up to all sorts. There are some ring-leaders who rope the others in. But they can do a huge amount of damage and you can see the damage they are doing to themselves (Newcastle health visitor).

Some schools try to create a kind of oasis for children whose greatest need is freedom from pressure.

There is a balance – [the children] are here to learn and achieve, but some of them need a place where they can come and just be themselves and have a time of relief, or rest (Manchester primary school governor).

All these extra difficulties can take a serious toll on staff, who sometimes feel very alone in their experience.

I want to say how very isolated it feels to be dealing with the results of housing and area abandonment. I haven't initiated it, I can't control it, I am dealing with the results of children disturbed by movement, the school reducing, maybe looking at redundancies for people who are doing a good job by every measure...and it's me who's doing this. The strain it puts on me is just a reflection of the strain it puts on the school (Newcastle primary school head).

'It feels really bad for local staff'

One housing manager we spoke to had lived until his early twenties in a Newcastle neighbourhood now earmarked for wholesale clearance. He felt terribly upset at this turn of events, and talked about shock-waves spreading throughout that community as people realised their streets were in proposed demolition areas. He felt the council's agenda could be summed up in the following terms: *'How do you get people with money to come into an area that's so stigmatised? Just get rid of everyone and flatten the place.'* But, he argued, *'the council seriously underestimated the strength of community spirit in this neighbourhood.'*

Another Newcastle officer, in the early days of Going for Growth, explained his concerns: *'...those long standing residents who have been here for a very long time, almost feel like it doesn't matter what they try and do, the writing is on the wall. Secret meetings are taking place – there is a hidden agenda.'*

It's hard for staff not to become deeply involved in neighbourhood problems, given that they are so acute.

A lot of the time I find I'm thinking about the families way beyond my working hours. There's not much of a balance here. Most families are very needy, and therefore require a lot of you (Newcastle health visitor).

Staff and residents valued continuity and stability, and were worried when turnover was high. But they also highlighted the need for regular injections of 'new blood', extra energy and higher expectations. People definitely got ground down by everything they were hit with, and particularly in schools, expectations could fall to match the problems they saw.

> *It does take a lot out of you, and there are some staff who have been here too long. You forget what children are like out there, become too short-sighted, forget what children can do. If you become too embroiled in the social aspects of the school, then you make excuses for the children all the time. You know what it's like in their house in the morning and it's just a miracle that she gets to school, let alone does anything once she's here. And that attitude can begin to prevail. And that's why I think that seven years in a school like this is about right. Then it's time to move on* (Newcastle primary school head).

The same process of 'grinding down' seems to happen in housing. For instance, a Newcastle estate manager said, *'There comes a time I suppose...when it will be good for [the estate] to have someone fresh.'* Often, people can only keep up the level of commitment required for a limited period. This doesn't help continuity or stability and does suggest how seriously debilitating the problems are.

Pooling efforts at the front line?

Council housing officers in area-based offices are among the most regularly accessible faces of local government. This means they often take on extra roles; both because people actively bring non-housing matters to them and because they can see with their own eyes that they will not be able to manage their housing stock successfully unless the areas' wider social and economic problems are tackled. Several housing managers expressed the view that 'we can't do everything!'

> *Sometimes I feel that housing is taking on all the ills of the world* (Newcastle council housing manager).

The housing service's lack of power to insist on the input of other services inevitably limits the effectiveness of their own attempts to tackle problems, and their potential co-ordinating role.

> *On some estates, housing officers do all they can to keep the tenants keeping their bit looking OK. But then, if operational services don't come and clear up rubbish when it's dropped, and respond to our requests to do so quickly, then it's not really a united effort* (Manchester housing manager).

One senior Manchester worker shifted out of housing into wider environmental and street services for exactly that reason. He believed that unless you could get the streets clean, you would never make unpopular neighbourhoods popular again.

Wherever we went, talking to housing staff quickly led us to the issue of policing and security. All the neighbourhoods have severe crime problems, in large measure a direct result of low demand, high turnover and instability, empty properties and a vacuum in control. The housing problems generate crime problems and vice versa. As a result, housing staff constantly call on the police for help with security, enforcement, protection. And police rely heavily on housing staff for information, local contacts and often a local base to call in to. In most of the neighbourhoods, the housing and police services work together closely in direct response to problems. The co-operation this entails has built up over a long period of time.

> *The main link that works is with the police* (Manchester council housing manager).

Residents are also involved in this link as they have explained quite clearly.

Relationships between housing and other services are often less well developed. However, in recent years, the national emphases on Best Value service delivery, and on 'neighbourhood management', have begun to change ways of working on the ground, and joint working between different services is becoming more structured. For example, on Ann's estate a wide variety of different service representatives regularly attend the community forum, and also co-ordinate the input they give to individual families who are experiencing (and causing) problems. On Tina's estate, the New Deal for Communities team is co-ordinating action on several fronts – including policing, jobs, and the environment.

> *[We are seeing the] integration of people who have worked incredibly hard but sat in professional boxes...all those barriers are crumbling now, and the partnerships are much, much stronger* (Manchester senior manager).

> *There's a real determination within the city to have much more joined up working within directorates and across directorates. I think there's been far too much territorial bickering in the past – with people saying 'that's not really my responsibility'...I already had a conversation with social services about how we can make stronger links and have much better service co-ordination...on the ground. It will be interesting times ahead* (Newcastle senior housing manager).

Manchester's urban regeneration company for East Manchester and its joint landlord agreement for the redesigned estate in North Manchester are two examples of creating this kind of 'seamless service' at ground level. The Riverside Community Partnership and the Byker Renewal Plan in Newcastle's East End both have the potential to create this kind of integrated and focused staff team, to tackle conditions on the ground.

Belief in the neighbourhoods and their communities

The basis on which any success in local services is built is, of course, the residents themselves. Nearly all the front line staff we spoke to felt this, and believed they had to work in partnership with local communities in order for their efforts to be effective.

> *I feel that...the people who live in [this area], the vast majority of the community are really committed to making it work. They are desperate to see the place turned round to the advantage of the local community so that their life chances are bettered. That is what makes me optimistic, that there are those people...* (Senior housing manager, Newcastle).

A number of the neighbourhood-based staff we spoke to had themselves grown up in the areas. Most have since moved out, but some still have parents living there. They care particularly deeply about what happens to the neighbourhoods – it's personal. One housing manager was born and grew up in the neighbourhood which she now manages. She started as a rent collector and worked her way up. Part of the neighbourhood is currently being cleared, and she emphasised the need for direct consultation all the way through the process:

> *It has to be a partnership [with the community] otherwise it won't work...* (Neighbourhood manager).

She was particularly worried about the destabilising effect of demolition and was greatly impressed by the strong response of the local community to the threat. She believed it had brought people who really cared and who believed in their community 'out of the woodwork'.

A Newcastle health visitor explained how impressive she found people's ability to manage the severest of problems: *'A lot of the women, particularly, I don't know how they manage. Year in year out, on their own on a very limited income. With children with quite serious needs, and yet they manage to keep going. I have a lot of respect for them.'*

Several staff emphasised that they had actively sought their current roles, and really relished the work that they were doing. It was the immense value that they placed on the community that was most striking.

> *When I was looking for a headship...I had very clear ideas about what I wanted and what I didn't want. It was to do with people – nothing to do with areas – it was to do with people and children. I felt that this would be right for me. Having chosen it, I think that everything I expected to be here is here. I love it! It is the sort of school that I want to be in. It's got good people – I love the parents. I get on well with the parents, more often than not. I like the way the children are – pleasant, grateful for things you do for them. For some of them, actually being in school is a relief* (Manchester primary head).

Some staff opted to work in these areas because of the challenge. There was a gritty determination to make something of it.

> *It is heavy-going. I wouldn't want to work anywhere that wasn't! There's a lot to be done here. It's an exciting time. I'm not looking to leave this estate...I don't think anybody appreciates the need to have people in post to see things through. But it does wear you out, mind!* (Newcastle estate manager).

Staff could often get so bogged down in day-to-day problems that they forgot just how much impact their efforts had. There was no way that residents could tackle the problems they faced without this help.

> *We are only now beginning to realise that maybe we should be blowing our own trumpet a bit more – there are actually lots and lots of good things that we have [done]* (Newcastle senior housing manager).

Conclusion

There have been some important gains in recent years, but problems often still feel overwhelming. The decision to keep a place going or wipe the slate clean gets closer to the surface all the time.

> *Supporting these areas is more expensive than knocking them down...[In the future] there will be a management of decline, a wind-down of entry-level [private housing] and social housing, until [levels are] more in line with national averages* (Manchester council officer).

But amongst both residents and front line staff, we frequently encountered a refusal to give in and a belief that these inner city neighbourhoods simply *have* to survive. Knocking down sound and potentially valuable homes in neighbourhoods so close to the city centre carries many costs, and may be deeply regretted as a statement of failure rather than positive change. As one senior housing manager in Newcastle put it, *'Don't abandon hope in the inner cities. They do have a future. There are so many good things happening to the City, we should be taking pride.'*

If cities are to work, they will work because of successful neighbourhoods.

> *You have to rebuild your neighbourhood and it can be done. There are so many success stories to prove that it can be done. It's what you make of it, and it's about what you're prepared to put into it* (Manchester housing association officer).

Much of the acute decline that we have documented in inner Manchester and inner Newcastle is driven by what is happening outside the city boundaries. Staff are extremely aware that a vast over-supply of housing in both the North West and

North East regions is driving the collapse of the poorest inner city areas. In this sense, local staff are trying to hold the baton for an orchestra that is playing elsewhere.

> *The answer lies in the future of the whole conurbation – not just in Manchester. Whatever you do might be undone by your adjacent local authorities* (Manchester council officer).

Ultimately, the sustainability of the whole country may depend upon the fortunes of our inner cities:

> *There is a point where you'd want to give up – the stock isn't productive for us and people are having awful existences in them. But if we give up, we're going to create havoc in cities. And cities are a major part of Britain. They have got to function, and we've got to work with people to make them function* (Manchester council housing manager).

CHAPTER 7:
Overview – abandonment
as opportunity

Around three thousand neighbourhoods in urban areas all over the country are difficult to live in and difficult to rescue. The overwhelming majority of the most difficult neighbourhoods are in towns and cities so that neighbourhood-based social exclusion, seen as the concentration of multiple problems in particularly disadvantaged areas, is primarily an urban phenomenon (SEU, 1998). Many of the most severely problematic pockets are in large council estates, which are also disproportionately concentrated in cities. But even the most prosperous and successful places have their small problematic neighbourhoods.

People with choice, money, jobs, know-how, energy, try to move out of such difficult areas. Even in London, many families in low income neighbourhoods want to leave their current homes for somewhere better (Mumford and Power, forthcoming). There are many long-run drivers of this wider collapse in confidence.

This final section is in two parts – the first, Part A, shows why many city neighbourhoods are still in trouble and why new ways of tackling their housing and social problems must be tried. We start with the root causes of abandonment in Sections 1 and 2, looking at what can work in 3 and 4, ending with the role of infill, organic regrowth and the potential for new investment in 5 and 6. The second section, Part B, presents the unique opportunity for regrowth. We argue for changing the way we manage neighbourhood problems in Sections 7 to 10, and look at ways for creating the potential for many more jobs in inner cities in Section 11. We conclude that refocusing growth through more sensitive and pro-city planning can lead to more sustainable cities and spare the countryside, in Sections 12 and 13.

Part A: Neighbourhoods in trouble

1. Why are inner neighbourhoods being abandoned?

Two historic factors underlie abandonment: outward sprawl and deindustrial-isation. As the first country in the world to become overwhelmingly urban – 90 per cent by 1900 – and industrial – only 2 per cent of the workforce in agriculture by 1900 – our cities paid a very heavy price for the huge wealth and international status that Britain acquired. The political consensus was to lead people *out* of them. Major efforts to tackle housing problems and slum conditions were driven over the following one hundred years by the idea that crowded and impoverished masses should be moved out of the city to new greenfield, suburban housing – council owned as well as private. The famous First World War One slogan *'Homes Fit for Heroes'* led eventually to a blunt and vast slum clearance programme targeting all inner cities across the country in an attempt to create space for better housing *within* as well as beyond city boundaries. The promotional poster for the Homes campaign showed a soldier pointing to the suburban semi as the dream home and spurning the monotonous, soot-blackened terraces of byelaw housing, many of which survive to this day, but which were built in their millions before the First World War as an orderly, low-cost remedy for the unsanitary and chaotic slums. Very few challenged the idea of large-scale demolition and exodus until the 1970s by which time the damage to cities and the communities they housed was immeasurable (Young and Wilmott, 1957).[1]

As the earliest industrial economy in the world, our dependence on old-style, heavy manufacturing was paramount. With the incremental decline in our factory-based economy from the turn of the twentieth century, and the virtual collapse of our mainstay heavy industries in the 1970s and 1980s, older urban areas were left high and dry, almost devoid of jobs, incrementally denuded of the more skilled and more ambitious who seized plentiful opportunities to carry on moving out (Turok and Edge, 1999). Slum clearance made this economic transformation harder and harsher. The large-scale blight and eradication of old inner areas left cities like Liverpool and Glasgow struggling to recover long after the population and jobs had been wiped out (Maclennan, 1997)

The process of 'housing exodus' was incremental and still continues today, certainly from the poorest neighbourhoods. The rate of outward migration has slowed, but is still significant (Holmans and Simpson, 1999). Industrial change gained rapid momentum under the impact of the 1970s economic recession, Thatcherism and international market forces. Both the housing and jobs transformation hit much harder in the major industrial cities of the north and midlands because here urban conditions were more dominated by dirty industry and the high population density of the industrial workforce. The slum clearance and estate building process, on a vast scale in these industrial regions, left some inner neighbourhoods with a third of their former population (Power, 1987).

Thus, Manchester and Newcastle, alongside Liverpool, Birmingham and almost all metropolitan areas, were by the late 1980s but shadows of their former wealth, population density and significance. The geographic spread of the conurbations was now wider, less concentrated and carved up by major roads. Old docks,

1. For more detailed accounts of the process, the reader could refer to Burnett, J (1991) *A Social History of Housing*; Briggs, A (1983) *A Social History of England*; Thomson, F M L (1990) *Cambridge Social History*; Rogers, R and Power, A (2002) *Cities for a Small Country*.

monuments to our world pre-eminence in shipping, lay idle in London, Liverpool, Glasgow and Newcastle (Harvey-Jones, 1994). The great rivers of the Clyde, Mersey and Tyne were deeply damaged by two centuries of grime and obsolete industrial relics. The first industrial workhouses of the world along the banks of the Manchester and Birmingham canal networks, were literally falling down or burnt down for insurance gains – a desecrated heritage of irreplaceable value.

It is against this backdrop of economic, social and geographical change that our work is set. The poorest neighbourhoods in our study, experiencing the most acute abandonment, are at the most extreme end of this long-run and extensive process, which embraced most of the country and certainly affected most cities. The Thames Gateway area, to the East of the City of London, shows remarkably similar signs to the eastern and northern areas of Manchester or the East and West Ends of Newcastle, albeit that new opportunities are closer to hand. Industrial closure, high unemployment, low-value housing and even, in places, signs of abandonment are clear (LSE Cities Programme, 2002). This pattern pervades Western European and North American former industrial cities as well as the United Kingdom (Core Cities Conference, 2002).

There is clearly a drastic need for change in direction. As inner neighbourhoods have become too depleted, with too little work, too much poverty, and eventually too few people, social conditions have unravelled. Schools close, buses run less often, shops and banks disappear and criminal networks thrive in the vacuum of left behind spaces (Home Office, 1999b). The one thing that does not decline is traffic. People who have forsaken the city still use the centre for its amenities and for work. As commuters, they now only drive through the areas they would probably have lived in, in earlier epochs. Congestion and the time involved in commuting are high prices to pay for allowing urban neighbourhoods to fall into such decay.

Housing built on the edges of cities, usually on greenfields, provides a popular alternative to city living for those that can afford to buy, but can destroy both countryside and inner cities simultaneously. At the most extreme, crude over-building outside cities fuels plummeting demand for lower value inner neighbourhoods within. This is exactly the process this report documents in the north where more homes are being built, almost all outside city boundaries, than there are projected households who might form to fill them. The over-supply of homes is a major driver of urban decline and abandonment (UTF, 1999; ODPM, 2002; GONW, 1999; DETR, 1999).

2. The link between housing markets and abandonment

Housing markets are driven by what people believe a home to be worth. People look for multiple signals of value, including confidence, care and the patterns of growth or decline. They also look at alternatives. Thus the long-run decline of inner cities and the acute decline of the poorest areas are matched by a pattern of falling relative demand and the availability of more attractive and affordable housing elsewhere. The withdrawal of owners without replacement occupiers – abandonment – is the strongest possible signal of a collapse in confidence and therefore value. Once housing abandonment is underway, even on a limited scale, the public statement of 'zero value' that it represents 'contaminates' the surrounding properties (DETR, 1999). Abandonment is a neighbourhood process, heavily concentrated in the least desirable urban areas even though it reflects wider trends. Reversing abandonment can only work if the neighbourhoods in which low-value properties are located are themselves improving. Property values and neighbourhood conditions are intimately related and this underlines a further aspect of abandonment. It often arises, not only because of property conditions per se, but because of wider neighbourhood decline. The process is interactive.

As potential buyers withdraw or simply fail to materialise, a 'shadowy private rented market' emerges. This conversion to private renting very often presages abandoment as it ekes out the use of properties, no longer readily saleable on the open market. Homes that were previously owner occupied, are converted to renting, an easier access, cheaper tenure, with shorter time-scales and lower commitments on the part of both owners and tenants (Bramley and Pawson, 2002). This sops up demand among the most marginalised households in low income areas. Police claim that it sometimes provides a cover for criminal networks in the areas we studied (GMP, 2000; Tyneside Police Authority, 2000). Social disorder can then take over the whole area. We witnessed this process in inner Manchester and inner Newcastle. It has happened on a vastly bigger scale in US cities (Wilson, 1987). Housing and regeneration workers in our cities are constantly on the look out for signs of an increase in private renting, often the first sign of market collapse. Alternatively they welcome signs of a reversion to owner occupation. This connection between private renting and decline need not happen in a more stable and balanced housing market (Power, 1993).

Tackling low demand council housing requires a different approach. This housing sector is targeted at those on lowest incomes, and in the inner areas of big cities there is often simply too much of it. Its values are already far below the city average. In Birmingham, one third of the stock is in low demand; in Manchester two thirds. The only alternative is demolition – often the favoured and easiest solution – unless the council tries to push it 'up market'. Councils often pioneer ideas for reversing abandonment of their own stock ahead of private owners who have often already lost too much and are too fragmented to try. Advertising unpopular council flats and homes has become the accepted method for attracting in people in work, often outsiders to the local community. These may be people with lower housing need but wanting to live in the city, people with some 'get up and go', willing to try it out. In Manchester this approach – the Manchester Homefinder – has been highly successful and could be widely copied. It rescues property with little or no demand, giving it new value. Newcastle has sold some property in unpopular inner neighbourhoods for a minimal sum to households with energy and resources to do it up – a form of homesteading.

Most inner city housing is at least a generation old and requires constant reinvestment. The value of the stock declines rapidly if it is not constantly upgraded. It needs repair, modernisation and general improvement to fit modern standards. Poorer households cannot afford this – particularly elderly owner occupiers. Nor can councils without special funding. If government does not step in, who will? Only a small portion of the stock in poor areas matches modern aspirations as it stands, particularly for younger households in work.

Neighbourhood decay often mirrors a general lack of care for the stock. Thus abandonment is triggered by a combination of over-supply, disrepair and neighbourhood decay. Some people question the sense of even attempting to rescue these areas following thirty years of 'failed effort' to reverse the long-run decline. We do not see it that way, but cities will only flourish if people want to live in them. At the moment too few do. We argue that the very areas that are being abandoned offer the best chance of city recovery. But only if we can attract new people into inner cities, and hold onto some of the households that currently choose to move out, will cities compete with the demand for out-of-town homes (Countryside Agency, 2002).

What would make city living more attractive? Can we learn from the rapid revival of city centres, in sharp contrast to most inner neighbourhoods? And what do more popular, more select urban neighbourhoods tell us about their appeal?

3. City centres and successful inner neighbourhoods

A key to the revival of cities as a whole is the vitality of city centres. This is because, far more than the proponents of the Information Revolution believed, we rely on city centres as the engines of the new economy. Proximity, face to face encounters, easy access to multiple back-up services, a concentration and clustering of related enterprises all generate new demand for space in cities. The centrality of financial services and requirements for high quality amenities in a modern economy, the need for accessible personal back-up from childcare, hairdressing, house maintenance through to interior design, ready prepared dinner deliveries and all kinds of specialist shops and repair, all help shape the revival of cities as our *'creative nerve centres'* (Rogers and Power, 2000).

British central and local governments in the 1980s adopted an innovative partnership approach to transforming the centres of our major cities from industrial relics into high-tech global connectors. Obsolete historic infrastructures were readily, if expensively, converted to new enterprises and housing. Neglected, often disused or under used landmarks such as canals, theatres, libraries, old transport infrastructures, have become exciting and appealing elements of the new as well as the old eras. As new businesses and new people have been attracted in, so have new values followed. Marketing city centre living has gathered its own steam.

On the back of this rebirth, shoppers from outlying Cumbria and Northumbria chose city centre shopping in Manchester and Newcastle ahead of the giant Trafford or Gateshead Metro shopping malls where the names, styles and atmosphere are predictable. People are also looking for 'street experience', for unexpected corners to explore, for recently restored side streets and bars where the 'city atmosphere' is a special, if almost forgotten, asset. The interaction of new 'urban tourists' and new urban dwellers is restoring the centres of every major city in the country.

So can inner city neighbourhoods catch this fever? The new, exciting urban walkway connecting Manchester's city centre with the heart of East Manchester 1½ miles away reinforces the link between the two. The truth is that the less decayed, more attractive neighbourhoods are already improving. Old Victorian or Georgian neighbourhoods, built for artisans and respectable working families have often recovered from industrial decay, where the poorest slum areas, housing a mass of casual workers, though upgraded many times over, have generally stayed poor and proved harder to regenerate.

Reputations are very long lasting (Lupton, 2001a). Our cities were long ago sectioned into poorer and richer areas and although people were physically closer together, because cities were denser and less spread-out, socially the distance between the poorest areas and the rest of the city was vast. The Booth poverty maps of London at the turn of the century show how concentrated poverty was and how strongly linked to specific areas. These patterns have survived almost intact to this day (Davey Smith *et al.*, 2000; *The Economist*, 2001).

It has been a lot easier to create the new economy and new prosperity in West London than in the East End. It is easier to see South Manchester gaining ground than the northern part of the city where property values are falling. So what helps the inner neighbourhoods that do recover take off again? Firstly, the intrinsic attractions of their housing. They usually have solid, old, semi-detached or terraced houses that are big enough to adapt easily to modern standards. People like old, but fully modernised homes. Previously multi-occupied, privately rented rooms and flats in large old houses, often deeply decayed and disrepaired, can be combined into spacious 'good as new' homes. The generous proportions and the simple, adaptable design of older housing allows for careful restoration, creating homes of character and style with the patina of time etched unmistakably on them, yet offering light, airy, up-to-the-minute conditions. Insulation, central heating, 'mod cons' combine admirably with old wooden floor boards, stripped, bevelled doors, ceiling mouldings and other attractive features that are signs of former wealth. Old gardens, even small ones, unlike back yards, often have mature trees that give a leafy green atmosphere and public streets become greener as the neighbourhood attracts young innovators. Infill sites created by loss of workplaces or other changes of use, create new, well designed, high quality housing opportunities and new uses make these recovering neighbourhoods more varied and interesting.

Secondly, new urban residents attracted by such recovering inner neighbourhoods often have civic connections and responsibilities and can lever in better services. Conditions improve, pubs and shops survive and go up-market. The historic, community-forming role of these neighbourhoods survives around the traditional street patterns while the moderately high density encourages street activity. These successful inner neighbourhoods have about 50 to 100 homes per hectare, one quarter to one half the density of the typical Victorian slums of East Manchester or Newcastle, but at least double to quadruple the density of modern suburban estates. This gives them a critical mass of people which supports services, making them highly sought after in every city including the inner areas of Newcastle, Manchester or Glasgow. Fast reviving inner neighbourhoods are intrinsically attractive urban locations, often near to major parks, close to old universities, on well-established public transport routes, created before the advent of the car. They are urbane in the best sense of the word.

All these elements make inner neighbourhoods of aging but solid structure highly attractive today. They offer all the advantages of city life and though they share many of the problems of other inner city neighbourhoods, particularly crime and poor schools, they have 'kerb appeal'. They have the major asset of a growing social mixture, which many people seem to prefer to more sterile, single-class suburbs. Notting Hill in London, or Victoria Park in Manchester, or Gosforth in Newcastle epitomise such areas.

Can the historically poorer neighbourhoods that are struggling to survive develop similar assets from a very different base? We would argue that they can. The building of the new Victoria line for the London Underground in the 1960s and the lifting of the large demolition plans hanging over much of Islington transformed it from a depopulating, decaying slum into a lively mixed tenure, multi-ethnic area. It still has by far the least open space of any London borough, the worst schools and very high crime – serious blights on its community – but it is *very* popular because of its density, its closeness to the centre, its mixed communities and its terraces! Many argue that Islington is a far cry from North Manchester or inner Newcastle, and this is indisputable. But a quick look back to the 1970s might suggest a more comparable history. Then it was fast depopulating, had extremely low property values, a high level of rapid turnover private renting, a serious loss of jobs, numerous school closures, and racial disorders provoked by rapid in-migration of ethnic minorities from abroad and provocative policing (Power, 1970). It had the worst council record on many fronts, particularly housing, and the majority of its wards ranked among the poorest in London on overcrowding, poor housing conditions, illegal landlords, as well as some of the most extreme social problems in the city (Shelter, 1974; Hamilton, 1978).

The turn-around came slowly, piecemeal, on the back of generous improvement grants to do up old, decayed property, environmental improvements street by street, tree planting involving residents throughout the borough, support for tenant co-operatives and a multitude of other community-based solutions to local problems. Local services have mushroomed on the back of its revival and many local jobs have flowed from its promising service sector. None of this made Islington into the gimmicky area of its newspaper fame. It is still one of the poorest urban areas in London with many difficult to manage council estates and it is beset with special needs and management problems. But it is so popular as a place to live, that its housing is now out of reach for most ordinary families. Integrating the very different communities that live alongside each other in Islington and urban neighbourhoods like it, is certainly a challenge, but a far more positive one than dealing with the decline and near collapse of its earlier history.

Under pressures of shortage and the fashionable revival of terraced houses in inner London, following the pioneers of the 1960s and 1970s, many of the poorer neighbourhoods in the East End are now recovering rapidly. This is a recent phenomenon of the last five years. Neighbourhood success depends on housing that is potentially attractive to some, not necessarily the most affluent sections of the community; that is well located and that offers transport links. Most old housing has the potential to be modernised and almost any urban area can be made greener and more attractive if there is sufficient demand and confidence.

Stratford, deep in the East End, and until very recently a severely declining, low value area with many economic, social, ethnic and environmental problems, is now recovering rapidly following new ultra-modern transport links and major environmental improvements. Changes in London's inner areas offer some clues to a brighter future for our cities. There is a new taste for city living, demonstrated by the high value of city centre apartments in Manchester and Newcastle, that we believe can be galvanised into housing demand in the urban core around the centre. We believe the northern cities can build on their success.

4. Recycled housing

Rescuing inner city housing has been a goal of government policy since the late 1960s when General Improvement Areas were first introduced as the slum clearance programme ran out of steam, its costs mounted and public protest began in earnest (Hamilton, 1978). Renewal policies have had mixed success. However, one thing is clear – inner city conditions would certainly be a lot worse, had it not been for virtually continuous attempts to maintain or improve conditions, equalise performance and target reinvestment efforts at the areas in most serious decline. The collapse of American inner city ghettos is a sharp reminder of the consequences of abandonment by government. It fuels further abandonment and accelerates sprawl (Katz, 2002). In Britain at least, the idea of keeping the poorest neighbourhoods within reach of the mainstream has retained some purchase (DoE, 1994; SEU, 1998).

Some successes in the regeneration of half abandoned housing point to a better future for inner cities, if only the approach to rescue was more consistent and more long term. Many of Glasgow's historic tenements, previously classed as slums, were converted in the 1970s and 1980s into popular, modern, mixed tenure flats through the creation of community-based housing associations. This model will now be used to help shape new community-run housing as the city of Glasgow transfers 100,000 run-down council homes into a series of independent community-based housing organisations. In cities like Glasgow and Newcastle, as well as London, tower blocks have been secured, clad, decorated and let to suitable households in a much more controlled way than on the basis of 'neediest' first 'access' rules. This package of improvements restores viability and actually makes tower blocks attractive in disparate neighbourhoods across the country. Urban Splash, the northern based development company most strongly identified with recycling obsolete industrial buildings into attractive, high-value homes, is proposing to renovate tower blocks in North Manchester for mixed occupancy. Of course, not all tower blocks are rescuable but they certainly do not justify blanket condemnation (Hunt Thompson Associates, 2001).

Victorian terraces, currently the target of major demolition plans in some cities and towns, have proved eminently reusable in reviving neighbourhoods. Their versatility and durability make their conversion into modern houses attractive and economic in more popular neighbourhoods, even in such 'low demand cities' as Manchester and Newcastle. In London, Edinburgh and Dublin, they are the prize options.

A number of combining factors could help to reduce the gap in the state of the economy between London and the south, and the rest of the country. The government's ten-year transport plan, changes to the planning system and a focus on regional economic growth may provide important opportunities for businesses and individuals to locate further afield. The alternative is becoming increasingly unsustainable as London runs out of space and high housing costs negatively impact on the labour market (*The Economist*, 2002c). Promoting the potential of their inner areas will help other cities to catch up. London got there first because it is the capital, has a more diverse economy and was less hard hit by industrial collapse, albeit its vast dockland areas plummeted in value and were semi-abandoned for nearly two decades (LDDC, 1981). It is also closer to other European countries giving it a strong economic advantage. A quick revisit to the Inner Area Studies of the 1970s will remind us just how close the parallels were between the decline of inner London and the decline of other cities such as Birmingham and Liverpool (DoE, 1976).

Northern city leaders need not hide behind the fact that 'its different up here'. The differences could turn out to be their greatest asset – a uniquely different atmosphere, heritage, style and therefore appeal. By stating their potential and vaunting their distinctiveness is how cities like Rotterdam, Hamburg and Lille recovered from being post-industrial backwaters, away from their thriving capitals.

Victorian warehouses came into vogue later than terraces and even more unexpectedly but they are now the urban property developer's golden egg. The flats they produce are futuristic as well as historic. This greatly adds to their appeal to the younger generation of would-be urban pioneers. The supply is rapidly drying up in the city centres and developers are applying the 'warehouse' approach to converting offices into flats. Some pretty unimpressive concrete 1960s office blocks offering few architectural or historic merits, are becoming 'luxury loft-style apartments' in inner Glasgow and inner London. 'Lofts' offer a style of 'non-housing' homes that works across a big range of building types and occupants. But more importantly, in Manchester, Glasgow and Birmingham at least, Victorian workshops, factories and warehouses spread out into the inner ring of poorer neighbourhoods far beyond the city centre. The scope for spreading the 'loft fashion' into these areas at lower cost is as yet largely untapped, though the new walkway out to East Manchester to reach the new stadium is studded with such relics. Developers are clearly snapping the best of them up and new homes are on the way. The Ouseburn regeneration in East Newcastle, scrambling up the old industrial valley from the Tyne, is generating new interest and already some beautiful live-work units are springing up. It will not be long before the spill over from the absurdly high prices for lofts in city centres begins to raise the value of abandoned, redundant industrial buildings beyond the central ring, creating more affordable 'loft' homes for more moderately paid workers.

The rescue of large run-down, inner city council estates has its own specific problems. Council estates get an increasingly bad press. The latest People's Panel survey shows satisfaction among council tenants plummeting from 70 per cent in 2000 to only 49 per cent in 2002, a worryingly low estimation of its value (Office of Public Services Reform, 2002). A dominant problem is the fact that council housing is built mainly in large, monotonous lumps. Poor management, poor security, disrepair, unattractive environments and an unsustainable concentration of social problems has made many estates highly off-putting to people with any choice. Yet often there are residents with strong roots in the areas who want to make them work and believe they can, who moved there in a different era when becoming a council tenant was a mark of pride and when leaving behind old slums seemed a route to progress. The commitment of established residents underlines their intrinsic value and potential under conditions of care, pride and competition for homes.

All over the country, particularly in some of the most difficult estates, tenants' groups have formed tenant management organisations, taking over responsibility for estates and forcing conditions up to a reasonable standard. Community-based housing associations within large, difficult estates in Scotland have had similar impact, invariably breaking up over-large estates into smaller, more varied groups of homes (Tunstall, 2000; Clapham and Kintrea, 1999). Some unpopular estates have transferred to a local housing company or housing association. These have also seen a major improvement in conditions. The most impressive turn-around has occurred through a combination of high resident involvement, significant physical upgrade, much tighter management and enforcement, and the recruitment of new tenants on a very different basis from the previous council lettings system – more choice-based, and carefully checked for compliance with basic tenancy laws.

It has proved impossible to run council housing as islands of need in an increasingly affluent society. This experience fits with evidence from all over Europe. Estates simply don't survive as *'social ghettos'* (Power, 1999). Some of the large outer and inner estates simply will not survive on this basis. Some demolition is inevitable. An important ingredient of turning around unpopular council estates is attracting a broader band of people on the back of improved conditions, diversifying the structure and tenure, and investing in meticulous ground-level management. As more city council homes are transferred to independent housing associations or housing companies, they begin to attract significant new investment from private lenders who generally regard inner city housing as a secure long-term bet. This should increase their appeal.

The overwhelming dominance of council housing in many inner city neighbourhoods – 40 to 80 per cent or more compared to a national average of 17 per cent – creates a ghettoisation of the poor which is problematic both in sustaining these areas and in attracting newcomers. The easy but expensive answer is to demolish whole estates. Investing in more mixed ownership and income patterns seems essential. In high demand areas, like London, where boom prices make affordability vital, reducing the overall supply of affordable homes through demolition is having serious consequences and is increasingly challenged by residents themselves. Many extremely decayed London estates, previously up for demolition, are now being restored. Broadening eligibility to people with less problems is critical to success. There are levers for upgrading these areas without displacing existing residents who want to stay – often with small-scale demolition of particularly difficult areas, and letting on a more up-market basis where demand is low.

5. Demolition and new housing

An incremental rather than bulldozer approach to changing housing conditions works its way carefully through neighbourhoods, avoiding years of blight and complete loss of function. Manchester City Council calls this more negotiated approach *'radical incrementalism'*. In Manchester one of the very worst estates has been turned around through the action of residents and the city council together with selective demolition and major improvements to the rest. Environmentally, socially and economically, this must make sense if it is possible. For the impact on the environment of demolition and rebuilding is huge; socially, it takes a generation at least to rebuild a wiped out community, and economically even the highest renovation costs rarely reach the full costs of demolition and rebuilding (Power, 1999).

Where an area has too much housing and severe abandonment, the 'scalpel' approach to demolition – careful removal of the harmful bits to protect the rest from 'contamination' – generally works better that the chain ball and bulldozer approach – laying flat whole areas. Too many bad memories of earlier clearances are still alive creating resistance to large-scale demolition; whereas removing specific eyesores to the benefit of residents reaffirms their security and their stake. Some demolition can be positive.

There are many ways of taking a 'scalpel' to an area and it is important to avoid 'creeping demolition' which triggers loss of confidence. An improvement plan needs to run alongside any selective demolition. If bits of streets are demolished whenever a cluster of voids appears, then given the inevitable time-lag with demolition, the empties generate more empty properties before they can be taken out. This approach can cast permanent uncertainty over the neighbourhood because as soon as one or two voids appear, people know their street could be next on the demolition hit-list and so they try and get out in advance. Demolition then encroaches further and further. Avoiding this atmosphere of blight is vital to recovery. A carefully negotiated renewal plan, small area by small area, becomes a critical tool in building new confidence. The urban village proposals for inner East Newcastle are starting to do this.

There are many techniques. The narrow two-up, two-down terraces with tiny backyards, and alleyways opening straight onto the pavements, are often considered beyond salvation. Their practical basic design to relieve atrocious overcrowding in the last century no longer fits modern needs. But they do offer an urban atmosphere that adds potential to a bleak area requiring major reinvestment. They also house within them some of the city's most committed residents, as New East Manchester showed during the Commonwealth Games (*The Economist*, 2002b).

Removing maybe one in four or even every other row of small, dense terraced streets can create a new small park or play area, more or larger gardens or a wider street with front gardens in place of surplus housing. Reducing the very high density of terraced houses in this way keeps street patterns and some homes intact. It allows residents who want to stay to do so. But it has to be brokered on a very local scale, house by house.

Willing investors and confidence in the location are prerequisites for these forms of renovation. In Leicester, some residents have joined terraced houses sideways, creating more spacious homes in its inner terraced streets. In most older rural settlements incomers have joined together terraced two-up, two-down cottages to make more spacious homes that sell for 'a bomb'. There are many other ideas for recycling housing. Not all will work everywhere. And not all housing is saveable. But it would help the restoration of inner city neighbourhoods if we started from a presumption of reusing what we can in new forms and often under new ownership, where previous patterns of ownership and use are clearly failing.

As for new housing, inner city areas are full of unused, empty spaces where buildings have fallen into disuse, homes have been demolished, or earlier plans unrealised. An aerial map of any major city will show up these spaces and their potential even in the crowded South East (South East Regional Development Agency, 2002, Survey of available urban sites). In fact at least one third to a half of all new development happens through the use of unplanned, uncounted, spare sites, many of them quite small (UTF, 1999). In addition, there are many large urban development sites, particularly in northern cities like Manchester, Newcastle, Liverpool, Glasgow, crying out for reuse. These sites often require remediation and sometimes there is serious contamination which deters investment for decades, as on the famous Dome site in North Greenwich.

The techniques for bringing difficult urban sites into productive use are now well-established and imaginative developers, engineers, architects, planners and regeneration managers are seizing the opportunity they offer (RICS, 2002). We now have new skills and tools including the pathfinding projects that more avant garde developers have used to prove the potential for inserting and grafting on to the existing urban space new housing and services as needed. This approach includes ways of incorporating solid, existing housing and other buildings, and embracing and winning over anxious communities under threat, thus reinforcing positive social networks (Glasgow City Council, 2002).

6. Attracting investment to inner neighbourhoods

How do cities make inward investment attractive? The northern city neighbourhoods often have lively, committed residents willing to invest energy, time and enthusiasm into recovery. Yet seemingly much money has been wasted on bricks and mortar (Newcastle, 2000). And many community efforts are undone by the constant exodus of more able bodied, younger residents and by the extremes of local anti-social activity. What would make a difference? Holding onto the small knots of community that have survived allows us to create new opportunities round them. Wiping areas clean of people and buildings, as the original Going for Growth strategy seemed to propose in Newcastle, is not only contentious and upsetting to community confidence, but it makes the time-scale for revitalisation longer and may even make the new planned neighbourhoods less attractive, more sterile and less urbane. Some developers such as Tom Bloxham of Urban Splash argue that success is more likely where it can be grafted onto existing communities, using existing infrastructure (Stevenson, 1999; New East Manchester, 2000). However, many in both Newcastle and Manchester, as well as other cities, argue that radical change is essential. We do not disagree. But how long and with what tools?

The secret of city centre regrowth has been to preserve, restore and rebuild as much as possible, and to add infill buildings and activities to the many spaces that have grown up, creating an atmosphere of renewal and focused activity that generates confidence. This approach can work in poorer neighbourhoods. It has already succeeded in small, successful, self-confident cities like Chester, York, Bristol,

Ipswich, Brighton, Oxford, where old former working class streets, increasingly abandoned by traditional residents, have been converted on the back of social and often ethnic mix, and proximity to the centre of the city. Attractive homes and multiple, small enterprises have sprung up. Terraced two-up two-down houses have extended into attic areas, backyards and side passages. These lower income communities were in steep decline. Their revival and success today is based on the decision not to demolish structurally sound but increasingly obsolete housing. A second chance worked wonders because those cities were themselves popular and short of cheaper old-style housing. As bigger cities regain their reputation as places to be, the same could happen to them. Already the evidence is there that younger households prefer converted, modernised property to newly built homes (JRF, 1998).

The growth in universities, mostly located in urban areas, is fuelling demand for student housing in inner cities. New build university blocks sometimes compete with available property. But some cities rescue older housing to meet this demand. Transient as students may be, if well managed, student housing offers a real chance for building a longer-term, higher skilled commitment to the city. Manchester and Liverpool are building on their educational assets to develop new enterprise clusters. Middlesbrough and Lancaster are rescuing some of their poorest terraces as attractive and marketable student accommodation. A better safer city environment is key to success, and close management and repair of the rented property is essential. Some city universities are playing a pro-active role in approving and registering landlords, thus helping combat the poor image of private renting.

Converting properties into modern homes in the neighbourhoods where space and housing are available isn't cheap. Private investors, either individuals or developers, will only come in after obvious risks have shrunk right back – like crime or drugs, or disorderly behaviour – and only after the public sector has committed itself to providing and paying for the right infrastructure and environment. London Docklands is a prize example of this approach. A lot of money went into the transport links. Several hundred council flats were demolished to make way for new road works and the overhead light railway. Public money levered in private support for all these changes.

So what should the government and the big northern and midlands cities do? The nine pathfinder programmes to combat housing market failure in the midlands and the north, including Manchester and Newcastle will push money towards authorities that can curb the building of outer homes in direct competition with failing inner neighbourhoods. The problem of surplus housing and concentrated abandonment are firmly on the agenda.

Local councils, housing associations and developers may say that areas of acute failure are 'clapped out', 'obsolete' and have to be cleared to make way for new communities in the hope of receiving large-scale regeneration funding. But the government will be sceptical about the huge costs involved. The renewal fund is unlikely to offer more than around £10,000 per property, whereas the housing improvement grants that rescued the decayed London terraces thirty years ago quickly rose from around £5,000 a home in 1968 to £25,000 a home in 1974 (Power, 1974). The equivalent in today's prices would be unthinkable.

Around £40,000 per property may be necessary to restore currently 'obsolete' housing. In other words, we are not seriously funding renewal of the existing housing stock and the government's efforts are likely to founder as outer greenfield building continues in the face of inadequate reinvestment in inner neighbourhoods and their 'unloved' homes. When we compare the cost of new build houses with full renovation, we must include not only the direct building costs, but full demolition costs, new infrastructure and service costs, environmental impacts, congestion costs, time-lag and rehousing costs.

Investment in the existing stock and the environments of these neighbourhoods is a prerequisite of change. Only in this way can we quickly start to attract more affluent households and hold onto existing residents as they become more affluent (Best, 2002). The balance of funding is currently strongly skewed against housing renewal and in favour of low density sprawl. Equally, fiscal incentives probably work better than cash grants (UTF, 1999; 2002) and the Treasury has begun to facilitate the renewal of older stock this way (DTLR, 2002). Improvement loans on favourable terms, environmental improvements, using planning to restrict outer building and facilitate inner conversions, cutting VAT on all inner city reinvestment would give strong signals to lenders and borrowers alike.

If new social housing was no longer built in places where there is clearly a surplus, such as Newcastle or Manchester, then the money saved from knocking down quality homes to build again, could be redirected to making inner neighbourhoods more attractive. Change in neighbourhood and housing investment patterns is an absolute key to winning people over to inner city living. Such a shift will involve block by block, street by street security, cleaning and maintenance, rapid, reliable transport links, quality shops, schools and health centres. In this way, housing and neighbourhood conditions need to go hand in hand.

Part B: Chance for regrowth

7. Demographic change and new demand for cities

Household and demographic change offers new opportunities for the recovery of inner city communities with the growth in smaller households. With only a slowly growing population, we are experiencing rapid growth in childless households at the younger and older ends of the age range (Maclennan, 2002), as well as in the middle ages. For some people, suburban housing may not be ideal – too spacious, too far from amenities, too much gardening, too few local buses, shops, health or other services. Inner neighbourhoods in contrast, offer accessible local firms, smaller homes, proximity, amenities, services and public transport. They need stronger marketing of these assets.

The shrinking size of households not only increases demand for new homes, but in turn is influenced by increasing supply. The fact that 70 per cent of projected new households are single people, many of them elderly, is a sign of the extreme social isolation into which we are building ourselves. It is unsustainable and socially unmanageable to house an aging population, often people alone, in ever more dispersed homes. Need for healthcare, family support, proximity to neighbours all suggest a surge in demand for smaller homes within easy reach of other people and main services. The dream of a large house and garden can become an excessive burden with increasing disability.

At the same time, many younger people, marrying and bearing children much later, do not necessarily want to live far outside the city where most new homes are built – quite the opposite in fact according to recent property surveys (*Sunday Times*, 2001). People who have less company at home often chose to live nearer to city amenities given the chance, the quality and the security. The very high prices paid for centre city apartments in part reflect strong demand from new style households. Some would-be occupants on more modest incomes who simply cannot compete for city centre apartments, could be attracted to near-abandoned housing close by if it can be booted into life.

Northern cities should be working out how to graft on new uses, new populations, new open spaces, new tree planting, new transport links, to existing communities in order to respond to demand from new types of urban household. It is surely much harder to secure that demand on the back of lost communities than on the back of 'streets with potential'. Holding onto existing communities as far as possible, as is now happening in New East Manchester, ensures that a viable, cheap housing stock and basic infrastructure is 'at the ready' for conversion and adaptation. After all this is what is happening with the old warehouses that no-one valued a few years ago.

8. Dealing with trouble in poorer neighbourhoods

If the way forward for inner areas is going to rely on grafting onto existing communities, what of the chaotic lives of difficult and anti-social families who have become concentrated in these areas? Public bodies and private investors often mistakenly type-cast a whole community on the basis of the chaotic extremes that are most commonly visible in these disadvantaged areas. Behavioural breakdown by a small minority leads to mistaken and ineffectual remedies. For example, demolition can be driven by social rather than physical disorder (SEU, 1998). This is because of the quite disproportionate impact of anti-social behaviour on declining, depopulating neighbourhoods as they become a haven and dumping ground for families no-one wants to live next door to, thereby escalating the problems out of control (Power, 1987). Trouble and disorder become self-magnifying as they become over-concentrated. Their impact becomes more intense as more ordinary people leave. Any recovery in urban conditions is premised on the urgency of overcoming the stigma of its criminal networks and its social disarray. The one feeds the other. These conditions result from very complex interactions which earlier studies have analysed in great detail (Power, 1987; 1999; Power and Tunstall, 1997).

A tough and all-encompassing anti-crime and law-enforcement campaign can shift the direction of a neighbourhood as long as residents will provide evidence and are protected from intimidation. Tackling rogue landlords, drug dealing, unregistered, uninsured cars and car dumping, street prostitution, child abuse, youth gangs, knife carrying and other violent abuse requires detailed local information and co-operation, swift action and strong security. Combating crime requires active policing, a visible street presence, supervision, repair and upgrading activity, all signals that the neighbourhood matters. These measures push back the boundaries of disruptive behaviour and reinstate controls.

Too many of the poorest areas have slid into a vicious circle of social decline where lettings policies have chased behind low demand, allocating homes on a panic basis to people who cannot cope with a tenancy. Far more sophisticated, multi-sided support is needed to help such households and cities like Manchester have long recognised that allowing the numbers of such families to build up in the poorest areas simply makes those areas prey to the grossest of social abuse. The devastating impact of anti-social behaviour on inner city communities has effectively ransacked parts of the neighbourhoods we visited. Bad private landlords and inadequate policing went hand in hand with careless, insensitive allocations. There are lessons to be learnt from the tough stance taken by Manchester on anti-social behaviour. Local housing experts like Steve Mycio, the former Director of Housing, and Tom Manion, Chief Executive of Irwell Valley Housing Association, have long been clear that tenants deserve, *'peaceful enjoyment of their home and neighbourhood'*. They mean it and have shown residents that it is deliverable.

During the Commonwealth Games, *'the usual yobbos were not to be seen'* (Manchester resident, 2002). Was it because so many people, so much activity, such care and supervision by 1,000s of volunteers cramped their style and drove them away? The vacuum was no longer there waiting to be filled maybe. And informal supervision was all around. So, containing trouble is possible if enough people work together to make it happen.

But troubled neighbourhoods are not easy places to manage and not all neighbourhoods can play host to the Commonwealth Games. Protecting and enhancing the essential services and the people who work in them, like schools, health centres, shops and streets, implies a level of supervision and investment such as does not exist in most poor neighbourhoods today. Without such a framework of supervision, it will be difficult to persuade newcomers they can safely invest in homes in the area or stable local families and good staff that they should hang on as things improve.

9. Neighbourhood management

The idea of neighbourhood management, covering fairly small areas of around 5,000 homes, is proving an invaluable tool for recovery (Power and Bergin, 1999). Piecing together all the service elements in a jigsaw of organisational progress, encouraging each element to operate with maximum autonomy but creating an environment of neighbourhood order, inter-organisational co-operation, and forward momentum, requires a strong organisational commitment, significant resources, a dedicated budget and people. Around £250,000 a year in revenue will provide for a local neighbourhood manager, a neighbourhood office, a warden team, a repair fund and a community fund for tackling local eyesores and providing local support.

Street cleaning and street care are critical signs of worth. Without closely supervised, hands-on management, it is hard to see decayed streets reaching the standards necessary for recovery. It requires extraordinary commitment and constant on-the-spot action. It also needs day-by-day problem solving which is the passion of doers, but the dread of bureaucrats. Places need to be cleaner, greener, tidier and fresher than average to overcome the major prejudices of risk-averse investors.

Street conditions will only hold up if crime is held down. So warden schemes – like the blue uniformed biking guardians of better conditions in New East Manchester – provide a people-link that make the streets feel safer. The Home policing initiative in the West End of Newcastle similarly created a sense of security that restabilised a small community. The difference in cost between neighbourhood management and large-scale demolition is startling; in cash the first runs into thousands, while reinstating social and neighbourhood conditions; the other into millions.

Under most scenarios, neighbourhood management pays for itself in reduced vandalism, lower insurance and better repair, increased values, more activity and enhanced attractiveness. It also acts as a conduit for government funding and private sector support. The true costs and benefits of neighbourhood management can only be estimated, but evidence to date, based on seven different models, suggests that it offers the prospect of making difficult areas work at moderate cost, in the way that city centre management has proved vital to the recovery of the downtown areas. It could provide exactly the vehicle that is necessary for the

National Neighbourhood Renewal programme to deliver on its targets. For it is relatively quick, relatively cheap and achievable with a combination of local authority leadership and an arm's length local management structure.

10. Restoring neighbourhood environments

Street conditions give the first signal of neighbourhood recovery. The identical urban landscapes, with the same contours and buildings, can emit totally contrasting messages: welcome, friendliness, care, value, connectedness, supervision, tolerance; or fear, problems, neglect, isolation, worthlessness. Streets provide a vital extension to our home life. They offer the shared spaces where people connect with each other and move into the civic sphere. Streets should be where children can play, adults can sit, and families meet. Too often streets have become the great dividers, deserted as residents withdraw behind front doors, away from unpleasantness.

Street decay is all pervasive in our cities and is strongly linked to vandalism, crime and fear (Home Office, 2000). For this reason the government instituted a cross-cutting review of this issue, arguing that making streets 'liveable' was a first step in restoring a sense of security and belonging to inner neighbourhoods.

Part of the battle is over visible, pro-active street policing. Soaring street crime reflects a serious gap in our method of supervision. The Americans paved the way in culling street crime and violence by adding hugely to the numbers of policemen on foot, on bikes and even on roller-blades, an idea we have now copied in Brighton. But we have a long way to go.

A relatively easy change that makes streets feel as though they belong to the people who live there are the creation of Home Zones. They use the very simple idea, borrowed from the Continent, that people and particularly children should be able to walk safely on streets, cross over, sit down, chat and play without fear of being run over. Home Zone streets allow cars, but only at walking pace, not more than 10 miles an hour. They create wider pavements and people have priority. They use benches, planters and street layout to slow cars and signal resident social life. They give priority to safe biking and walking. All this generates a family atmosphere that makes young couples more likely to invest and stay. It is much harder for crime to go undetected in a Home Zone because so many more people patrol the street. Home Zones are relatively easy, relatively cheap and have shown how easy it is to reinforce rather than sever community links.

The role of street wardens in supporting and supervising, not just Homes Zones, but residential streets and estates more generally is now widely recognised. There are several hundred warden schemes in 2002, compared with just 50 in 1999 when the idea first caught the eye of government (SEU, 1999). Slowly but surely ways of 'managing out decline' are being tried out.

Turning backyards and alleyways behind terraced housing into enclosed private spaces that residents control makes people feel at lot safer, inspires more clean-ups, painting, planting and sharing than any amount of public pleading. It is also possible to create private back gardens using yard and alleyway spaces, negotiating with residents for a redesign of backs into green areas. New East Manchester's ambitious 'alley-gating' programme targeting over 200 small areas is driven by resident demand, and holds out hope for local control and beautification of seriously run-down environments.

There are many ways in which the environment of older, poorer neighbourhoods can become attractive. Doing up the frontages and roofs of houses – 'enveloping' as it was christened in Birmingham – provides a strong visual signal of value and care. It leaves internal problems unresolved, but it transforms the appearance of a street. Sheffield is doing it in Burngreave, on the edge of its city centre and stimulating new demand for older housing on the back of it. Tree planting, tubs, hanging baskets and window boxes along the front of terraced houses that open straight onto the street, help residents lay claim to street spaces that were previously neglected, ugly and menacing. All these approaches work if residents are truly behind them.

11. Jobs and the economy

What about the jobs that are needed to fuel growth and higher demand for housing? Although unemployment is higher than the national average, northern regions are generating new jobs at an impressive rate. But their industrial base, shrivelled as it is, is still shedding workers, or at best regaining them at a much slower rate than the service sector or than outer city jobs more generally (Turok and Edge, 1999). Higher wages and more job opportunities in suburban and semi-rural areas in the north are helping people to move out of the city and buy new homes. Even where people work in the city, they often opt to live outside it. So unless inner city conditions improve remarkably, people given the opportunity will continue to leave. This simply reaffirms the need for greater urban investment (Rogers, 2002).

There are two hopeful signs. Firstly, in spite of deep national cynicism about fast rail links, the West Coast mainline link to Manchester from London will start running up-to-the-minute Pendolino trains in 2002, and by 2003 the track will be sufficiently upgraded to cut at least half an hour off the journey and double the number of inner city trains. Already, for the opening of the Commonwealth Games, the first new Voyager trains were appearing. Ten years hence, journey times may shrink by an hour, but meanwhile Virgin Cross Country and mainline services between northern cities and to the south are set to double their frequency and greatly increase comfort, reliability and speed. This should shift business thinking northwards, currently hampered by congested roads, failing railways and inadequate airport capacity. The fast rail links to Europe currently under construction will then form part of a revitalised international rail network. All over Europe, this development has accelerated the recovery of provincial cities.

A related prospect is that the boom in the congested South East will start to hamper prosperity in that region. It must be encouraged to spread out to the midlands and north. Many communities in the over-built south are fighting against further expansion in housing, traffic or road capacity. Often portrayed as selfish Nimbyism, public protests against over-development are a predictable reaction to living in one of the most congested regions in the world, only an hour to two from depleted regions with spare capacity.

Already according to industry experts, major multinationals are eyeing a range of developments and opportunities: the spaces in East Manchester, the new light rail links now being laid, the future extension northwards from the fast channel tunnel rail link through Kings Cross, the attractions of the Peak District National Park and the Northumbrian coast, a stones-throw from the housing problems of North Manchester and East Newcastle. The sheer challenge of making things work where there's space to expand rather than sitting in inescapable traffic jams in the South East must begin to have some appeal (Serraga, 2000).

Economic development does not stand still. If industry can move away from overcrowded mega cities like Calcutta to the foothills of the Himalayas in search of space, more reliable water and electricity, then it can likewise move from the overcrowded South East of Britain, one of the most densely peopled areas of the world, to the over-sparse but historically pre-eminent cities of the north which offer immeasurable assets in their people and in their urban infrastructures. The Japanese have indeed already chosen to invest in the midlands and the North East because of the readily available workforce, housing and infrastructure. The rash of northern call centres, often unfairly classed as dead-end enterprises, tap the 'people and place' assets of areas that have lost their earlier rationale, on the back of new communication industries. Both Manchester and Liverpool are gaining ground in 21st century media, music, and arts industries.

One really crucial lesson of reviving neighbourhoods is that repopulation generates jobs. Attracting more mixed urban communities with some better off people generates demand for urban services. Running city neighbourhoods and their public spaces properly means multiplying the numbers of front line jobs. The localisation of services, the creation of neighbourhood management, the reinstatement of street policing and neighbourhood warden services, the reinvestment in repair, renovation and conversion of existing buildings, implies many local jobs – about 100 for every neighbourhood of 1,000-1,500 homes (Power, 1991).

Currently too many public resources are tied up in layers of bureaucratic management. Yet evidence from the city of Birmingham suggests that three front line jobs cost around the same as one middle manager (Birmingham, 2002). If 50 per cent of all direct service budgets (police, parks, cleansing, environment, repair) went on direct front line staff and services, we would see around a doubling in the number of neighbourhood jobs, thus killing two birds with one stone, improving neighbourhood conditions and security, simultaneously with creating new forms of work. It is only one strand of economic activity, but it is hugely important (Power and Bergin, 1999; Power and Tunstall, 1997; Power, 1999). Many government pronouncements support this more intensive approach at the lower cost end of the service (SEU, 1999).

Tim Brighouse, the Chief Education Officer for Birmingham, proposes the use of *'paraprofessionals'* in education, health, neighbourhood management and other front line services. This enables residents with little formal education or training to contribute to the services on which they depend. Neighbourhood wardens are one example. These jobs are quick and relatively cheap to create, yet they offer a route to learning and skills, a support for hard pressed services, and a community reinforcement that helps families, schools, other public services and neighbourhood conditions. They involve residents in training alongside work, they pay them and often lead to a career progression from a low skill start to semi-professional status (Mumford and Power, 2002).

In Birmingham, parents in the Small Heath area are involved in reading programmes, education extension work and school home liaison in an attempt to drive up literacy and school performance. This 'Parenting in Partnership' has not only brought some of the more active parents into schools, education and work, it has also led to a whole different focus in city education services, tapping skills that were previously ignored and greatly extending teachers' capacity. The city wants to apply this approach to neighbourhood renewal (Birmingham, 2000). Super-caretaking on estates where on-site staff develop repair, supervision and community liaison skills; warden services where staff act as information conduits and first point helpers for vulnerable residents and a link to the police; youth, after school activities, elderly care all offer this potential for local employment.

As poorer neighbourhoods come to house a larger proportion of people with jobs, so demand for services will grow. Day-to-day 'spin-off' jobs are a very important consequence of more mixed, more generally affluent communities. Mixed areas support multiple small businesses and generate scores of micro enterprises, as Will Hutton persuasively argues in his book, *The World We're In* (Hutton, 2002). Many recovering city neighbourhoods now boast small supermarkets, newsagents, cafes, hairdressers and other 'locals'. We may see more of this regrowth in urban enterprise as cities gradually re-densify.

12. Housing markets and neighbourhood renewal

Housing and job markets tend to work together and both are central to the way neighbourhoods, towns, cities and their surrounding regions work. Both markets are different from most other markets because of the human and social factors that influence them. They are not only driven by money, even though that dominates most decisions. Jobs are a major influence on housing, but housing is our main concern. Other studies cover the vast and critical area of 'work' (Turok and Edge, 1999; DTLR, 1999).

Housing markets are influenced by many factors outside a simple buying and selling process, otherwise we would not be experiencing within a small country, within single cities even, both boom and abandonment. A strong economy and job market pushes up demand for housing, thus fuelling the current galloping boom in the South East. Strongly growing house prices give buyers confidence and increase competition to enter the local housing market. The opposite is the case in declining regions, cities and neighbourhoods where lower, and even falling, prices deter would-be buyers. The offer of new detached four bedroom homes on greenfield land for under £70,000 with no deposit, full mortgage arranged, in the troubled regions of the north suggests a difficult and vulnerable housing market – and not just in the poorest neighbourhoods actually experiencing abandonment (Nevin *et al.*, 2001). Since the pattern of sprawl and building abandonment is far more entrenched, long-running and documented in North America, we must learn from their experience *before* our poorest neighbourhoods reach the level of decay and distress of US city neighbourhoods, with all their concomitant costs (Katz, 2002).

Housing differs from other consumer goods in being vastly more expensive to produce and maintain, longer lasting and physically immobile. As the economy, population, standards and availability of suitable housing change, so demand shifts. But the stock of homes only adapts slowly. Many argue that this problem justifies a much faster rate of demolition than currently happens. However, we argue that demolition is not an easy solution in existing communities – and rarely does abandonment happen across whole areas, unlike in the States. In the US, rather than face the cost of demolition, private landlords have simply abandoned property on a huge scale, leaving semi-abandoned urban neighbourhoods of unparalleled misery (Wilson, 1987; Jargowsky, 1997). Cities work best when neighbourhoods, buildings and communities adapt organically to new conditions (Brandes Gratz, 1990; Jacobs, 1972).

The supply of housing is driven by many non-market factors such as the availability of land and planning consents, the provision and maintenance of wider social and physical infrastructure for settlements, the use of population projections to force local planning authorities to release land, the trade-offs in local authority decisions between developer and community interests (*Observer*, 2002). This combination of influences often results in long-run, large-scale mistakes in the allocation of resources and permissions to build. Evidence from the north, is now overwhelming that the overall supply of homes exceeds potential household growth, thus fuelling abandonment (Bramley, 2002; Nevin, 2001; SEU, 1999; Rogers and Power, 2000; Power and Mumford, 1999; GONW, 2002b). While we can save much of the existing stock, not all of it will survive as cities struggle to rationalise and revitalise these areas.

Because housing is so problematic in built-up, urbanised societies, governments are invariably interventionist. In Britain, not only is around 25 per cent of our stock at least partly funded through government (including brick and mortar subsidy and housing benefit), but large areas of inner cities and some outer areas too, are virtually government owned and controlled. Subsidised council and housing association housing has rules of access, methods of management, standards, costs and charges that generally bear the stamp of public and social provision, dislocating it from the private housing market. Queuing and allocating points are blunt instruments for dealing with people in search of homes.

Even with widespread advertising, social landlords are still obliged to follow public rules of access, using the legal definition of homelessness as a priority access route, rather than as an emergency measure. This helps in ensuring low income people are housed, but it excludes other potential occupiers and it influences job opportunities, employer investment decisions, the availability of shops and other amenities – all the elements that help create and sustain vibrant neighbourhoods within dynamic cities (Rogers, 2002). Even if all the demand problems of social housing disappeared, we would still need to integrate council estates more closely into the wider housing market in order to make them work. This implies breaking them up, diversifying them, mixing their intake, marketing them and integrating them (Gregg, 2002).

How do all these influences on housing markets shape poorer urban neighbourhoods? In the short term – even for a generation – people often resist moving from familiar places. Having your rent paid by government removes any financial incentive, and only the availability of other subsidised and better quality housing may change that. Inertia also applies at the more affluent end of the market. Hence the conclusion of Nevin *et al.* that northern housing markets are segmented and they are unable to pinpoint the connection between more successful suburban growth markets and collapsing inner city markets (Nevin *et al.*, 2002, Chs. 5 and 6). However, the overall supply of homes, fuels a very long and slow moving chain of multiple choices of invisible complexity, linking outer building and inner decline, boom and abandonment (Bramley and Pawson, 2002). Twelve thousand new homes a year in the North West has a big, if indirect impact on demand in North Manchester (ODPM, 2002a).

If the resources that currently support sprawling housing developments at low density are diverted to the urban renaissance agenda, as the government is now proposing, will this be enough to entice people into cities in sufficient numbers to fuel a rebirth of the poorest neighbourhoods? Many measures are in train (NRU, 2000) and there is broad consensus that conditions can and must improve. Building on the back of improved neighbourhood infrastructure and more equal incentives for investors to operate in existing urban areas, there is no reason why the shift should not be rapid and visible. In the three years since *The Slow Death of Great Cities*, we observed major transformations underway in both Newcastle and Manchester.

The two cities are vigorously pursuing policies of regrowth. To succeed this will require several elements:

- continued household growth and new demand for more compact, more urban lifestyles;
- major improvements in security and crime prevention, premised on different kinds and levels of visible policing and supervision;
- environmental investment that enhances, reuses and embellishes the ex-industrial urban and waterside landscapes that are the unique hallmarks of these impressive cities;
- a stop to the subsidised over-supply of outer homes and a charge on new development that matches the real cost of new infrastructure and environmental impact;
- fast, reliable trains and other transport links, making Scotland, the north and midlands easily accessible to Europe as well as London and the south, encouraging inward investment;
- new forms of community governance and management that capture the commitment and energy, not just of existing residents but of all investors in inner neighbourhoods;
- holding strategies that keep inner areas going while their problems are tackled in manageable chunks.

Neighbourhood renewal depends on a local project organisation within each neighbourhood that can tackle collective and communal concerns. In Spain, by law, such organisations exist and take responsibility in every small neighbourhood (City of Barcelona, 1999). In Brazil, the cities of Curitiba and Porto Alegre have successfully combated appalling urban problems through neighbourhood and community structures. It requires strategic visionaries at the centre to go out and tap local social networks, heed community priorities, and establish community level programmes. This will then allow *'a thousand flowers to bloom'*.

In the past we have relied heavily on state intervention to manage our urban crises (Power, 1987). In the future, local authorities will be working for, and will often have to create, other, more imaginative tools for delivering the multiple changes that will make urban communities work successfully. 'Big Bang' plans will have to be carefully negotiated into neighbourhood regeneration projects.

There is no reason why we should endorse abandonment as 'the housing market at work' or fund sprawl as 'people's choice', if the community as a whole pays too high a price for these choices. For much of the boom and abandonment is fuelled by policies and practices, now obsolete, but still driving a pattern of development that makes little environmental, social or economic sense. The following Figures 7.1 and 7.2 show the process of decline and reversal.

Figure 7.1: Neighbourhood and housing decline

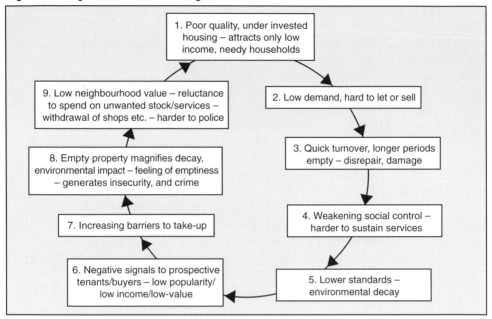

Figure 7.2: Neighbourhood and housing recovery

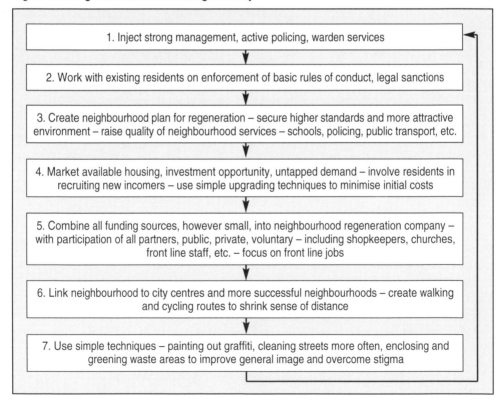

13. Government planning

So what should the government do? It has passed new planning guidance for housing, laying down a sequential test for new house building similar to the sequential test for out-of-town shopping centres that stopped developers in their tracks (DETR, 2000). If there is empty property or space in an already built-up area, then out-of-town greenfield building should not go ahead. On this basis, both Manchester and Newcastle would soon see signs of recovery. Yet as both cities assert, they have no power to stop surrounding authorities from building (Urban Sounding Board, 2002).

There are two barriers to sequential testing for housing achieving the impact that it had on shopping. The first is the determination of authorities surrounding cities – ten in Greater Manchester, five in Tyneside – to operate in their own interest and against the common interest of the city region. Increasing their often weak population base, improving their local tax base and enhancing their status through growth are strong motivators. Government is struggling to come up with powerful enough tools to combat this damaging and in the end, self-defeating game of numbers on the basis of sub-regional plans (DTLR, 2002).

The second barrier is the large supply of land with planning permission already in the pipeline. However, developers respond eagerly to incentives. An environmental levy, or simply VAT, on all greenfield homes which currently are zero-rated, and tax incentives for higher moderate density, better designed brownfield homes to help fund the longer-term supervision costs, could shift the balance. There should be an equalisation of VAT on conversions and renewal with new build. The proposed reforms of the planning system do not go nearly far enough in controlling unnecessary development or helping cities to prevent damaging sprawl; clearly a lot more work is needed. But the proposed stronger controls, if enforced, should ripple quickly through the housing market. The new Housing Market Renewal pathfinder areas will only work this way.

Both Manchester and Newcastle are stuck in the heart of regions, *'determined to build each other out of business'* (Northern Chief Executive, 2002). It needs more people looking for homes than actually exist if poorer, more run-down, older areas are to acquire new value. This is now happening in South Manchester but not yet in the northern areas of the city. It is happening on the Quayside of Newcastle but not in the inner neighbourhoods of the East and West Ends.

At the same time, the government's proposals for neighbourhood planning within the more flexible local planning framework offer the chance for neighbourhood managers to work out how to tackle as a whole the under-utilised neighbourhood environments, design Home Zones, create cycle and bus links, develop new uses for empty spaces and buildings, prioritise green pocket parks, supervise children's play areas, restore shopping streets and so on (DETR, 2000a; DETR, 2000b; ODPM, 2000c).

There is scope within the fast changing planning system to make better use of scarce urban land – but only if we greatly increase the value of greenland as protected countryside, rather than as building potential, thereby greatly pushing up the value of abandoned, currently almost valueless, brownland and empty homes. The failure to charge owners council tax for holding urban land and buildings empty, while charging active citizens full council tax for using urban spaces constructively is very costly to urban communities.

Working against the recovery of northern cities is the government's fear that Britain's investors will move abroad if they can't develop where and how they want in Britain. This fear works in favour of already strong cities and regions. Eventually it will become self-defeating as over-development undermines the very assets investors seek to protect. Figure 7.3 shows how we can regrow cities more sustainably.

Conclusion – urban renaissance

All over the world, cities are booming. In Britain, many are lapsing far behind. We need to get to the bottom of the problem. The government's Neighbourhood Renewal Agenda could help if taken and implemented seriously. It advocates neighbourhood management, local wardens, community investment and development, inter-racial contact and cohesion, better schools, more visible policing, more direct public health jobs and skills development. Sure Start, the government's support strategy for young mothers and children at risk, is cropping up in most deprived neighbourhoods affected by low demand and abandonment. It offers strong support at the point when families most need it – the beginning of a child's life. It could help prevent the drastic behaviour problems that make classrooms in inner cities such a challenge. But solving neighbourhood social problems is only half of the agenda.

Redesigning inner neighbourhoods, so they are modern yet rooted in their history, green yet dense enough to feel safe and mixed enough to support good shops and schools, linked by transport routes to the centre yet traffic-tamed in their local streets, requires technical as well as organisational skill. Urban design is in short supply. People like Richard Rogers have shown how better design of the public realm changes the value and atmosphere of cities – streets, pavements, squares, gardens, play areas, cycle tracks, parking and speed controls, fast buses and trams, are vital to liveable neighbourhoods.

The Urban Regeneration Companies, like New East Manchester, draw together many strands of urban renaissance activity under a unifying umbrella. Funding is beginning to flow and they may lever forward the type of renewal we propose, as long as they are not defeated by sprawl. Similarly the ambitious Newcastle-Gateshead Partnership forged across the Tyne may create a new centre of gravity for the North East. The government may help cities to advance sustainable

Figure 7.3: Potential for city regrowth and sustainability

Regional loss of jobs – hits cities hardest

Population decline – hits cities hardest

Chronic urban decline/slow regional decline – hits poorest neighbourhoods first

Job regrowth
• new economy
• develops in outer and non-urban areas

Housing demand and building – in outer, more attractive areas

Exodus of younger, economically active households
• sustains demand for new build
• leaves emptying inner areas

Role of cities as nerve centres of new economy
• recovery of city centres
• new attraction of city centre living
• high prices for centre city apartments
• growth in service jobs
• faster more reliable transport connections

Inner neighbourhoods caught in downward spiral
• new city workers commute in
• demand grows in recovering neighbourhoods – 'urban pioneers'
• abandonment extends its reach in poorest areas
• demolition blight fuels further exodus

Potential for regional regrowth
• congestion in South East
• new transport investment
• stronger Core Cities focus

Neighbourhood reinvestment becomes urgent
• neighbourhood renewal gains priority
• new neighbourhood management vehicles
• change in government and developer emphasis
• household patterns change
• smaller households, less children, wanting proximity
• higher density building generates mixed uses
• partnership investment becomes more familiar
• new style design and supervision generate demand

↓

Environmental pressures change urban agenda
• traffic and commuting
• land shortages/flooding
• compounding impacts of development
• resident objections in outer areas to more building
• brownfield priority and availability
• historic buildings and street patterns sought after
• poorer neighbourhoods offer under-valued assets
• recycling becomes central
• new approaches to urban living
• proximity, compact neighbourhoods gain popularity

development in a closely linked and urgent new emphasis on urban regrowth. For in a land-short, land-hungry country where we are reaching the limits of environmental tolerance, we have no choice but to reuse and recycle what we so badly damaged in the last 200 years.

The inner city streets of Manchester and Salford enter most living rooms every day as Coronation Street. The alleys, yards, terraces and allotments bordering the Tyne are captured by the most prolific and popular novelist of the north, in a hundred best-selling books by Catherine Cookson. When developers conducted a Mori survey in summer 2001 for the *Sunday Times* of housing preferences among young potential buyers, their top choice was terraced housing, followed closely by apartments, at high density in urban areas. If the government enforces the priorities it has set out for urban land use, then North and East Manchester, and the West and East Ends of Newcastle will acquire new value. Their beleaguered communities may survive, revive and offer some of the space that we need for our urban future. They reflect a much wider problem and often much greater potential than we have yet recognised.

References

Bankside and City Council Going for Growth Partnership (2001) Press Release, 07/03/01.

Bankside Neighbourhood Profile (2000) Compiled by community housing manager, 15/08/00.

Bankside resident (2001) Personal communication with the author, 12/09/01.

Barcelona, City of (1999) *Delinquency in Barcelona City*. Barcelona: PSC-Secretaria.

Bate, R, Best, R and Holmans, A (eds.) (2000) *On the move: The housing consequences of migration*. York: Joseph Rowntree Foundation.

Beacons (2001) *Beacons for a Brighter Future – Annual Report 1999-2001*. Manchester: New Deal for East Manchester.

Benjamin, A (2002) 'Storm warning' in *The Guardian*, 07/08/02.

Best, R (2002) Evidence from visit to Liverpool – personal communication with author.

Birmingham City Council (2001) *Housing Strategy 2001*. Birmingham: Birmingham City Council.

Birmingham City Council (2002) *Housing Strategy 2002*. Birmingham: Birmingham City Council.

Birmingham (2002) *Flourishing Neighbourhoods: report of Highbury 3*. Birmingham: Birmingham City Council.

Blackman, D (2002) 'Insurance plan could combat market collapse' in *Inside Housing*, 08/03/02.

Boylan, E (2002) Response to 'Boom and Abandonment'.

Bradford (2000) *City Vision 2000*. Bradford: Bradford City Council.

Bramley, G, Pawson, H and Third, H with Parker, J, Hague, C and McIntosh, S (2000) *Low demand housing and unpopular neighbourhoods*. DETR: London.

Bramley, G and Pawson, H (2002) 'Low Demand for Housing: incidence, causes and UK national policy implication' in *Urban Studies*, Vol. 39, No 3 393-422.

Brandes Gratz, R (1990) *The Living City*. New York: Touchstone Books.

Brauner, S (2001) 'No going back to slum clearance' in *Regeneration and Renewal*, 16/11/01.

Briggs, A (1983) *A social history of England*. Harmondsworth: Penguin.

Bright, J (2001) ''Trapped' minorities stay Midlands' decay' in *Housing Today*, 10/05/01.

Brown, A (2001) 'Who wins when stadiums come to town?' in *Regeneration and Renewal*, 23/11/01.

Burnett, J (1991) *A social history of housing 1815-1985*. London: Routledge.

Buzzin Supplement (2001) Special supplement produced in conjunction with the *Evening Chronicle*, Newcastle and Gateshead.

Byker Asylum Seekers Support Group (2001) Minutes of a meeting, 05/04/01.

Byker residents (2001) in *The Byker Way Forward – Report of the Working Party in conjunction with the Byker Listing Residents Working Group*, January 2001.

Cabinet Office (1999) *Sharing the Nation's Prosperity: Variation in economic and social conditions across the UK: A report to the Prime Minister*. London: Cabinet Office

Champion, T (2000) 'Flight from the cities?' in Bate *et al.* (eds.) *op cit.*

Chief Executive (2001) Meeting with the authors, Manchester, 23/10/01.

CIH (2000) *Sustaining Success: Registered Social Landlords, Financial Risk and Low Demand*. Coventry: CIH.

Citylife (2001) 'City centre's throbbing heart' in *Citylife* October 2001. Newcastle: Newcastle City Council.

Clapham, D and Kintrea, K (1999) *Evaluation of Glasgow's Housing Co-operatives*. Edinburgh: Scottish Homes.

Cole, I, Iqbal, B, Slocombe, L and Trott, T (2001) *Social Engineering or Consumer Choice: Rethinking Housing Allocations*. Coventry and York: CIH/JRF.

Community and Housing Director (2001) Interview with the authors, Newcastle, 03/10/01.

Conway, E and Green, J (1996) *The Story of the Bankside Area Strategy*. Newcastle: Social Welfare Research Unit, University of Northumbria.

Cooke, M (2002) 'Londoners on their way up' in *Inside Housing*, 17/05/02.

Core Cities Group (2002) *Core Cities Conference Proceedings*, Manchester City Council, April 2002.

Council officer (2001) Meeting with the author, Manchester, 22/10/01.

Council officer (2002) Personal communication with the researchers, 14/03/02.

Council manager (2002) Statistics supplied to the authors, July 2002.

Countryside Agency (2002) *Submission to DTLR on demand for affordable housing in the countryside*. London: Countryside Agency.

Cox, P (2000) 'Trends in household formation and migration: the policy dimension' in Bate *et al.* (eds.) *op cit.*

Creasey, S (2002) 'Retail rebirth' in *Property Week*, 24/05/02.

Cullingworth, JB (1979) *Essays on housing policy: the British scene*. London: Allen and Unwin.

Davey Smith, G *et al.* (2000) 'Inequalities in health continue to grow despite government's pledges' in *British Medical Journal*, 320, 582.

DETR (1999a) *Unpopular Housing: Report of Policy Action Team 7*. London: DETR.

DETR (2000a) *Planning Policy Guidance Note No.3: Housing*. London: DETR.

DETR (2000b) Urban White Paper, *Our Town and Cities: The Future – Delivering an Urban Rennaisance*. London: DETR.

DfEE (2000) *Jobs for All, Report of Policy Action Team 1*. London: Home Office.

DoE (1974) 'Difficult to Let'; unpublished report of postal survey.

DoE (1977) *Inner area studies: Liverpool, Birmingham and Lambeth: summaries of consultants' final reports.* London: DoE.

DoE (1981) *Difficult to Let Investigation.* London: DoE.

DoE (1994) *Assessing the Impact of Urban Policy.* London: DoE.

DTLR (2001a) *Housing in England 99/00: A report of the 1999/2000 Survey of English Housing.* London: DTLR.

DTLR (2001b) *Planning: Delivering a Fundamental Change.* London: DTLR.

DTLR (2002a) *Revised household projections for London and the South East. Spring 2002.* London: DTLR.

DTLR (2002b) *Government welcomes select committee report on empty homes.* Press release May 8. London: DTLR.

DTLR (2002c) *Dealing with dereliction – £25 million boost for pathfinder projects.* Press release May 16. London: DTLR.

DTLR (2002d) *Action to tackle housing abandonment.* Press release April 10. London: DTLR.

DTLR Committee (2002) *Sixth Report: Empty Homes.* London: HMSO.

DTZ Pieda Consulting (2000) *Demolition and New Building on Local Authority Estates.* London: DETR.

East Manchester News (2001) 'We're beating the crooks' in *East Manchester News*, Issue 3, September 2001.

Economic Research Services Limited (2001) *Final Evaluation of Reviving the Heart of the West End.* March 2001. Newcastle: Reviving the Heart of the West End.

Economist, The (2001) 'Down-wind and out' in *The Economist*, 11/01/01.

Economist, The (2002a) 'Economist Britain Section' in *The Economist*, 31/05/02.

Economist, The (2002b) 'Ready and Steady' in *The Economist*, 18/07/02.

Economist, The (2002c) 'Recession in Scotland?' in *The Economist*, 22/08/02.

Estate agent website (2002) East Manchester estate agent's website, 25/02/02.

Evans, R (2001a) 'Players divided over low demand plans' in *Inside Housing*, 14/12/01.

Evans, R (2001b) 'Biggest homes swap could blaze a trail' in *Inside Housing*, 16/11/01.

Ford, T and Pawson, H (2001) *Sector Study 7: Low demand for housing association housing. Measuring low demand: the national picture.* London: The Housing Corporation.

Ford, T and Pawson, H (2002) *Sector Study 13: Characteristics of low demand housing association housing.* London: The Housing Corporation

Glasgow City Council (2002) Transfer Proposals. Glasgow City Council

Glennerster *et al.* (1999) *Poverty, Social Exclusion and Neighbourhood: Studying the area bases of social exclusion*, CASE 22. London: CASE.

Government Office for the North East (2001) Interview concerning housing demand. Newcastle: GONE.

Government Office for the North West (2002a) *Draft Regional Planning Guidance for the North West* (RPG 13). Manchester: GONW.

Government Office for the North West (2002b) Response to 'Boom and Abandonment'. Manchester: GONW.

Government Office for the North West (1999) Evidence of over supply of homes submitted to the Social Exclusion Unit Policy Action Team 7 on Unpopular Housing. Manchester: GONW.

Grainger Townlife (2001) 'The story so far' in *Grainger Townlife*, Issue 13, Summer 2001.

Greater Manchester Police (2000) Interview with author.

Gregg, P (2002) *Neighbourhood Effects, Causes and Policy Responses*. Bristol: University of Bristol.

Guardian, The (2000) 'Street Drama' by Hilary Wainwright, 13/09/00.

Guardian, The (2002) Manchester July Sports Section.

Halifax (2002) Halifax Building Society statistics on mortgage to income ratios, 1984-2002.

Hamilton, R (1978) *Street by Street*. London: Shelter.

Harvey-Jones, J (1994) *Making it Happen: reflections on leadership*. London: Collins

Hebden, P (2001) 'Younger generation see their future away from social sector' in *Inside Housing*, 28/11/01.

Hetherington, P (2001) 'Dirty old towns' in *The Guardian*, 12/03/01.

Hills, J (2002) Personal communication with the authors, 26/03/02.

Holmans, A and Simpson, M (1999) *Low Demand – separating fact from fiction*. Coventry: Chartered Institute of Housing.

Home Office (1999) *Neighbourhood Wardens: Report of Policy Action Team 6*. London: Home Office.

Home Office (1999b) *British Crime Survey 1999*. London: Home Office.

Home Office (2000) *British Crime Survey 2000*. London: Home Office.

Hooper, A, Dunmore, K and Hughes, M (1998) *Home Alone, volume 1*. National House-Building Council.

Housing (2001) 'Barcelona upon Tyne? The Grainger Town regeneration project in the centre of Newcastle aims to turn the city into a European regional capital' by David Gilliver, May 2001.

Housing Corporation (2002) Personal communication with the authors, 08/07/02.

Housing Director (2001) Meeting with the authors, Manchester, 23/10/01.

Housing Manager (2001) Interview with the author, Newcastle, 03/10/01.

Housing Team Leader (2001) Interview with researcher, Manchester, 10/09/01.

Housing Today (2000) 'Rogers turns back on Going for Growth' by Paul Hebden, in *Housing Today*, 07/12/00.

Hunt Thompson Associates (2001) *Project Profiles of Tower Blocks* (unpublished).

Hutton, W (2002) *The World We're In*. London: Little Brown.

Inside Housing (1997) News article in *Inside Housing*, 25/07/97.

Inside Housing (2000) 'Newcastle demolition plan faces West End showdown' by Janis Bright in *Inside Housing*, 25/08/00.

Inside Housing (2001a) 'Cities should be targeted to combat low demand' in *Inside Housing*, 16/11/01.

Inside Housing (2001b) 'Demolition plans face opposition' in *Inside Housing*, 02/11/01.

Inside Housing (2001c) 'Demolition backing puts Newcastle renewal on track' by Paul Humphries in *Inside Housing*, 13/04/01.

Inside Housing (2002a) Leader comment in *Inside Housing*, 15/02/02.

Inside Housing (2002b) 'Deal aims to change high-rise preconceptions' in *Inside Housing*, 01/02/02.

Inside Housing (2002c) 'Rooker launches relocation scheme' in *Inside Housing*, 02/08/02.

Islington (2001) Report on rehousing from the Marquess Estate, Islington Borough Council.

Jacobs, J (1972) *The death and life of great American cities.* Harmondsworth: Penguin.

Jargowsky, P A (1997) *Poverty and Place: Ghettos, Barrios and the American City.* New York: Russell Sage Foundation.

JRF (1998) Evidence to the Urban Task Force on the CASPAR project (City Apartments for Single People at Affordable Rents).

Katz, B (2002) 'Smart growth: the future of the American metropolis'. London: LSE CASEpaper – forthcoming.

Konttinen, S (1983) *Byker.* London: Jonathan Cape.

Lee P, Leather P, Murie A, Phillimore J, Goodson L (2002) *Yorkshire and Humberside: changing housing markets and urban regeneration.* Birmingham: Centre for Urban and Regional Studies, University of Birmingham in conjunction with the Housing Corporation, National Housing Federation and Yorkshire and Humberside Housing Forum.

Lipman, C (2002) 'Boulevard of broken dreams' in *New Start*, 15/02/02.

Locally-based researcher (2001) Interview with the author, 02/10/01.

London Dockland Development Corporation (1981) Housing and Employment Reports. London: DTLR.

Lowe, S, Spencer, S and Keenan, P (eds.) (1998) *Housing Abandonment in Britain: studies in the causes and effects of low demand housing.* York: Centre for Housing Policy, University of York.

LSE Cities Programme (2002) Barking Case Study presentation. 25/07/02.

Lupton, R (2000) *Descriptive profile of Shipview (Newcastle).* London: CASE.

Lupton, R (2001a) Internal fieldwork report, 09/11/01.

Lupton, R (2001b) *Places Apart: the initial report of CASE's areas study* CASEReport 14. London: CASE.

Lupton, R and Power, A (2002) 'Social exclusion and neighbourhoods' in Hills, J, Legrand, J and Piachaud, D (eds.) *Understanding Social Exclusion.* Oxford: Oxford University Press.

Lupton, R *et al.* (2002) *A Rock and a Hard Place: Drug markets in deprived areas.* Home Office Research Study 240. London: The Home Office.

Lupton, R (forthcoming) *Poverty Street.*

Maclennan, D (1997) *Britain's Cities: a more positive future.* Lunar Society Lecture, November 1997.

Maclennan, D (2002) Personal communication with author.

Manchester City Council (1994) *[Estate] Baseline Study, 1994.* Manchester: Manchester City Council.

Manchester (1999) *Manchester's Corporate Housing Strategy 1998 – 2001: Update 99.* Manchester: Manchester City Council.

Manchester (2000a) *Manchester's Corporate Housing Strategy, 2000.* Manchester: Manchester City Council.

Manchester (2000b) Housing report, March 2000, based on information available for three developments in the regeneration area. Manchester: Manchester City Council.

Manchester (2001a) *Economic Development Statement*, Manchester City Council website last updated 18/04/01.

Manchester (2001b) *'All change at Piccadilly' – Manchester Update*, Manchester City Council online archive.

Manchester (2001c) *'Lofts on the up and up' – Manchester Update*, Manchester City Council online archive.

Manchester (2001d) *Manchester's Corporate Housing Strategy, 2001.* Manchester: Manchester City Council.

Manchester bid (2001) *Bid for Choice Based Lettings Pilot Scheme*, 11/01/01. Manchester: Manchester City Council.

Manchester Housing (1999) Information supplied to the authors by Manchester housing department.

Manchester Housing (2001) *Housing Strategy – Review 2001/2002; Private Sector Housing (North).*

Manchester Housing (2002) Information supplied to the authors, July 2002.

Manchester Housing Demand Team (2001a) *Manchester Housing Stock – Overview of Demand Update.*

Manchester Housing Demand Team (2001b) Statistics supplied to the authors, November 2001.

Manchester Housing Demand Team (2002) Statistics supplied to the authors, July 2002.

Manchester and Newcastle City Councils (2001) Interviews with council officers, October 2001.

Manchester Planning Studies (2001) Population figures supplied to the authors by the Planning Studies Department, 2001.

Mapstone, A (2001) 'Don't pull the plug' in *Axis*, August-September 2001.

Martin, D (2001) 'New funding rules to favour north' in *Inside Housing*, 23/11/01.

Martin, D (2002) 'Northern Toll' in *Inside Housing*, 01/02/02.

Mumford, K and Lupton, R (1999) *Low demand for housing and area abandonment: compounding effects of areas on life chances*. Paper presented to ENHR-MRI Conference, August 1999.

Mumford, K and Power, A (forthcoming) *East Enders: Family and community in East London*.

Neighbourhood Manager (2001) Interview with researcher, 23/08/01.

Neighbourhood Renewal Unit (2000) *Action Plan for Neighbourhood Renewal*. London: DTLR.

Nevin, B (2001) *Securing housing market renewal: A submission to the comprehensive spending review* produced for the National Housing Federation in collaboration with the Key Cities Housing Group and the Northern Housing Forums. Birmingham: University of Birmingham, November 2001.

Nevin, B, Lee, P, Goodson, L, Murie, A and Phillimore, J (2001) *Changing housing markets and urban regeneration in the M62 corridor*. Birmingham: Centre for Urban and Regional Studies, the University of Birmingham.

Newcastle City Council (1999) Internal memorandum, Community and Housing Directorate.

Newcastle City Council (2000a) *Going for Growth: a green paper...a citywide vision for Newcastle 2020*, January 2000.

Newcastle City Council (2000b) *News Release: East End and West End options pave way for radical change*, 06/06/00.

Newcastle City Council (2000c) *Draft masterplans for the East End and West End of Newcastle,* Newcastle City Council in collaboration with Richard Rogers Partnership and Andrew Wright Associates with DTZ Pieda Consulting.

Newcastle City Council (2000d) *Bankside Area Neighbourhood Profile*, website, prepared September 2000.

Newcastle City Council (2001a) *Delivering an Urban Renaissance for Newcastle: executive summary*. Newcastle: City Council.

Newcastle City Council (2001b) *Delivering an Urban Renaissance for Newcastle: Regeneration Plan East End*. Newcastle: City Council.

Newcastle City Council (2001c) *Delivering an Urban Renaissance for Newcastle: Regeneration Plan West End*. Newcastle: City Council.

Newcastle City Council (2001d) *Byker Conservation Plan Day*, 07/07/01. Newcastle: Capital Investment Section, Newcastle City Council.

Newcastle City Council (2001e) *Byker Strategy – the Way Forward*. February 2001, Newcastle internal report.

Newcastle City Council (2001f) *Byker Ward Profile: Social perspective*, 10/09/01, Newcastle internal report.

Newcastle City Council (2001g) *Byker: Report for the Outer East Area Committee*, 28/06/01, Newcastle internal report.

Newcastle City Council (2001h) 'Regional planning guidance: response to proposed changes', Cabinet report, 18/07/01.

Newcastle City Council (2002) Personal communication with the authors, July 2002.

Newcastle Education and Libraries Directorate (2001) *Newcastle School Organisation Plan*. Newcastle: Education and Libraries Directorate.

Newcastle Gateshead Initiative (2001) *Newcastle Gateshead Buzzin supplement*, produced in conjunction with the *Evening Chronicle*, 2001.

Newcastle Housing (1998) Figures on residential demolitions supplied to the authors, 1998.

New Deal (1999) *New Deal for Communities Delivery Plan*, September 1999, Manchester: New Deal for East Manchester.

New East Manchester (2000) *Prospectus Manchester*. Manchester City Council.

New East Manchester (2001a) *Development of local area strategies*, report to Board Meeting, 18/07/01.

New East Manchester (2001b) Interview with senior manager, 23/10/01.

New East Manchester (2001c) *East Manchester Regeneration Framework Consultation Review – March 2001*. Manchester: New East Manchester.

New East Manchester (2001d) *New East Manchester A New Town in the City; Regeneration Framework*, March 2001.

New Start (2001a) 'On your marks' in *New Start*, 10/08/01.

New Start (2001b) 'End in sight for daylight robbery' in *New Start*, 22/06/01.

Nexus (2001) Information from website, supplied by Newcastle City Council, 19/10/01.

North Manchester News (2000) The newsletter of North Manchester Regeneration, Autumn 2000.

North Manchester News (2001) The newsletter of North Manchester Regeneration, Spring 2001.

North Manchester Regeneration (2001) Information pack, updated 27/02/01.

ODPM (2002a) Housing Construction Statistics.

ODPM (2002b) *Prescott outlines £1.5 million vision for communities*, Press release 18 July 2002.

ODPM (2002c) Planning Green Paper, *Planning: Delivering a Fundamental Change*. London: Office of the Deputy Prime Minister.

Office of Public Services Reform (2002) *Monitoring Satisfaction: Trends from 1998 – 2002*. People's Panel Final Wave. London: Cabinet Office.

Ouseburn Partnership (2000,2001) Various information supplied to the author by the Partnership.

Oxley, D (1997) Letter in *Inside Housing*, 01/08/97.

Power, A (1970) 'Black and Blue' in *New Society*, 03/09/70.

Power, A (1974) *David and Goliath*. London: Shelter.

Power, A (1987). *Property Before People: The management of twentieth-century council housing*. London: Allen and Unwin.

Power, A (1991) *Housing Management: A guide to quality and creativity*. London: Longman.

Power, A (1993) *Hovels to High Rise: State housing in Europe since 1850*. London: Routledge.

Power, A (1999) *Estates on the Edge*. London: Macmillan Press.

Power, A (2000) 'From unlettable homes to urban sprawl' in Bate *et al.* (eds.) *op cit.*

Power, A and Bergin, E (1999) *Neighbourhood management.* London: LSE CASEpaper 31.

Power, A and Mumford, K (1999) *The Slow Death of Great Cities? Urban abandonment or urban renaissance.* York: Joseph Rowntree Foundation.

Power, A and Tunstall, R (1995) *Swimming against the tide.* York: Joseph Rowntree Foundation.

Prescott, J (2002) Prescott outlines £1.5 billion vision for communities, 18/07/02. London: ODPM.

Prescott-Clarke, P, Clemens, S and Park, A for the DoE (1994) *Roots into Local Authority Housing: A Study of Local Authority Waiting Lists and New Tenancies.* London: HMSO.

Project North East (2001) *Bolam Coyne – A feasibility study (draft report),* August 2001.

Ratcliffe, P with Harrison, M, Hogg, R, Line, B, Phillips, D, Tomlins, R, Power, A (2001) *Breaking Down the Barriers: Improving Asian Access to Social Rented Housing.* Coventry: Chartered Institute of Housing,

Regeneration and Renewal (2002) 'Salford and Newcastle: Two alternatives to dereliction' in *Regeneration and Renewal,* 01/03/02.

Regeneration manager (2001a) Interview with Reviving the Heart of the West End manager, 23/08/01.

Regeneration manager (2001b) Meeting with Manchester regeneration manager, 23/10/01.

Reid, Margaret (2000) *Living in [two neighbourhoods in East Manchester]: A survey examining neighbour nuisance and racial harassment.* Manchester: Centre for Applied Social Research, University of Manchester.

Research visit (2001) Fieldwork visit to Manchester, October 2001.

Reviving the Heart of the West End (2000) *Annual Report 1999/2000.* Newcastle: Reviving the Heart of the West End.

Riba (2002) Jonathon Dimbleby talking on sustainable development at the annual public lecture.

Richard Rogers Partnership *Strategic Masterplanning Framework for East Manchester* – proposal submitted to English Partnerships. London: Richard Rogers Partnership.

Richardson, L and Mumford, K (2002) 'Community, Neighbourhood, and Social Infrastructure' in Hills, J, Le Grand, J and Piachaud, D (eds.) *Understanding Social Exclusion.* Oxford: Oxford University Press.

RICS (2002) Conference on Sustainable Regeneration, London, May 2002.

Rogers, R and Power, A (2000) *Cities for a Small Country.* London: Faber and Faber.

Rogers, R (2002) 'Urban Renaissance' speech to *Observer* conference on regeneration, June 2002.

Sandercock, L (1998) *Towards Cosmopolis.* London: Wiley.

Schoon, N (2001) 'Non-decent proposal' in *Inside Housing,* 23/11/01.

Select Committee on Transport, Local Government and the Regions (2002) *Sixth Report – Empty Homes.* London: HMSO.

Senior housing officer (2001) Personal communication with the author, 08/10/01.

Senior LA strategy officer (2001) Interview with researcher, 10/09/01.

Serraga, P (2000) Personal evidence on inward investment.

Shelter (1974) *A Better Place*. London: Shelter.

Social Exclusion Unit (1998) *Bringing Britain Together: A National Strategy for Neighbourhood Renewal*. London: The Stationery Office.

Social Exclusion Unit (2000) *Neighbourhood Management*. Report of Policy Action Team 4. London: SEU.

Social Exclusion Unit (2001) *A New Commitment to Neighbourhood Renewal: National Strategy Action Plan*. London: Cabinet Office.

Stevenson, B (1999) Personal communication with author.

Summer Ben Gen (2001) 'CityWest – Things are Building Up' and 'Reviving the Heart's Training Strategy', summer edition 2001, Reviving the Heart of the West End.

Sunday Times (2001) Special Property Supplement in the *Sunday Times*, August 2001.

Thomson, F M L (1990) *The Cambridge social history of Britain 1750-1950*. Cambridge: Cambridge University Press.

Times, The (2002) 'Property bubble set to burst as race for houses drives up prices' in *The Times*, 22/05/02.

Travis, A (2001) 'Largest fall in crime for 20 years' in *The Guardian*, 26/10/01.

Tunstall, R (2000) *Participation: the example of tenant management organisations*. PhD thesis London University.

Turok, I and Edge, N (1999) *The Jobs Gap in Britain's Cities – Employment Loss and Labour Market Consequences*. Bristol: Policy Press.

Tyneside Police Authority (2002) Interview with authors.

UNCHS (1996) *An Urbanising World: Global Report on Human Settlements*. Oxford: Oxford University Press for UNCHS.

UNCHS (2001) *Cities in a Globalising World: Global Report on Human Settlements*. London: Earthscan Publications.

Urban Sounding Board (2002) Report on low demand urban recovery (unpublished).

Urban Task Force (1999) *Towards an urban renaissance: final report of the Urban Task Force*. London: The Stationery Office.

Urban Task Force (2002) Delivering the urban renaissance. Observer conference on regeneration, June 2002.

Young, M and Wilmott, P (1957) *Family and Kinship in East London*. London: Routledge and Kegan Paul.

Wilcox, S (2001) *Housing Finance Review 2000/2001*. Coventry and London: CIH and CML.

Wilson, W J (1987) *The truly disadvantaged: the inner city, the underclass, and public policy*. Chicago: University of Chicago Press.

Wilson, A *et al.* (2002) *Heroin and Crack Cocaine Markets in Deprived Areas: Seven local case studies*, CASEreport 19. London: CA.

Photo gallery

Bankside, Newcastle

Pleasant views from the Bankside terraces, awaiting clearance.

A brightly coloured mural in Bankside. This main road will be cleared.

The decision to demolish the housing along this main road came as a shock to Bankside's community, as most homes are occupied.

Demolition starts.

Council housing: one of the few Bankside streets to be staying.

Newcastle city centre

Revitalised buildings in Grainger Town, now Yates wine bar.

The Gateshead Millennium Bridge.

Grainger Town shops: 'The Bond Street of the North'.

City-Edge, East Manchester

City-Edge sits within the shadow of the Commonwealth Games Stadium.

The Commonwealth Games Stadium.

Ungated alleyway: insecure, with dumped rubbish.

Gated alleyway: clean, secure and well looked after.

Demolition in Lower City-Edge.

Housing association sheltered housing scheme in Lower City-Edge built circa 1990, awaiting demolition.

Council homes in City-Edge due to be cleared.

Semi-detached council houses in City-Edge, less than 15 years old.

Community garden in City-Edge, created from derelict land by residents with the support of Groundwork Manchester.

Valleyside, North Manchester

Selective demolition and a crack-down on crime has improved this Valleyside council estate.

Improved housing on a revamped council estate.

Owner occupied newly built homes in Valleyside adjacent to a revamped council estate.

Popular new private flats on an arterial road.

New private housing being built in the midst of Valleyside's abandoned streets.

Demolition has started in this Valleyside street. Two houses are still occupied.

Site after selective demolition, like this since April 2001, photographed in November 2001.

Many residents want to stay here. A rescue plan is being developed.

Riverview, Newcastle

Lower Riverview council houses with views across the Tyne, awaiting demolition.

These attractive Lower Riverview council streets are staying for now.

These Lower Riverview tower blocks will be retained and refurbished.

Private housing in Lower Riverview awaiting clearance.

Manchester city centre

Castlefield redevelopment around the waterway.

Castlefield redevelopment around the waterway.

New retail development in Manchester city centre, anchored by Harvey Nichols.

Prime development site, Manchester city centre, May 2001.

The same site had been developed as an upmarket café by September 2001.

Byker, Newcastle

Instead of being demolished, Bolam Coyne will be redeveloped as live-work units for artists.

Views of Byker.

Just over 6 per cent of all properties are empty in Byker.

A street in Byker.